more

terrible

than

death

ALSO BY ROBIN KIRK

The Monkey's Paw: New Chronicles from Peru
The Peru Reader: History, Culture, Politics (coeditor)

more terrible than death

MASSACRES, DRUGS, AND
AMERICA'S WAR IN COLOMBIA

Robin Kirk

PublicAffairs
New York

The quote from General Giap Vo Nguyen is from Stanley Karnow's *Vietnam, a history* (New York: Viking Press, 1983) and Wisława Szymborska's quote is from her *View with a grain of sand: Selected Poems*. Translation by Stanisław Barańczak and Clare Cavanagh (San Diego: Harcourt Brace, 1995).

Published in the United States by PublicAffairs™,
a member of the Perseus Books Group.

Printed in the United States of America.

Book design by Jane Raese

Library of Congress Cataloging-in-Publication Data
Kirk, Robin.
More terrible than death: massacres, drugs, and America's war in Colombia/Robin Kirk.–1st ed.
p. cm.
Includes bibliographical references and index.
ISBN 1-58648-104-5
1. Drug traffic–Colombia. 2. Cocaine industry–Colombia. 3. Human rights–Colombia.
4. Narcotics, Control of–Colombia. 5. United States–Military relations–Colombia.
6. Colombia–Military relations–United States.
I. Title.
HV5840.C7 K57   2003
363.45'09861–dc21
2002036609

FIRST EDITION

10 9 8 7 6 5 4 3 2 1

TO ORIN

... Hope
is not reason or logic,
but tough as the fingerpads
that draw the gut bow.

"In war, there are two factors—human beings and weapons.
Ultimately, though, human beings are the decisive factor.
Human beings! Human beings!"

General Giap Vo Nguyen,
commander, People's Army of Vietnam

Conspiracies aren't the only things shrouded in silence.
Retinues of reasons don't trail coronations alone.
Anniversaries of revolutions may roll around,
but so do oval pebbles encircling the bay.

Wisława Szymborska, "No Title Required"

CONTENTS

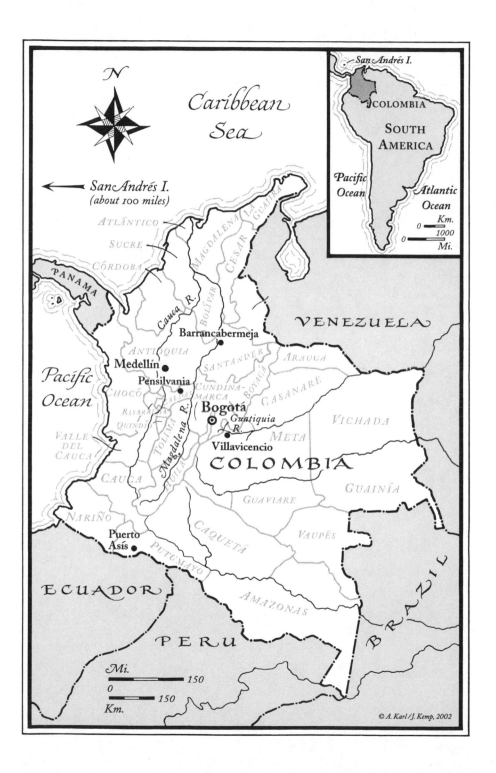

N

Caribbean Sea

San Andrés I.
(about 100 miles)

ATLÁNTICO

SUCRE

CÓRDOBA

PANAMA

Pacific Ocean

ANTIOQUIA

Medellín

Pensilvania

CHOCÓ

RISARALDA

QUINDÍO

VALLE DEL CAUCA

CAUCA

NARIÑO

Cauca R.

Barrancabermeja

SANTANDER

CALDAS

CUNDINA-MARCA

TOLIMA

Magdalena R.

HUILA

Bogotá

Guatiquia R.

Villavicencio

META

COLOMBIA

GUAVIARE

CAQUETÁ

Puerto Asís

PUTUMAYO

AMAZONAS

ECUADOR

PERU

MAGDALENA

LA GUAJIRA

CESAR

BOLÍVAR

VENEZUELA

ARAUCA

BOYACÁ

CASANARE

VICHADA

GUAINÍA

VAUPÉS

BRAZIL

Mi.
0   150
Km.   150

San Andrés I.

COLOMBIA

SOUTH AMERICA

Pacific Ocean

Atlantic Ocean

Km.
0   1000
0
Mi.

© A. Karl / J. Kemp, 2002

1525   Spain begins conquest of Colombia.

1819   Simón Bolívar defeats the Spanish at Boyacá, Colombia. Republic of Gran Colombia formed with Ecuador, Panama, and Venezuela.

1849   Conservative and Liberal parties founded.

1928   FARC leader Pedro Antonio Marín's stated year of birth.

1948   Jorge Eliécer Gaitán is assassinated in Bogotá. One year later, Laureano Gómez is elected president. The next year, some Liberal rebels join with Communists at El Davis.

1953   General Gustavo Rojas Pinilla leads a military coup d'état and is deposed four years later with the formation of a civilian-military alliance that divides power between Liberals and Conservatives.

1964   Attack on the "independent republic" at Marquetalia.

1965   The ELN makes its first appearance. The campaign against the "independent republics" is declared a victory.

1966   The FARC is formally organized, with Pedro Marín as its leader. Carlos Castaño is born.

1970   Misael Pastrana is elected president in a questioned election; end of the National Front. Four years later, the April 19 Movement (M-19) announces itself, formed to protest this election, and steals the sword of Simón Bolívar from a Bogotá museum.

1980   Jesús Castaño is kidnapped and killed, followed the next year by the kidnapping of the Álvarez children and Martha Nieves Ochoa and the formation of MAS. The children are killed by the M-19. Ochoa is released in February 1982.

1984   The FARC agrees to a cease-fire that lasts six years.

1985   The M-19 seizes the Palace of Justice. Eleven justices and
        dozens of others are killed when the army retakes the
        building; the Patriotic Union Party is founded.

1989   Presidential candidate Luis Carlos Galán is assassinated; M-19
        becomes a legal party after reaching a peace agreement with
        the government. A judicial commission is massacred near La
        Rochela, prompting the government to outlaw paramilitary
        groups.

1990   Presidential candidates Bernardo Jaramillo (Patriotic Union)
        and Carlos Pizarro (M-19) are murdered by Castaños. The
        government-FARC cease-fire ends with the attack on Casa
        Verde.

1991   Pablo Escobar negotiates his surrender. He leaves his luxury
        prison a year later, then is shot dead while trying to evade
        arrest on December 2, 1993.

1994   Ernesto Samper is elected president after a campaign tainted
        by contributions from traffickers. Carlos Castaño takes over
        paramilitaries after his elder brother is killed by guerrillas.

1997   The Mapiripán massacre takes over three dozen lives;
        Castaño forms a paramilitary alliance called the AUC.

1998   Andrés Pastrana is elected. Three leading human rights
        defenders, among them Jesús Valle, are murdered. The ELN
        provokes the Machuca disaster.

1999   New peace talks between the government and FARC are
        formally launched; drug czar General Barry McCaffrey
        (retired) declares the country in "near-emergency"; the
        Clinton administration proposes millions in military aid.

2000   The United States authorizes almost US$1 billion in mainly
        military aid to fight drug trafficking in Colombia.
        Paramilitaries murder at least thirty-six people at El Salado.

2002   President Pastrana ends peace talks. The United States orders
        the extradition of guerrillas and paramilitary leader Carlos
        Castaño for drug trafficking. Álvaro Uribe is elected president.

I SET OUT TO WRITE THIS BOOK BECAUSE I WANTED TO TELL STORIES. After working for a decade in Colombia as a human rights advocate, I have notebooks full of stories that I have never been able to tell at more than the occasional party. Even then, I usually refrain. For most, Colombia is just another one of those places where a lot of bad things happen and there is no cure.

These places run together in our minds: Bosnia, Soweto, Dili, the Congo, Chechnya. One friend calls them the "vowel places," since so many seem to end that way.

Everyone who travels has stories to tell. If my only purpose were to entertain, I could satisfy myself over cocktails or in the conferences that loom like rain clouds over my schedule. I want to do more than entertain. I want to tell these stories because for me, they are where the truth of things lies, whether in Colombia or in my backyard. By that, I mean truth not like a shiny coin, but as a fabric of perceptions and lived experience, disappointments and moments of disgust and revelation, that wraps the heart of things and the unmistakable shiver of life. The human rights reports I have written are true. But it is a simplified truth, a truth of dates and quotes and judicial decisions stripped of emotion and complication. They are like the directions on how to assemble a bicycle, not a chronicle of the joy of riding.

I want to tell more complex stories because Colombia matters. It matters to me, since I have dedicated much of the past decade to thinking about it and trying to understand what is happening there. But I also believe that it should matter to anyone who is American, for reasons that are rooted in the way Americans think and live and do business in the world. This is why: Our pleasures are tearing Colombia apart. Our leisure funds terror. Our parties pull Colombia under, as surely as a stone sinks cloth in water. Our addictions and experimentations ensnare not just ourselves and our families, but a nation. Most of all, our unwillingness to acknowledge our behavior and examine its real consequences threatens to sink Colombia.

Perhaps more than ever, Americans are aware of the impact our actions have in the world. Yet we are still largely deaf and blind to the havoc we have created in Colombia. It is ironic, given that Colombia is only a movie's-length from our border (the way I measure airplane flights). The Colombian pop star Shakira entertains us, Colombians stock our Starbucks with coffee, adorn our weddings and homes with fresh flowers, and mine the emeralds that glow in the belly buttons of our movie stars.

Of course, all that is beside the point. What Colombia really does is supply the cocaine and heroin that millions of Americans ingest. Colombia is the main producer of the cocaine and heroin used in the United States. Currently, the roughly 6 million Americans considered "chronic" or occasional users of cocaine and heroin spend at least $46 billion annually on the drugs.

Meanwhile, we have sought to suppress these drugs with bullets and helicopters and herbicides and ads and prisons and patrols and mandatory sentences. Over more than two decades, the United States has spent over $150 billion trying to wipe out the sources of illegal narcotics (the *coca* bush used to manufacture cocaine and the opium poppy plant), to interdict illegal drugs on the way to U.S. shores and identify and jail the people who traffic in and buy cocaine and heroin. But the drug war was never won. Today, cocaine and heroin are plentiful, affordable, and more pure than ever. The "war on drugs" is one of the most spectacularly failed government programs in the history of the United States.

To give just one of many examples, in 1984, the authorities seized a drug lab in Colombia called Tranquilandia and its fifteen tons of cocaine, a huge amount at the time. Police had never before seen so much cocaine in one place. Two decades later, seizures of similar quantities are routine. The amount seized at Tranquilandia is but 2 percent of Colombia's current annual cocaine production, estimated in 2001 at 640 tons per year.

Drugs are cool. No advertising campaign will change that. The havoc drug use creates is part of the attraction, built in like a whirling light. Drugs are sexy, they are fashionable, they are new (and at the same time as old as humankind). They will always attract youth and risk takers and the frankly bored. Our politicians point the finger south to avoid pointing it squarely at the noses and veins and mouths of their constituents.

As long as people want illegal drugs, they will be able to get them. They will pay lots of money for them. As long as there is demand, there will be supply. As long as there are buyers, there will be sellers. It's a truth that is so unquestioned, so obvious to all, so completely and utterly proven that it is neatly ignored. Or perhaps not ignored, but made invisible, like the force of gravity.

The drug trade persists and is robust. That much is not news. Neither is the fact that it has corrupted much of Colombian life. In the 2002 Colombian elections, controversy surrounded dozens of congressional and even presidential candidates, accused of tolerating or even profiting from the trade in cocaine and heroin. One Colombian president, Ernesto Samper, had his term poisoned by evidence that his campaign staff knowingly accepted contributions from traffickers. Current president Álvaro Uribe Vélez is himself shadowed by allegations.

What is news is this: The criminal drug networks of the 1980s are no longer the only beneficiaries in Colombia. Illegal armies now reap a healthy profit. Kingpins still spend their fortunes on costly jewelry, cars, and alcohol-soaked parties. But their partners on the ideological left and right invest their percentage in bullets and bombs. The street price of a single kilo of cocaine in New York—roughly $110,000—buys a month's worth of salaries for 250 fighters, or 180 AK-47 semiautomatic rifles, or 120 satellite telephones, or full camouflage uniforms for 1,000 men.

The United States extradited the first Colombian guerrilla for alleged trafficking in 2002. The reason was that the Drug Enforcement Administration (DEA) said it found the guerrillas' stamp on blocks of purified cocaine leaving Colombia for American shores. Over the years, guerrillas have climbed up the ladder of the business, advancing from security guards and tax collectors to wholesalers.

The guerrillas' enemies, the paramilitaries, have been at the top of the trade for over two decades. A number of the chieftains are themselves traffickers, responsible for shipping hundreds of tons of cocaine and heroin into the United States and Europe. In 2001, paramilitaries began a novel auction. In exchange for protection, they sold blocks of Colombia under their military control to traffickers willing to pay fees based on cocaine production. In September 2002, the United States filed extradition papers on Carlos Castaño, the top paramilitary leader, and two associates.

It's no surprise that cocaine has been as effective in penetrating Colombia's five-decade-old war as any other element of Colombian society. The country has narco-mayors, narco-police, narco-malls and narco-hotels, narco-highways and narco-airlines, narco-universities, narco-nuns and narco-NGOs, narco-parks, narco-beauty pageants, narco-singers, narco-horses, and narco-dogs. There are narco-children, among them the five-year-old caught carrying two pounds of heroin caught at New York's John F. Kennedy International Airport in April 2002. Americans are not immune. There are even narco-soldiers and narco-soldiers' wives, among them the American wife of the head of the U.S. military attaché's office in Bogotá, convicted of shipping cocaine home like a souvenir of her tour.

My point is not to level blame. I propose no cure. Libraries are filled with papers and studies and polls about America's addictions and their cost to society. Many worthy books have been and will be written about the war on drugs and the dramas that are its juicy bits; this is not one of them. To write this book, I read some of those books, mainly to ensure that I steer a different path. Colombia's conflict predates cocaine, so Americans did not cause it. But we amplify it with our consumer behavior and give it a devastating scope.

I hope to show that what looms in Colombia is more than a familiar tale of Latin corruption or savagery. It has as much to do with us as it does with Colombia. If viability in the world can be likened to a shelf, there hangs Colombia, its fingers slipping and the twisting of its torso antic with dread. We watch as if it had nothing, really, to do with us. Yet it does, intimately. Our failed policy–dramatically failed, epically failed, and failing with a numbing, annual frequency–is largely responsible.

I've done my bit, as a human rights activist, to show why and how and where the innocent and defenseless are harmed. At the same time, though, there is more to be said beyond the lists of atrocities and body parts that fill human rights reports. The stories here go beyond the necessary limits of the human rights world and aim at the bigger truths of the American relationship to Colombia and the need to change it.

The point of this book is to lay bare the context of what lies behind and within America's war on drugs in Colombia and show how the United States, through its consumer habits and official policies, has provoked Colombia's home-grown demons. The book does not argue that the United States is responsible for all of Colombia's ills; certainly, there is blame to generously share. Yet there is one conclusion I hope most readers will take away from these pages: American habits and ideas and actions on the ground give speed and bite to the wars now gripping Colombia. We share responsibility. But we have yet to acknowledge this, or to think deeply or truly about how to stop. To the contrary, we delve ever deeper into Colombia's conflict. In 2002, the Bush administration was granted permission by the U.S. Congress to use training and weapons formerly provided to Colombia's military to fight illegal drugs in operations that targeted guerrillas and paramilitaries even when these operations were not drug-related. The change in mission reflected the facts on the ground; yet it also meant a step deeper into a conflict that remains one of the most tangled and treacherous in the hemisphere.

I also argue that there is no such thing as an immutable "culture of violence" in Colombia. Rather, violence is an amalgam of identifiable decisions and the behavior of known individuals and relationships. Human beings are the engines and fuel of this war. By that I refer not just to the personalities whose names appear in newspapers but also to many whose fame never transcends a family or town. As General Giap Vo Nguyen said of another distant conflict, "Human beings are the decisive factor." Human beings make the war; they are the only ones who can unmake it. Colombia's hope lies in human minds and hearts and hands.

This book tells the story of one Colombian who risked his life for peace, Josué Giraldo Cardona. He was a friend and colleague with whom I worked in Colombia. The first and last thing I want readers to see in their mind's eye is Josué, a Colombian dedicated to peace and nonviolence. He is the one who told me that to give up on the hope for change in Colombia would be "more terrible than death," which gave me the title for this book. Although it may be hard for American news consumers to believe it, most Colombians are more like Josué than they are like Pablo Escobar, a better-known figure. My focus on Josué is a way of recognizing all of those brave individuals who continue to work for peace and justice in Colombia.

Most Colombians want nothing to do with illegal drugs. Most Colombians abhor murder. Most Colombians want honest, hard-working, and careful leaders. They want quiet neighborhoods, good schools for their children, occasional vacations. They want to leave their homes each morning with a better than average chance of returning home alive. They want guns off the streets, criminals in jail, and a police and army that they can be proud of. So what they desire is not, in the end, much different from what you or I might want. Yet they live differently, because not a single one of those things is assured for any of them.

Colombian history is intricate and, to many, impossibly tangled. There are too many acronyms; there are not enough periods of excisable calm. Where possible, I have cut out the knots and intricacies that lead many of us who follow Colombia into a kind of despair of our own (since one never, ever reaches an end or beginning of any tale). Certainly, some readers will find gaps infuriating or suspicious. My intention is not to mislead but rather to keep to a narrative path that will lead most readers to the book's end. As one friend once remarked to me, Colombia is complex but never confused. I hope to flavor the book with that fascinating tangle, yet not lose my readers in the process.

Also to ease the reader's way, I have adopted several space-saving or confusion-reducing conventions. Where possible, I say "paramilitaries" or "guerrillas" to avoid overloading the text with acronyms that add up to the same thing. Suffice it to say that both have sets and sub-sets and sub-subsets that at times act and make pronouncements in distinctive ways. When identifying Colombians for the first time, I use their full name except in cases where the person has not customarily done so. Countries colonized by the Spanish use two last names that derive from that individual's parents. For instance, Pablo Escobar Gaviria has a father whose last name (from his father) is Escobar. His mother's last name (from her father) is Gaviria. Subsequently, I drop the matrilineal name.

In one case, I have employed an unusual way to identify a very well-known person: Pedro Antonio Marín, the leader of Colombia's largest guerrilla insurgency (whose mother's last name I have been unable to confirm). This is his real name. However, in news reports and books, he is identified by an assumed name that he took when he rebelled against Colombia's government as a youth, Manuel Marulanda Vélez. I made this decision deliberately. Like everyone else in this drama, I want Marín to appear first as a person, not a legend, and explain where he came from, what forces turned him into what he is today, and why. One of those forces turned him into Marulanda. But it is not the sum of him and does not account entirely for the man who continues to fight from Colombia's hinterlands.

Spelling is sometimes more a matter of choice than rule. The last name "Loayza," for example, can also be spelled "Loaiza," fruit of a rich oral, not written tradition in Colombia (they sound the same, *low-AYE-za*). Many people asked me not to use their real names, out of fear. In these cases, I note that I am using a pseudonym and the reason for that is always obvious.

Finally, I want to make it clear that this book reflects only my views and not those of Human Rights Watch. By this, I suggest no hidden controversy between myself and the organization I admire and have worked with for the last ten years. I owe a great deal to the men and women who are my colleagues there. I value immensely the organization's history and contributions to human rights in Colombia and elsewhere. This book represents something I felt I needed to do to understand and come to terms with the breadth of my experience in Colombia, which often breached the necessary limits of a human rights focus.

Durham, North Carolina

more

terrible

than

death

JOSUÉ

THERE IS A CURIOUS QUIET THAT TAKES HOLD OF COLOMBIAN TOWNS. These are towns with central squares and junker cars and open air restaurants that play salsa tapes or, depending on where you are, tapes featuring the harps or accordions that accompany Colombian folk music. Often, the square will have a fountain or statue. When I conjure in my mind what I am writing about, I see a wrought iron fence to protect grass that is already punished by litter, spit, piss, the feet of children, trash, and dogs. An elderly man sits on a bench, a newspaper vendor waits in the shadow of a kiosk. There are flies. The pace of passers-by ebbs and flows with the hour. A few vehicles pass, perhaps a motorcycle. In my imagination, it is always sunny.

Yet there is something in the air. If a farmer happens by, the clop-clop of the horse marks a beat like a racing heart. At midmorning, the shops are open, the coffee brews, and women in flip-flops carry the makings of lunch in plastic mesh bags. The portent is a palpable, almost human presence. Everyone feels it. Something has altered the course of a day. Plans are made. Even the dogs seem poised to run.

On just such a morning in just such a town, Josué Giraldo Cardona wondered whether he would make it home alive. His first name is pronounced with a musical lift, *hose-WAY*. A chime, a greeting. The name of the town is Pensilvania and it is where Josué was born. The town is neither unique nor particularly prone to acts of violence. Its houses have red tile roofs. There are white churches sunk deep in the grass green of an Andean valley. Thinned by altitude, the air gives color a special intensity, as if tinted by an artist.

1

Pensilvania is at Colombia's coffee-growing center. The coffee-advertising symbol known as Juan Valdez could walk with his donkey across the square and look oddly fastidious, like a man in a bowler hat, but still perfectly attuned to his surroundings, even among the Toyota Land Cruisers and blaring stereos. It was in the square that Josué saw men preparing to kill him. He saw them from a seat in a coffee shop. They saw him from a spot on the square.

That moment is part of the story I want to tell. Many of the murders in Colombia are like the one that was planned for Josué that day–deliberate, visible, slow. There is plenty of time to know and see what is happening. The human target may even recognize the face of the killer for what it is long before any word is spoken or shot is fired. For Josué, it was the death foretold in Gabriel García Márquez's tale. It wore a dress shirt and khakis, with a windbreaker to cover the pistol tucked in the small of the back.

It may be a childhood playmate, as it was in Josué's case. Or a student in a class. Or the young man who has been hanging around on the corner for the last several days. It arrives in the course of a day, as the target is shopping or buying a newspaper or maybe walking home from work or dropping the kids at school. There is one moment, a terrible, terrifying moment, I imagine, when the body registers that death is near. For the human target, time slows. There is space to see and know and consider what is happening.

That morning, someone on the square–a square just like the ones I have seen again and again in Colombian towns–had told Josué that the police had been ordered back to their station. In Colombia, this is a sign that a murder is imminent. The police withdraw, to give the murderers room and time. The police are either part of the plot or see themselves as bystanders, unable to halt other, more powerful interests.

After the shots are fired and the murder is committed, the police return to their posts. They supervise the viewing of the body and make sure, with exquisite attention to procedure, that its shape on the ground, its exact location and attitude, face up or face down, is recorded. Josué reviewed his options. He recognized Amado, his childhood playmate. Everyone in Pensilvania knew that Amado was an assassin. It is a recognized occupation, like butcher or thief.

Amado chatted with the police chief, who stood beside him. He was the only officer not in the station. Josué also saw the two men who had been loitering for the past several days in front of his office. These must be, he concluded, Amado's men. Josué thought he might still be able to slip out of the coffee shop. When he did, he saw that two other men, Amado's men, were on the side street and blocked his escape. Around him, people began to hurry. They saw what was happening. In Colombia, it is an old and familiar story.

Josué stopped in the doorway of the local priest. He caught his breath. The assassins made insulting gestures with their hands. "They wanted to leave no doubt that it was me they were searching for," he said to me as he described that day.

Ironically, the gestures confused him. "It didn't seem logical that they would announce my death so blatantly." The men conferred, then vanished. Josué fooled himself into believing that every sense and premonition registered by his brain was in error. They didn't want to kill him, he thought. Such is the power of life. He left the priest's doorway. Around a corner, he almost bumped into one of the gunmen. Frantic, he veered into the open door of a restaurant. Again, he waited. Even killers so blatant, Josué thought to himself, would grow nervous with so much time passing and so many people watching, knowing. He convinced himself that he had prevailed, had fooled them. Again, he started walking.

It was then he discovered that the killers had waited for him all along.

ooooo

I WAS A HEAD TALLER THAN JOSUÉ. HIS BLACK HAIR WAS SHORT AND neatly trimmed. He wore a gold chain bracelet and a gold watch. He favored the pastel Oxford-collar shirts and tasseled loafers of a provincial Colombian lawyer. His ease and the confident way he carried himself made him seem larger than he was. Josué had a habit of pressing his tongue against his front teeth to make a soft thwacking sound. He never quite got my name straight, calling me "Kick" even the last time we spoke.

Often, while traveling in Colombia, I thought I glimpsed him. Josué looked like a thousand other men his age and size and class. Colom-

bians come in many sizes and colors, from the Afro-Colombians of the
coast to the tall and blond Euro-Colombians of the cities and the short
and broad indigenous Colombians of the Andes and the Amazonian
jungles. Yet there is wide middle, a combination of skin tone and features and manner of dress. If one were to pick a Colombian type,
someone who represented the general category of what Colombian
men look like, Josué would have been it, no question.

On the last day that we spoke, rain fell in thick sheets over Bogotá,
Colombia's capital. I was in the office of a human rights group to the
north of the city's colonial-era center. Bogotá sits at 8,000 feet, yet is
near enough to the Equator to elude snow on all but its peaks. With
the telephone to my ear, I watched rain drench the Tequendama Hotel
across the street on Carrera Décima, a busy artery. Buses hunched lop-
sided over their axles. The downpour did not cleanse them, but made
their grime smear and liquefy and drip onto the clothing of the passengers. The windowpane I gazed through was tempered to resist an explosion blast, installed after the drug trafficker Pablo Escobar Gaviria
had ordered a car bomb detonated in front of the leather shop eleven
floors below. I don't think Escobar had anything against the briefcases
and women's purses displayed in the shop window. Like many things
he harmed, the shop qualified as collateral damage. The windowpane
gave the city a bluish tint, like an Ektachrome photograph.

Over the phone, I listened to Josué's voice and the thwack of his
tongue against his teeth. A radio played salsa music. I couldn't tell
whether the radio was somewhere in the office where I was or where
Josué was or perhaps in another office, where the people listening to
our conversation sat. I had been told that there was a wiretap on the
telephone line, though it seemed that all the Colombians I had ever
met were convinced that the telephones they used were not secure.

For four years, I had covered Colombia for Human Rights Watch, an
American-based international human rights group. On one of my first
trips to Colombia, Josué had welcomed me when few others had. My
citizenship, I had learned, was an issue for many Colombians. For
some, I was the physical manifestation of a U.S. policy that they considered to be a wholly malevolent force. Others looked to America as the
only force capable of exterminating Colombia's demons. They told me
that America should send troops and airplanes to Colombia to settle

matters once and for all so that Colombians could dedicate themselves to business and parties, things for which they claim a genetic talent.

These contradictory expectations often left me dizzy. In one meeting, I would be made to feel like the agent of imperialism quashing a noble peasantry. In the next, I would be expected to favor the prompt delivery of the weaponry necessary to wipe that peasantry from the face of the earth.

In contrast, the American perception of Colombians tends to be brutally simple. Colombians are drug traffickers. Once, I flew from Bogotá to Miami on the same flight as Colombia's police chief, General Rosso José Serrano. A hero in Colombia, he had helped dismantle the drug trafficking Medellín and Cali Cartels. My drug warrior friends in the U.S. Congress proposed him for a Nobel Peace Prize. Seated in first class, he hobnobbed with a famous singer, a famous writer, and the man who would later become the country's president, Andrés Pastrana.

Yet once the general reached Miami baggage claim, he was treated like a Colombian, which is to say, suspect. The general is short and round, with the brown skin of a man risen from peasant stock. Alone and in civilian clothes, he looked as tender and lost as a grandfather separated from his family chaperone. A customs service beagle separated him from the other passengers. With its tail wagging like an antenna in a Florida hurricane, the beagle backed General Serrano against a pile of shrink-wrapped suitcases. The incident lasted only a few seconds. But the general's face was a mixture of mortification and outrage. All eyes turned on him, the suspected drug mule (the term used for people who transport illegal drugs on their bodies) caught in the act.

The beagle must have signaled to the handler that what it smelled was not drugs. With a tug on its leash and no apology, the handler moved on.

Occasionally, I hear Americans say that Colombia has a "culture of violence" that no amount of financial aid or military intervention or human rights advocacy will change. Of all the mutual misperceptions, this is the one I abhor most. For much of its history as a nation, the United States was immersed in a "culture of violence" practiced against African and Native Americans as well as new immigrants. Only time and deliberate action ended that culture; Colombia (and all other countries dismissed as hopeless) is capable of the same transformation.

When I found myself the target of a prolonged and spitty harangue—anti-Yanqui or pro-imperialist, referenced to the innocent collective the speaker claimed to represent and focused on the guilty collective the speaker meant to eliminate—I came to consider it as much a part of my work as collecting evidence of abuses. I advocated human rights, but I also aspired to practice them. I wanted to show by deed and, just as important, by my physical presence that there were other forces at work in the world that could produce what we could agree were better results for Colombia. Among those forces was the human rights movement. In other words, I tried to navigate these tensions with a very American assumption that time and goodwill and product in the form of hard-hitting reports, personal commitment, and tangible improvements on human rights protection would convince the skeptical of my ultimately fine and true intentions.

It is not easy to hang on to this assumption when facing the fury of a person who is aiming it squarely at your well-meaning self. No one trains for this in human-rights-worker school. I've never actually trained in anything but English lit. The skill of word-to-word combat in Spanish, in a blanket of cigarette smoke, in a windowless office, late for my next appointment and not sure how to get there, and with odd bacteria roiling my bowels was definitely a skill I had to learn on the job.

As I write this, I'm dismayed by the naïveté that shines through. Of course, I was naive. I am American to the core, guilty by passport. Like a Peace Corps volunteer laden with admirable projects or a missionary sure of carrying God's one true word, I came to Colombia small and willfully ignoring my status as a dust speck on the big history of the world. Once, Josué suggested that I buy an amulet for the extra protection that he was sure would come in handy. Many Colombians swear by them, little pouches or packets that have been assembled by a folk healer or shaman.

The problem was, as I saw it, that knowing I was small changed nothing. There was still something I was convinced I could do to make the world a better place. If circumstance made that place Colombia, I was willing. As for the amulet, I saw it as a funny little custom. Colombia is low on exotic products to haul home as trophies of travel, so I made a note to look into the amulet question some day, when I needed gifts.

This digression is a long way of saying that, with friendships rare, I had a special appreciation for Josué. Like so many of his colleagues, he was committed to a political cause and fiercely critical of the United States. Yet his manner with me was easy. Josué never made me feel irrelevant; he accepted me as a person with something of value to offer.

When I spoke on the phone with him that wet afternoon, Josué told me that more death threats had been made against him. He was collecting cases that showed links between businesspeople, Colombia's army, and the paramilitary groups responsible for most of the killings in the region where he lived. The emerald dealer and rancher alleged to be the main financial supporter of the paramilitaries was also one of Colombia's richest men, Víctor Carranza. Josué's work documenting crimes and the help Carranza got from the authorities threatened to land Carranza in jail. That meant that Josué was a prime target for Carranza, who did not hesitate to kill his critics.

Josué was no longer able to go home to see his wife and two girls. With many others, I urged him to leave Colombia, get some rest, and gather strength for a return when things were calmer. Earlier in the year, Josué had spent several months in Europe. He hoped that the threats would dissipate, the drizzle that ends the storm. But upon his return, the threats began again. This time, though, he said that he would not leave Colombia again. I knew that our telephone conversation might be the last time I would hear him speak. I told him that if he needed help, if he needed a ticket, a visa, a destination, beds for his girls, to let me know. I could help. I wanted to help. But what I offered wasn't, in the end, what he thought he needed.

ooooo

THE FIRST TIME I MET JOSUÉ, IN 1993, I TRAVELED THREE HOURS IN a car that I thought would become my coffin. The trip was from Bogotá to the city of Villavicencio, at the western edge of the plains that reach all the way to Venezuela and Brazil. In Colombia, the plains are known as the *llanos*, the flats, a largely unpopulated savannah that ends at the Orinoco River. In some areas, trucks cross the *llanos* like schooners, following only compass directions and instinct.

I had bought a seat in a Dodge Dart that did the round trip several times a day. The highway climbs out of the Andean valley that holds Bogotá, crosses the Eastern Range of the Andes, then dives into the *llanos*. From the last height, the *llanos* stretch like a vast green and brown sea. They make up one-fourth of the country's land mass. That journey covered an abrupt and uncomplicated topography–ups and downs, valley, mountain, and plain all the way to the Atlantic Ocean.

During the trip, I thought a lot about Colombia's geography. It kept my mind off the junk heap of a Dart and the driver, who had a lush, black, Fu Manchu–style mustache. He used the crumbling edge of the pavement and every blind curve to pass other vehicles. The road was framed by a wall of rock and vegetation on one side and on the other a straight and fast drop to a river glinting below. Maybe it was a stream. When I saw it, out of the open window and with just a slight lean of my body, it looked tiny, a length of thread. I felt elevated enough to crave a pretzel pack.

Foolishly, I asked the driver why all the Dodge Darts belonging to the same company that were returning to Bogotá were draped with purple ribbons.

"They are mourning the death of a driver," the driver said. He looked at me over his shoulder. Panicked, I stared at the curving road, willing his gaze to return there. "He went over the edge with his passengers this morning. I'll show you where they broke through the weeds."

Minutes later, he pointed at a spot. There were pink impatiens and a car's width of flattened grass. The driver looked again at me, eyes twinkling. "Women are like brakes," he said. "They never warn you before they go."

I had him deposit me well before the transportation terminal in Villavicencio. My worst fear when traveling in Latin America is the prospect of dying in a tangle of metal and flaming rubber, with the tang of excess testosterone still pungent in the air. I did not want to know the name of the stream so far below, since it would have made me think of the opening lines of my obituary and the identification of the place where I had met a senseless death.

I headed toward the high-rises that mark the city center. The offices of the Meta Civic Committee for Human Rights, which Josué helped found, were on an upper floor. The heat of the plains rose in a breeze that fluttered the leaves of the acacias and ceibas that left patchy shade on the sidewalk. The committee members were having their weekly meeting. At the time, the committee was virtually under siege. Unidentified people phoned in threats every day. Mysterious men lingered outside the building lobby, then followed committee members to the post office, to the photocopy store, to lunch. Armed men shot colleagues and supporters in nearby towns; funerals had become a regular item on their schedules.

In the conference room, about fifteen members of the committee were seated around a large table. Josué waved me in. To my eye, they looked like average, middle-class Colombians, who dress well even on weekends. There was one nun, in a formal white habit. Sister Nohemy Palencia had been sent by the Catholic Church to help coordinate the committee's activities.

That day, the committee was discussing what to do about the hundreds of families that had fled attacks by paramilitary groups working with the support of the Colombian army. Many had congregated in the muddy flats along the Guatiquia River, which bordered the city to the north. They were terrified, sick, and starving. The Catholic Church and the committee were trying to get emergency help from the government and local charities, with only small success.

The city's leaders did not want the refugees, seen as a burden on the budget as well as a source of political contagion. The refugees came from towns near or in areas controlled by the guerrilla group known as the Revolutionary Armed Forces of Colombia (Fuerzas Armadas Revolucionarias de Colombia, or FARC). Refugees were the vanguard, they feared, of a guerrilla invasion.

Members of the committee knew many of the families from visits made to the countryside to investigate human rights cases. They were bakers, farmers, truck drivers, street vendors. There may have been guerrilla supporters among them. But it was absurd, Josué said, to imagine that a father would put his children through the misery of the mud flats just to infiltrate a city that he could more easily penetrate as a day laborer or salesman. The committee adjourned after agreeing on a plan to use Caritas aid, provided by the Catholic Church, and to continue to appeal for help from Bogotá.

Josué invited me to accompany him on a visit to the refugees. At the time, he did not have a bodyguard. In his car, he put in a cassette featuring music typical of the eastern plains. The combination of guitar and harp gives it a delicate texture, strings and rhythm woven like a piece of aural lace.

The contrast between the beauty of the music and the misery of the settlements was stark. They were damp and buggy, enveloped in a stink no picture could capture. People had left their homes and farms at night, carrying little so as not to awaken suspicion. Their shelters were built of scrap lumber, black plastic, and flattened soda cans. Without their own clothes, they wore the ill-fitting dregs of some charity depository—thin T-shirts and flip-flops repaired with plastic strands pulled from sacks of donated flour.

Josué worried that the rains predicted for the afternoon would cause the river to flood the shelters. The skyscrapers of the city center were on higher ground. But moving the families closer to them and safety would provoke a violent reaction, Josué feared. On the one hand, the families risked an inundation and losing the little they had managed to save from their homes or collect from charity. On the other hand, they risked being beaten or shot and losing everything. "So far, we haven't been able to find another place to relocate them," he said.

Faced with equally poor choices, Josué and his colleagues had opted to pray for sunshine. At least this time, their prayers were answered. The rain clouds massing to the north dissipated by evening. The sun emerged. Its intense heat drew a steam from the damp hovels as if cooking them in someone's massive, invisible pan.

ooooo

THE ROUND BELLY THAT STRETCHED OUT JOSUÉ'S POLO SHIRT INDIcated that he was not an ascetic. He rewarded me for this thought by pulling into the parking lot of a restaurant that featured steak cooked in the style favored on the *llanos*. As far as I could tell, that meant large and charred, served on a blue plastic plate with air on the side. It was Meat, simplicity itself. Except "simple," in this context, is not what gourmands mean when they praise certain dishes. I was served what could have been the knuckle of a diplodocus. A hot wind blew in the windows. Smoke from the hissing grills surrounded us.

Over that lunch, Josué began the story of his encounter with Amado, his childhood friend. On that day in Pensilvania, he left the restaurant thinking that he had outwitted his pursuers.

"Behind me, I saw the shadow of a movement," Josué said. The gunman came walking, pistol cocked and aimed. "I went to the center of the street and in this same moment he shot at me for the first time, hitting me in the back at the height of my shoulder. The bullet buried itself in my collarbone, where I carry the lead to this day."

With his finger, he pulled the collar of his shirt down. Near where the polo player raised his thread mallet was the pucker of a scar.

Josué fell. He said that it felt like he had tumbled from the highest cliff in the Eastern Range. With his eyes, he marked the receding trees, the stones of the square, and the black earth that sustains the coffee bushes of Pensilvania. It was the longest fall of his life.

The shock of hitting the ground was what may have saved him. It demonstrated that he was not dead. He struggled to his feet. By then, the gunman was so close that he could have grabbed Josué. The man fired again. "The bullet scratched my head and split one ear. Although the bullet took off part of my scalp, I remained conscious."

Josué stumbled forward. The assassin covered his left eye with his hand to aim the third shot at Josué's legs. "I jumped just as the gun exploded, and a young woman passing by was hit in the leg."

The gunman shot a fourth time. The bullet sheared off another length of Josué's scalp. He shot a fifth time and missed. He shot a sixth time, hitting Josué in the stomach. It was his last bullet. "He assumed that I would die, so he fled."

Josué propelled himself into a restaurant and grabbed a chair. He fell. A teacher at the local community college called for help. "I was still conscious, in my hand I carried a book of Benedetti's poems, I never dropped it, I was still holding on tight, thinking that as long as I did, I would not lose my grip on life. On the way to the hospital, I said to them repeatedly to prevent the police from coming into my room, since they were responsible for the attack. When I arrived at the hospital, I passed out."

Mario Benedetti is a well-known Uruguayan writer who wrote a poem titled, "You Won't Be Saved" (*No te salves*). The poem criticizes the decision to remove oneself from pain and danger for selfish reasons. It is a poem that Josué prized. Josué regained consciousness several days later. He learned that Amado and two gunmen had attempted to enter the hospital and kill him in his bed. Josué's brother thwarted them by shooting into the air at the hospital's entrance, forcing them to flee.

Death itself was not denied, Josué was quick to add. Eight days after the attack, gunmen killed the president of the Pensilvania town council. Josué later learned that the man had opposed the plan to kill him. The man's death was supposed to compensate for Josué's survival.

Several killings followed. Amado's men rolled an explosive beneath the police chief's car, killing two officers but leaving the chief unharmed. Amado was upset, it turned out, because the police chief had refused to pay him for the attempt on Josué. Apparently, Amado believed that effort alone was sufficient. The police chief disagreed. Later, Amado himself was shot and killed.

As Josué's story unfolded, I had many questions. Why would a childhood friend accept money to kill him? What did the president of the town council have to do with it? Why would a police chief consort with a murderer? It was as if, in every instance, Josué had purposefully chosen the oddest, most contradictory thing to say. Was he testing my credulity? Perhaps he had other loyalties, other debts, that he was not admitting.

Nothing in his manner betrayed cunning. Josué gnawed on a cow thigh. My shirt was wet with sweat made the color of the smoke that enveloped us. The knuckle on my plate glistened.

To explain why the assassin attempted that murder in Pensilvania, Josué said that he needed to explain some things about the past. I peeled away a tendon that I could have used to tie my shoes. Thus began my first good lesson in the truth of Colombia.

BASILISCO

LIKE MANY FROM COLOMBIA'S COFFEE-GROWING CENTER, JOSUÉ HAD a large family. There were sixteen siblings and a brother who died in infancy. At mealtime, Josué told me, they lined up for food. After loading each plate, Josué's father would mark the child's forehead with ash from the kitchen fire. In this way, he prevented the child from bolting the food, then returning to the line for seconds. Josué was child number thirteen.

Josué insisted that the name "Pensilvania" had nothing to do with the Quaker William Penn, deriving instead from an American admiral who fought in one of Colombia's nineteenth-century wars. Later, I spent a morning searching for this elusive admiral, only to conclude that as far as I could determine, Josué's hometown had indeed taken its name from "Penn's Woods," the land grant that had sheltered dissidents from religious persecution.

Yet Josué's point of view made perfect sense for him. It allowed him to be purely proud of who he was and of the people who had made him and the country where he was raising his family. Colombia does not have the legendary ancient civilizations of Peru, whose empires were among the most advanced cultures of pre-Columbian America. The Chibchas were the most highly developed of the groups that lived within the boundaries of modern-day Colombia, but they existed beyond the borders of Incan, Mayan, and Aztec rule.

By the time the Spanish arrived in Colombia, Hernán Cortés had already conquered Mexico. Fortunately, Francisco Pizarro, the ruthless

Extremaduran who would, a decade later, conquer Peru, visited only briefly, then headed south. Gonzalo Jiménez de Quesada was the conquistador who finally penetrated Colombia's interior via the Magdalena River in his search for El Dorado. In contrast to Pizarro and Cortés, Jiménez de Quesada was a lawyer by training. The natives had told him about a ritual involving a man dusted with gold who would leap into a lake every year to insure prosperity. The lake was rumored to be filled with gold idols. In his search for it, Jiménez de Quesada lost most of his men, at least 600, to starvation, fevers, wild animals, and the poisoned-tipped arrows of warriors they often never saw or heard. When Jiménez de Quesada finally reached what is now Bogotá, he saw a prosperous valley of corn and potato farms. The Chibchas decorated their doors with wind chimes made of beaten gold. It was, as one Spanish chronicler wrote, the "sweetest melody" they had ever heard.

But the Chibchas didn't mine gold. They obtained it through trade for salt and emeralds, using it to make trinkets. Tisquesusha, the Chibcha chief, briefly fought the Spaniards, then fled. To consolidate control, Jiménez de Quesada manipulated the rivalries between the leaders who remained, much as Pizarro later did in Peru. One by one, they were flattered, caught, tortured, and executed for failing to produce the locations of the fictional gold mines. Jiménez de Quesada did not kill his captives without first submitting them to trial, in correct lawyerly fashion. But his was a law that compelled submission.

Overall, Colombia was a disappointment to the conquistadors. Its riches were disguised in its temperate climate and fertile land. Jiménez de Quesada had a brother who tried to drain the legendary lake, called Guatavita, to recover the fabled treasure. He found some objects on its shores but was unable to reach the bottom. In 1912, a British company made a final attempt to recover the gold, emptying the lake completely and creating a giant mudhole that threatened to suck in anyone who dared cross it. The company recovered 10,000 gold objects before the mud hardened into a surface as hard as granite.

When Jiménez de Quesada returned to Spain to argue that Colombia be placed under his governorship, he brought back many curiosities. One was a tuber prized by the natives that he called a *batata*, a potato, which later became a valuable tool to ward off famine in Europe. Unusual among his cohort, most of whom died violently, Jiménez de Quesada eventually succumbed to old age.

Josué prized these quirky, surprising details about Colombian history—markers, he believed, of its true greatness. He adored his country. He told me that he could not survive outside it. He spoke with such conviction that I imagined he secretly suspected the country's borders to be cloaked in ammonia and patrolled by hostile species. That kind of pride may surprise those who think of Colombia only as a place of chaos, death, and drugs. But it is quite common among some Colombians, convinced that they live in the greatest country in the world, perhaps the greatest country ever. For Josué, the presence of great men like the American admiral, for however brief or fictitious a time, showed that they perceived the brilliance at the country's core.

Josué's siblings followed tradition and became nuns and wives (the six daughters) and priests and businessmen (the ten sons). Josué chose law. Once he obtained his degree, he returned to Pensilvania and began to involve himself in politics.

For most of its history, Colombia had two political parties. The Conservatives claim their roots as supporters of Simón Bolívar, the Venezuelan general who ended Spain's rule over Colombia in 1819 and led the liberation of its other American colonies. In practice, the party defended a Spanish-bred aristocracy and a fundamentalist Catholicism. Their rivals, the Liberals, backed Bolívar's rebellious vice president, Francisco de Paula Santander, and spoke for Americas-born businessmen and local power brokers.

For much of the nineteenth century, the Conservatives and Liberals scuffled, provoking thirteen coups and uprisings, the "petty tyrannies of all complexions and races" that Bolívar himself had presaged as he watched his vision for a unified America tear apart. Families from opposing parties did not mix. Although they might eat the same foods and enjoy the same music and worship the same god and even live in the same town, Conservatives and Liberals viewed each other with hostility, the Capulets and Montagues of the Andes.

Josué absorbed that history like language. Pensilvania was a loyal Conservative town. Josué's father was a Conservative and a town councilman. When Liberal politicians came to Pensilvania, Josué's father would grab his machete for the street fighting that inevitably ensued. "My father was a Conservative and partisan, his blood boiled blue and he could not stand even seeing a Liberal rally," Josué told me. In Colombia, blue is for Conservatives and red for Liberals.

To outsiders, however, differences were virtually invisible. Difficult in its topography and essentially farm-based both in economy and culture, Colombia was a country of regions, each with its local elites and its twists on the prevailing traditions brought from Europe and leavened with indigenous and African beliefs, from slaves bought to work the haciendas. Although the Colombian state existed as a word and a constitution, backed by the occasional presence of a police officer or tax collector, in practice it was more concept than real power. Colombia was an inward-looking country, with few immigrants (especially when compared to the United States or Brazil) and widely shared traditions. Well into the twentieth century, Colombia frowned upon outsiders and cleaved to custom.

In his novel *One Hundred Years of Solitude*, Colombian writer and Nobel Prize winner Gabriel García Márquez has a character conclude, after much confusion, that "the only difference today between Liberals and Conservatives is that Liberals go to mass at five o'clock and the Conservatives at eight." For both parties, the focus was on the town or village, the Catholic feast days, and the periodic visits of the political stars of the day, for the most part "*doctores*." These were cultivated people with higher education, mostly lawyers and intellectuals. Their skills lay more in literary criticism and cocktail banter than the dirty work of running a nation. While disputes between Liberals and Conservatives in the countryside could lead to blows, the *doctores*, wrote General Rafael Uribe Uribe, a Liberal politician and war hero, remained in their clubs, "chatting delightedly among enemies."

What was at stake was not, fundamentally, ideology, but power. Historian David Bushnell wrote that "one often needs a magnifying glass and an aptitude for refined hair-splitting" to distinguish between the parties' political ideas. More relevant were questions like who would reap the rewards of power. Only the president was vulnerable to a vote. Once elected, he and his party appointed everything from governors and mayors down to highway inspectors. Winners got jobs, land, economic help, and status. Losers plotted how to seize it all back.

Reliably, the juiciest rewards went to a very few, who filled their own pockets and those of their families and friends. It was as if with each election, most Colombians either had the vicarious satisfaction of seeing their *doctores* become wealthy and renowned—without themselves reaping many benefits—or would become virtual refugees in their own country, without secure homes, jobs, or any hope that grievances would be resolved fairly.

As the civilians fought among themselves, the Colombian army remained largely aloof. Bolívar had used soldiers to free Latin America from Spain and guard its independence. But they were not, in his plan, meant to meddle in civilian affairs. The generals concentrated on what they considered a permanent threat to the country's borders. Perhaps Venezuela would invade or the United States would try to grab more than Panama, once a Colombian province. Even the changes wrought by World War II did little to change the way Colombians thought. Latin America's third-most-populous country remained intent on itself, like a customer nursing a beer while brawlers fight in a bar.

As 1946 presidential elections approached, the Liberals bickered. For the first time, a renegade vied for the party nomination to run for president. Jorge Eliécer Gaitán Ayala was as Colombian as *ajiaco,* the potato stew served in Bogotá to ward off the mountain chill. Even his face—darker than many, with sharp angles and a prominent nose—marked his difference from most *doctores.* Gaitán was the son of a poor Liberal family whose allegiance to the party had been the keystone of his upbringing. Yet he had also managed to leave Colombia as a young man for studies in Italy. While there, he traveled widely in Europe, immersing himself in the wider forces reshaping the postwar world.

Unwilling to play by the rules of the *doctores,* Gaitán built support by appealing directly to the party rank and file, people like his parents. They had never been included in backroom deal making, where most business was accomplished. Gaitán also drew in Colombians without strong ties to politics. There is a strong entrepreneurial streak in the Colombian character, and Gaitán appealed to it by promising to remake the country, using the ingenuity and muscle of the middle and lower classes. In public, Gaitán berated Liberal leaders for enriching themselves and not their country. Behind closed doors, he bested them with his wit and European ideas.

Party leaders failed to quash his challenge, so they backed a rival candidate, Gabriel Turbay. It wasn't an easy decision. Turbay was a "Turk" in Colombian parlance, the son of Lebanese immigrants. To some, that meant he was not truly Colombian. His Lebanese parents had been part of a wave of immigration, first from the Ottoman Empire, then from Syria, Lebanon, and Palestine. These families came between 1880 and 1930 to set up businesses, particularly along the country's north coast.

Gaitán's message also upset the Conservatives, who feared that he would loose rabble in the halls of government. To both Liberal and Conservative leaders, Gaitán was no more than an Indian thug. They believed that his disdain for "delighted chats" made him unworthy of the presidential sash. There were also murmurings about Gaitán's true allegiances, to the red banner of the Liberals or the yellow hammer and sickle of the small Communist Party.

Gaitán was not a Communist, though he did select ideas from Marxist theory that appealed to him, like fruits in a market stall. He was equally choosy about capitalism and fascism, though some wags nicknamed him "Il Duce." He once described himself gleefully as a "demagogue who has read some books." Gaitán's recipe was never violence, though the marches and outdoor meetings he organized struck the *doctores* as manifestations of a barely contained fury. Historian Herbert Braun portrayed Gaitán this way:

> To neither friend nor foe was it clear whom he represented. In the eyes of many Gaitán was a socialist; some saw in him the makings of a fascist; others perceived him as the ugly face of resentment aimed at a cultured society from which he felt alienated; still others saw him simply as an *arriviste* whose sole concern was his own career. For many, Gaitán was all of these at one time or another. For his followers he was the savior who would redeem them from all earthly ills.

The split within the Liberal Party gave the advantage to the Conservatives, who easily won. Nevertheless, it was clear that Gaitán drew on a powerful new constituency, people who had never voted before, weren't counted in the polls, and had been inspired by his eloquence.

If Gaitán had been the only Liberal candidate, he would have won in a landslide.

ooooo

JOSUÉ'S CONSERVATIVE FATHER WAS THRILLED. THE NEW PRESIDENT, Mariano Ospina, was now in a position to repay favors generously. This meant money and prestige for Pensilvania and for his family, the Giraldos. For his part, Gaitán interpreted the election as an incentive to complete his takeover of the Liberal Party, which he did. In the countryside, violence spread as Conservatives began to seize what they felt was their due, driving out or killing Liberals.

In 1948, President Ospina prepared to host the Ninth Pan-American Conference in Bogotá, which drew Latin leaders as well as Secretary of State George C. Marshall of the United States. It put Colombia on the world stage for the first time since the Allied victory. Publicly, Marshall said that the conference would strengthen regional alliances and establish mechanisms such as the Organization of American States that would prevent another world war. Privately, he worried that the Soviets had introduced a seed into the fervor that Gaitán had generated and were coaxing it to flower. The conference reaffirmed American hegemony in the region and American determination to block Soviet efforts to mount any challenge.

There were Communists in Colombia, and the Colombian Communist Party, formed in 1930, was active among trade unionists and some farmers in the central Andes. However, their size and influence was small. A CIA report completed prior to the conference noted that the Communists in Bogotá aspired only to "embarrass" Secretary of State Marshall by "turning off lights and hurling miscellaneous objects at delegates" during his stay. The Liberals and Conservatives also feared the Communists, though for different reasons. Several leading Colombian families (including the Liberal Santos family, which continues to publish the most influential daily newspaper, *El Tiempo*) were sympathetic to General Francisco Franco and shared his conviction that communism was a direct attack on faith, a countercrusade meant to kill priests and destroy and profane churches.

Gaitán, too, was suspicious of them. Although the Colombian Communist Party had supported his presidential candidacy, it did so grudgingly and only because it had no other option. Gaitán understood world events well enough to realize that the Americans were alert to any sign that communism was gaining adherents in Colombia. The Communist presence in his campaign would complicate matters with the Americans, to little apparent gain.

The mistrust was mutual. Gilberto Vieira White, the Communist Party leader, told confidants that he feared Gaitán would swallow them whole. He believed Gaitán had robbed and twisted their message to fit Liberal rhetoric. Three years earlier, Vieira had even placed guards in front of his office in preparation for a rumored coup d'état by Gaitán. Vieira feared that he would be among the first imprisoned or killed. The coup never materialized.

The devastation pictured in newsreels shot in postwar Europe seemed otherworldly to the Colombians who prepared the hotel rooms and restaurant tables for their illustrious guests. This was to be Colombia's moment to shine as a valued member of the new alliance shaping the globe. It is clear that none of the diplomats, journalists, and activists who converged in Bogotá in 1948 suspected how profoundly Colombia would change during the week of the conference and how powerless, in the end, all of them would be in the face of it.

ooooo

FIDEL CASTRO WAS AMONG THE THRONG ARRIVING FOR THE PAN-American Conference. Still a decade away from declaring himself a Communist, Castro planned to attend a meeting of Latin American university students. He had lost an election a year earlier for the leadership of the Havana University student federation. He hoped to maneuver his way back in by making his case directly to his countrymen gathered in Bogotá.

Castro met Gaitán and was impressed by him. Later, Castro described the Colombian as "an Indian type, his countenance quite intelligent . . . brilliant politician, brilliant speaker, brilliant lawyer, all of these things caused a great impression."

Castro planned a second meeting with Gaitán on the afternoon of

April 9. But as Gaitán was on his way to lunch that day, a man shot him with a pistol at point-blank range. Gaitán survived the trip to the hospital, only to die as doctors frantically tried to stop the bleeding. Since, Colombians have tendered their own grassy-knoll theories about why Gaitán was murdered. Was the assassin the relative of a man whose alleged murderer Gaitán had won an acquittal for just the day before? Or was he a provocateur, sent by the Conservatives or disgruntled Liberals to eliminate the agent of change? Many Colombians still believe that the death of such a charismatic and powerful man could not have been the result of passion alone; there had to have been dark forces at work, perhaps even the United States. A mob seized and killed the alleged assassin, silencing his version of events forever. They tore off his clothes and dragged his battered body to the presidential palace. The event marked what some have called Colombia's brutal entry into the twentieth century.

Conspiracy theorists delight in Castro's proximity to what became Colombia's first and most wrenching *magnicidio*, the word Colombians use to describe the murder of a leading political figure. But he seemed as disoriented as the Colombians who heard the news shouted from the street: Gaitán was dead. For hours, there was rage on the streets. Some shouted anti-American slogans. But the mob flung itself relentlessly against Conservatives and their symbols, among them a Conservative-owned newspaper and government buildings. Rioters also attacked churches, since the Catholic hierarchy was viewed as closely allied with the Conservative cause.

Swept up, Castro observed and then embraced what he later called the spontaneous combustion of the *pueblo* that had loved Gaitán as one of their own. Castro tried to steal some police boots, but they were too small for his feet. He grabbed a tear gas gun, which he later traded for a rifle and bullets. But he never fired a shot. "No one can claim to have organized what happened on April 9 because what was absent on April 9 was precisely that, organization. This is the key, there was absolutely no organization," he later said. On April 10, the Cuban ambassador helped Castro leave Colombia.

Certainly, the Communists took advantage of what became known as the Bogotazo. A few agile comrades even managed to raise a Soviet banner over the town hall in faraway Barranquilla, on the Caribbean coast. A single army officer pulled it down. In fact, the Communists were as shocked by the *magnicidio* as anyone. Looters even sacked their tiny office. City blocks smoldered after rioters torched the wood and straw buildings. Nevertheless, within hours, the Conservatives had blamed Communists for Gaitán's murder and the riots that followed. Rioters, charged President Ospina, were inspired by "a spirit alien to us, a movement of communist inspiration and practices."

Americans found Ospina's words intoxicating. They seemed to confirm every suspicion circulating in Washington of the Soviet plan for domination in the hemisphere. On April 14, 1948, the *New York Times* reported on a statement by Secretary Marshall, which struck a new and ominous tone:

> Backing up the findings of the Colombian Government, Secretary of State Marshall and other delegates to the Inter-American Conference have now likewise accused Soviet Russia, and its tool, international communism, of instigating the riots that wrecked Bogota and cast a pall over the whole Western Hemisphere. Basing their judgment on first-hand information and personal observation on the spot, they see in the tragic events which interrupted their deliberations the same powers and patterns at work as in attempted insurrections in France and Italy. And that makes Bogota, as Mr. Marshall said, not merely a Colombian or Latin American incident but a world affair, and a particularly lurid illustration of the length to which Russia is willing to go in its no longer [cold war] against the democracies.

U.S. election-year politics had a strong influence on Marshall's view. At the time, the Republicans were calling President Harry S. Truman naive in the fight against communism. Campaigning for the Republican nomination, Governor Thomas E. Dewey said in a stump speech on April 12 that Truman's mismanagement of American intelligence was to blame for the failure to detect what he called "Communist plans" for revolution in Colombia, "just two hours' bombing time from the Panama Canal." The dispute eventually settled on the question of whether the fledgling CIA had adequately warned Marshall about potential threats.

Eleven days later, New York *Herald Tribune* columnist Walter Lippmann described Marshall's assessment as well as the fears of an imminent Communist rebellion as based on faulty logic. The Americans
were engaging in what he called "the very human propensity to insist
on making the facts fit one's stereotyped preconceptions–in this case
to treat a South American revolution as a phase of the Russian Revolution, and then to suppose that all revolutionary conditions in the
world begin and end in Moscow, but for Moscow there would be no
revolutions."

But Lippmann's voice of reason was lost. The United States would
not retreat. In the American view, communism was afoot in Colombia
and it had to be stopped. The Colombians were ill-equipped to face
the Soviets. President Ospina hadn't even been able to save his own
capital, much of which lay in ruins. Only through more active intervention–meaning military support and picking leaders who firmly
shared Washington's views–could the menace be stopped, the Americans concluded. Influential Americans like Marshall were convinced
that Gaitán himself and the events that followed his murder were unmistakable symptoms of a political infection.

The immediate violence touched off by Gaitán's assassination
quickly subsided in the capital. But his absence created a vacuum in
the Liberal leadership that the *doctores* could not fill. They distrusted
the rank and file as much as the Conservatives did, perhaps more so,
since Gaitán had used them to take over the Liberal Party. Without direction, the Liberals, particularly the party faithful in Colombia's
towns and villages, were vulnerable, and the Conservatives sensed it.

There were no more "delighted chats" among enemies. Senators and
representatives went armed to their floor seats. The November following Gaitán's death, a Conservative shot and killed a Liberal on the floor
of Colombia's House of Representatives, touching off a shoot-out as
dozens pulled out their loaded pistols. But things were much worse in
the countryside. Corpses began to appear, dumped on the sides of
roads or in village squares. Often, the only identification on the body
was a card showing the person had belonged to the Liberal Party.

Liberals refused to put forward a presidential candidate for the 1950
elections, to protest the violence waged against them by the Conserva-

tives. The field was open for Conservative Laureano Gómez to win unopposed after the vote was moved up a year, to 1949. He won all but fourteen of the votes cast. A fervent Catholic and skilled orator, Gómez had lost both his newspaper and home to the mob during the Bogotá riot, proof of his status as the Conservative most reviled by the Liberal faithful.

Gómez returned the sentiment, accusing the Liberals of being morally corrupt and unfit to hold any government post. For Gómez, only an embrace of the kind of strict Catholicism then practiced in fascist Spain and a radical reorganization of Colombia's political structure to favor business and exclude the *populacho*–the uneducated, poor, and rural majority–could save Colombia. Otherwise, he warned, a monster would devour them. Gómez called the monster a "basilisco," communism transported by Liberal ideas to Colombian soil.

According to European legend, the basilisco is a lizard with the crest of a chicken and the wings of a bat who kills with a mere glance. It hatches from any unusually small eggs laid by hens. Its small size is deceptive. Once released, it is inexorable and impervious to attack. For Gómez, the basilisco was liberalism and the communism that he claimed was its secret brain. "Our basilisco walks with feet of confusion and naïveté, with legs of blows and violence, the stomach of the oligarchy; its breast is fury, its arms Masonic and it has a small, diminutive Communist head, yet it is the head," Gómez once said.

The Americans never described it in such vivid terms. But what became known as Gómez's "basilisco theory" fit their view of the Communist threat in Latin America. After all, red banners had already been unfurled during the Bogotazo (the color, the Americans should have known, used by the Liberals long before the Bolsheviks stormed the Winter Palace). The Americans agreed with Gómez that the only way to defeat the beast was to slay it wherever it appeared.

For the Conservatives, this meant eliminating Liberals who refused to abandon their party or who simply protested Conservative attacks. With such seemingly high stakes, no measure seemed too extreme. Conservative leaders like Gómez did not take direct part in attacks on Liberals, depending instead on lower-level militants to make plans and find men to carry them out. In control of the government, the Conservatives made the police one of their most effective weapons. Party leaders also recruited hundreds of young men willing to kill on command. The men were called *pájaros*–birds–because of their rapid movements from place to place and their ability to flock together for certain tasks, then fly apart and resume their lives.

Some *pájaros* became famous, and stories about them sound like myths, brutal and fantastic. Colombian writer Alfredo Molano Bravo collected testimonies about one *pájaro* known as the "Silent One," or El Silencioso. "His vice was killing Liberals, but he didn't just kill them. Once his 'client' was dead, the 'Silent One' would castrate the man, toss the testicles into his pocket, and sip a little of the dead man's blood so that the spirit wouldn't do any harm to him in the next life. When he came across a dog, he would throw what was in his pocket at it, saying, 'Swallow this Liberal, whoring son of a bitch.'"

Soon, Conservative attacks were answered by Liberal counterattacks. These were not crimes between strangers, but acts of astonishing violence between people who had known each other their whole lives. Called "La Violencia," the struggle that rapidly consumed Colombia, was personal. Grand political fortunes were at stake, but so too were simmering land disputes, municipal rivalries, indiscretions, ambitions, and affairs of the heart and gonads. Most of the killers were town men or of peasant stock, immersed in a world little different from that of their parents, grandparents, or even great-grandparents. So were the victims. The people who killed often knew their victims well, had known them since childhood, and had even been playmates, friends, family, or neighbors.

Once blood had been shed, it was answered with more blood, in a spiral that devoured whole families. Vengeance is a theme that runs deep and true through Colombian history, the "scorpion in the breast," to quote Colombian novelist José Eustacio Rivera, that "stabs at any instant with its stinger." People killed to pay back other killings, to even the score left by Gaitán's death, the War of a Thousand Days a half century earlier, the loss of land, of pride, of control. Often, killers left notes claiming responsibility for atrocities, ensuring that the survivors were clear on their authorship.

There was also greed behind La Violencia. Before La Violencia, most of the arable land in the town of Caicedonia, to take one example, had belonged to small farmers. Afterward, Caicedonia, known for producing a particularly desirable variety of coffee bean, belonged to a few wealthy families from the nearest city. "Violence became an excellent business for a very few," said journalist Germán Castro Caycedo, who wrote a long report on La Violencia's legacy there. "It meant murdering in order to buy on the cheap or simply take what belonged to the poor peasant."

Historians debate whether La Violencia was a civil war, but it was uncivil in the extreme. Historian Gonzalo Sánchez called it "an incessant war of neighbor against neighbor, district against district, towns and hamlets." Crossing any boundary could be fatal. "For Liberals, to wear a red tie or shirt or paint a door red was an invitation to death. For Conservatives, to possess an identity card indicating participation in the last, Conservative-only elections could result in the same fate."

Anthropologist María Victoria Uribe is one of a group of academics known in Colombia as *violentólogos*, or "violentologists." In Colombia, violentology is a broad and complex field, with subspecialties and the internal disputes common to academic disciplines. Uribe has argued that atrocity itself was not new to Colombia. During Colombia's War of Independence, for instance, one general was known for beheading the Spaniards he defeated in battle, thus leaving them, in his eyes, without a soul. However, La Violencia took it a step further. Bodies not only sent a message, they became a message, a language. La Violencia spawned a macabre dialect in which body parts and their arrangement were the letters, grammar, and words:

> Generally, victims were killed with a single shot, which caused death through massive blood loss. Next, the victims would be decapitated, then mutilated post-mortem. Until the cadaver was dismembered ... Most of the cuts were made with the idea that the people who had been sacrificed would be "well and truly dead."

The "cuts," as Uribe described them, became language when they went beyond the relatively common mutilations like the removal of breasts, ears, and penises. During La Violencia, cuts were elaborate, inventive, even artistic. There was the Colombian necktie *(corte de corbata),* when the killer cut a deep groove under the jawline of the victim and pulled the tongue muscle down and through it, so that it lay like a necktie on the chest. In the flannel cut *(corte de franela),* the killer severed the muscles that keep the head forward, thus allowing the head to fall backward over the spine at a ninety-degree angle, like a sailor's square collar. In the flower vase cut *(corte de florero),* the killer dismembered the victim and inserted the head and limbs into the trunk or the neck of the body, arranged like flowers in a vase. The monkey cut *(corte de mico)* took its name from a killer who decapitated the pet monkey of a victim and left the head in the man's lap. This cut was reproduced by killers who would decapitate their victims and place the victim's head on the chest of the body. In the French cut *(corte francés),* the killer would peel back the skin on the head while the victim lived, exposing the skull. Occasionally, the killers would leave bodies arranged in a mise-en-scène, sitting as if waiting for the next truck along a road, their heads like overnight bags in their laps.

The point, of course, was not just to kill, but to communicate. The blood-splattered *tableau mort* was meant to demonstrate that there were absolutely no limits to what would be done. In a strange way, gruesome displays by the Conservatives were also proclamations of faith. The Conservatives were most closely associated with the Catholic Church, and some church leaders supported their political aims, even justifying attacks that decimated Liberal villages. One bishop once ordered the army to burn a village to the ground, since he viewed it as a Liberal haven (to this day, it is called Pueblo Quemado, Burned Town). Acts of violence were therefore not a violation of belief but a proclamation of it, a way to defend and elevate the faith.

The horror became a testament to faith, to how far the faithful were willing to go. After all, the sacred heart, the body around it flayed, is pictured on the walls of thousands of homes in Colombia. The basilisco had rooted into the body of the enemy. By eviscerating it, laying it open to the light, the beast was vanquished.

ooooo

AMONG THOSE WHO FELT THE CONSERVATIVE ONSLAUGHT MOST directly was the family of Pedro Marín. He is better known now as Manuel Marulanda Vélez, or Tirofijo (Sureshot) and is the FARC leader. In 1948, he was an energetic, independent youth who had just left home to make his way as a traveling salesman. Marín was good with people, a natural leader, with a talent for making the kinds of friendships that, if he had continued in the work, would likely have led him to become a prosperous merchant, perhaps the mayor of a town or the chairman of the local chamber of commerce and the sponsor of a soccer team.

Like Josué, Marín is not physically imposing. He has a peasant's broad, low build. His features are slightly Asian, with flat cheekbones and narrow eyes. As is the custom in the central Andes, Marín often drapes over his shoulder a towel or peasant's light *ruana*, the poncho-like garment equally useful for warding off a chill or wiping sweat from the brow. Contemporaries said that he had an excellent sense of humor, though he rarely smiled. Traveling Colombia's back trails and haggling at its dusty cattle auctions, thousands looked just like him.

About the only thing that distinguished Génova, where Marín was born, from Pensilvania, where Josué was born, was politics. Pensilvania was Conservative, Génova Liberal. The towns had the same traditions and climate, food and rhythms. They profited from the coffee farms that covered the mountainsides in deep green. They suffered occasional floods and droughts, rejoiced when the harvest was plentiful, and resigned themselves to more beans than meat when times were bad.

On the day Gaitán died, Marín was in a town called Ceilán. Blaming their rivals for the assassination, the Liberals there seized Conservatives who held government posts and jailed them. They killed one Conservative official in his office. Then the Liberals chose a new mayor and new police officers, who began patrolling with guns seized from the police station.

But the rage passed. Within a week, they had released the Conservatives and returned the guns.

The Conservatives were less forgiving. Weeks later, *pájaros* seized Ceilán and killed the Liberals who resisted. Liberals were forced to sign papers renouncing their party affiliation. After looting stores, the *pájaros* set fire to Ceilán. Survivors later recounted how the flames lit the hills until a miraculous rain extinguished them, saving the town. Some killings were reported in the Liberal newspapers, but most went unrecorded even by the authorities who picked up the bodies. Much later, Marín said that he had wondered if the Conservatives meant to exterminate every last Liberal in Colombia. At the same time, he also wondered about the Liberal *doctores* in Bogotá, who seemed not to care about rural brethren like Marín. He felt abandoned. Where was the call to resist? Who had silenced the *doctores*? Where were the guns to fight back?

Hundreds of poor Liberals fled to the cities, but found little help. Some *doctores* argued that Gaitán's unruly *pueblo* was responsible for the violence. Not only did the leadership seem to want no part of what was happening in the countryside, but in Marín's view, they didn't even want to know that it was happening. But to anyone who lived it, the carnage was impossible to avoid. "I began to think differently," Marín told his biographer, Arturo Alape, years later. "I said to myself: this situation is very complicated, it seems that everything has changed, so I must find a solution. So I said to myself: who will search for it with me? Who will help? Weapons, where are they, how do we get them? If we just remain calmly in place, they will kill us all. But I could not bear more humiliation."

Targeted because of his affiliation to the Liberal Party, Marín went into hiding. It became an opportunity to reflect on events. He slept in a makeshift shack on his Uncle Manuel's coffee farm. Every week, Manuel would deliver food and cigarettes. A radio delivered the news, always grim. The Liberal leaders were nowhere to be found. Conservatives traveled openly with police on their rampages. The army stood by, collecting bodies. The reeds along the Tuluá River stank with the remains that caught there—men, women, children, even their dogs. Gradually, Marín came to a decision. As much as the Conservatives and the Americans would have liked to see proof that the basilisco of communism had poisoned Marín's mind, what appears much more likely is that he simply got tired of doing nothing. And he got mad. As a Liberal and as a man, he craved action.

Years later, he described his decision to "[n]ot allow [the Conservatives] to tie and kill us, to take us prisoner and walk us alive to the river bank, not permit them to take our lives on the bank of any river and let the waters carry us floating as the dead." There was no abstract cause, like land reform or social justice. Marín did not even have a name for what he planned or who his allies would be. "We did not call our group guerrillas, we had no idea what a guerrilla was."

Uncle Manuel gathered thirteen cousins. Several neighbors joined them. Liberal families rounded up what they had—Remington rifles, machetes, pistols, knives, ammunition, clothes, food. They were taught how to ambush by the elderly farmers who had fought and survived previous wars, men who barely recognized as weapons the automatic guns used by the police. But these veterans were experts in irregular war, a birthright handed down to generation after generation.

Marín and his band began by killing a Conservative judge in Génova. In his interview with his biographer, Marín did not say "*asesinar*," to murder, but "*ajusticiar*," to bring to justice. The word is not borrowed from any Soviet text but has its origin in the gristle and blood of La Violencia. Since Conservatives had killed, Liberals would kill. It was an Old Testament brand of vengeance.

With words like *ajusticiar*, Colombians created their own evolving vocabulary of murder: to take down, to crown, to fumigate, to organize, to break, to cleanse, to peel, to grate or tear, and to fish. To carry out a murder is a "business," a "piece of work." The victims are "dolls" or "cold ones," have "marked a skull," "marked a cross," or "failed a grade."

Marín said that he and his band went on to murder twenty-five men, "workers like us, but corrupted by their thirst for violence: Conservatives living in villages, farmers, cattlemen and horsemen, with little wealth, the same kind of men as we were." Marín also killed people who helped the Conservatives—those who gave them shelter, women who slept with them, owners of the restaurants they patronized. For him, the basilisco had blue skin, emerged whole and frightening from the breast of President Laureano Gómez. People soon lost the thread of where it began or who had started it. "This was the result of something that emerged that was not our fault, something that overwhelmed us, even against our will," Marín said. "It wasn't, as they say, the force of destiny, but let's say that we were swept up by events."

Marín believed that at some point, Liberal Party leaders would send guns and money. But from the cities, there was silence. Without Gaitán, the Liberal *doctores* had no way of or perhaps no interest in communicating with the peasants and rural townsfolk. Above Génova, Marín faced the army for the first time. Although forced to retreat, he managed to seize some weapons, a small victory. With eighty men, Marín decided to do something grand, seize Génova itself. On August

7, 1950, he tried but was quickly routed. Led by *pájaros*, the army chased him into the hills. Terrified, some of his fighters deserted. Marín was left with nine men. He managed to make contact with a Liberal family in a neighboring state. Then he slipped away, the first— but not the last—time he would vanish in the Andean wildness.

ooooo

THE LIBERALS FEARED THE CONSERVATIVES. THE CONSERVATIVES feared the Liberals. Both sides accused the other of being worse or more extreme, though clearly the Conservatives had greater resources to kill and force people to flee.

Josué told me that he grew up terrified of Liberals like Marín. "As a child, I heard local farmers and my mother talk about the terrible acts of violence that were linked to names like 'Black Blood,' 'Tarzan,' 'Revenge,' and 'Captain Vengeance,'" all Liberal guerrillas like Marín. For a Colombian boy, these were not comic book villains but real men who could burst into a home at night and kill you in your bed. "People remembered with revulsion the massacre of thirty people in Marquetalia, Caldas, among them ten Pensilvanians who had gone to a cattle auction. 'Black Blood' caught them one by one, took them to a room, beat them, then killed them all. One Pensilvanian managed to escape. They were killed because they belonged to the Conservative Party."

Before I met Josué, La Violencia seemed distant and marginal to my education in Colombia. So much had happened since then. But as he spoke in the grill in Villavicencio, its effects were as visible as the smoke that billowed around us.

Josué lifted his arms to take in the families gathered at the tables near ours, the sons and daughters of families who had fled La Violencia for the relative safety of the plains. Before their parents had arrived, the *llanos* were thinly populated by a few mestizo families and the native communities that had for centuries lived off the region's abundant animal and plant life. Expelled from their homes by La Violencia, refugees arrived in long columns that filled the mountain trails, with wagons and pigs and children in tow. New towns and villages prospered from the energy and drive of the refugees, who brought their entrepreneurial spirit.

The day after my lunch with Josué, I traveled to a community founded by Liberal refugees. To get there, I rode in one of the Jeeps, called *camperos,* that provide public transportation over the dirt roads that connect Colombia's cities to towns and villages. A friend of Josué's, Neptalí, had agreed to guide me. The child of refugees, Neptalí had careful, hooded eyes that contrasted with his dashing Errol Flynn mustache. He rarely spoke, leaving me to absorb the landscape as the *campero* churned over the dirt roads. Low hills rolled under a carpet of grass and scrub occasionally punctuated by a ceiba tree. Most of the trees had been cleared to make pasture. Cattle grazed alongside scrawny horses. There were a few fields of yucca, corn, and beans. Houses sheltered in the folds of the land, linked to the road by faint footpaths.

I must have been the first *gringa* Neptalí had ever spent any time with. He treated me like a placid but potentially dangerous buffalo, allowing me ample space even as he kept me under constant surveillance.

At one point, the road dipped straight into a river that had swollen with a week's worth of rain. Ferrymen loaded the *campero* onto a wood raft and poled us across. It was a journey that, in an instant, combined ancient Colombia with the technology that permeates the country to its most violent and primitive corners. In Colombia, killings are ordered via satellite phone; bodies are dismembered with chain saws; mass murderers log into Hotmail accounts and dabble in French modernist art. *Pájaros* may have been provincial assassins. But even in the 1950s, their bosses dined with the American ambassador and could converse about geopolitical trends and existentialist theory. This is a Colombian trait as distinctive as an accent or manner of dress. Modernity adorns but does not fundamentally alter the country's way of settling a score.

Our destination was El Castillo, part of a region known as the Ariari. Settlements at the foot of the mountains were predominately Liberal. The farms were large, with sometimes as many as 50,000 acres. Higher up, where the land was poorer, the settlements were more mixed and included families that belonged to Colombia's Communist Party.

I discovered that the region's political legacy was not hidden but remained proudly on display in the offices of the El Castillo mayor and town council. Above the council meeting table hung a large portrait of Lenin, flanked by Karl Marx and Friedrich Engels. Across from it hung the Colombian flag. I met one municipal official whose parents had named him Eixenhover, after the American president they admired. Others remained proud members of the Communist Party (and bore names like Lenin).

In El Castillo, refugees thought they had found a kind of paradise. They could work without fear of being ambushed on the way to a field or finding their family slaughtered. Zacarias, a resident with whom I spoke in his house, had been forced with his family from his home in 1948, right after the Bogotá riots. Zacarias had the kind of body that a life of backbreaking labor whittles from flesh and bone. His fingers were thick and calloused but caressed the air as he spoke, with a gentleness I often saw in Colombian men capable of splitting a log with one ax swing. "My father was a Liberal and we were forced from our home at gunpoint. We fled on a river and made it all the way into the jungles east of here, to save our lives."

In the Ariari, life was never easy, Zacarias said. At first, there were no schools or hospitals. Even after four decades, most people did not have formal title to their land. Once, Zacarias and his family had attempted to return to their original home. They discovered that it had been sold by the Conservatives who seized it.

In the center of El Castillo was a sculpture that the municipality had recently installed at the urging of Neptalí, my guide. It had been his dream for years, a quiet man's passion for a work of art that expressed his hopes for the future. The sculpture was over ten feet high. It was shaped like the swirl of a soft-serve ice cream cone. The name of it was as exuberant as a Colombian dance tune: "Infinite and Irreversible Wishes for Peace."

At the time of my visit, El Castillo had become enmeshed in another war, as desperate as La Violencia but far more intractable. Although the new residents of El Castillo had meant to flee La Violencia, trouble had followed them like an overdue bill. But I am getting ahead of my story. Zacarias shrugged when he reflected on that brief moment, as a young man, when he believed that a new life without fear was possible. "I don't remember how many times I moved with the idea of finding a place of peace for my family. Now, I'm getting too old."

Neptalí reminded me that we had to leave before dark. The road was known for its massacres, like other roads might be known for promising barbecue shacks. There was one particularly bad spot. There, an El Castillo mayor and her municipal team had been slaughtered by gunmen hidden in a streambed. All told, twenty-two people had been killed in that one spot over the previous five years.

Neptalí didn't have to tell me where it was. As we approached, he tensed, like a rabbit that has spotted a dog. The stones chittered under the *campero* wheels. Neptalí relaxed. This time, only the wind lay in wait.

CHAPTER THREE

THE ALCHEMIST

IN 1960, ARTURO ALAPE, PEDRO MARÍN'S BIOGRAPHER, MET HIM for the first time. Just returned from Cuba and a member of the Communist Party, Alape was fascinated by Marín's direct gaze and manner of speaking. With a companion, Alape stayed in the house of one of Marín's allies, a man known as Charro Negro. *Charro* means "cowboy" in Mexico. The name can be translated as "Black Rider," a sign of the man's admiration of the Mexican cowboys and mariachi music popular in the movie theaters of the time as well as his skill with a horse.

One night, Alape gave a talk to Marín and his followers about Cuba's revolutionary land reform. Alape later wrote that his audience responded with silence. He interpreted it as the reaction of men used to action, not words. Compared to what these men had already gone through, Castro's journey on the *Granma,* the boat he used to transport his men to Cuba to begin the revolution, must have seemed a pleasure cruise. Had Castro ever personally executed a *sapo,* a snitch? Had he gathered the body parts of neighbors and relatives fallen like fruit? Castro spent less than four years fighting in the Sierra Maestra before toppling Cuban president Fulgencio Batista. The day that Alape arrived, Marín had eleven years of killing behind him. What could Cuba teach Marín, after all, about war? Among them, the rebels as yet had no lawyers, no student leaders, no intellectuals. They were farmers or men like Marín, who had won their bread by traveling Colombia's bone-rattling roads.

The night before Alape was to leave, Marín and Charro Negro decided to play a practical joke on this soft intellectual. Charro Negro's house was one of several that formed the nucleus of the camp. When Alape was asleep, shots rang out. People screamed. It was the kind of dark where there are no electric lights for miles around and even the fires and the kerosene lamps have gone cold.

Alape leaped out of bed. He ran outside and found a hole to crouch in.

Carrying a light, Marín loomed out of the darkness. As Alape later wrote, the hole where Marín found him was the camp urinal. Alape shook uncontrollably. Marín laughed so hard that tears dripped down his cheeks. This, Marín said, was "an exchange of experiences, a political lesson by assault."

ooooo

UNLIKE THE HILLS AROUND GÉNOVA OR PENSILVANIA, THE DEPARTment of Tolima, which sheltered Marín after his escape, had a history of peasant organization and protest. For centuries, Colombia maintained a system centered on a small number of families and their control over huge tracts of land, much of it kept fallow. In the 1930s, Tolima laborers began to press for better wages and working conditions. Others tried to stake out their own plots. Both attempts met a violent response, often supported by the police.

In the unrest, the Communist Party saw opportunity. Organizers recruited men to form "self-defense" groups to confront landowners and the police and to try to buy enough time to win legal right to the land or a decent wage. Among those who joined the Communist Party was Isauro Yosa, who had established a farm on uncultivated land bordering the spread of a rich family. At first, Yosa tried to use the law to protect his claim. The law failed him. After listening to the Communists, he began to fit his personal battle into the larger picture they painted of the world. Eventually, he took the "war name" Major Lister, to honor a Spaniard who had been killed fighting General Franco, and joined a group pledged to defend its members against the landowners and their allies, the government. For weapons, they used farm tools like machetes and guns they used for hunting.

La Violencia transformed these disputes. Farmers–Liberals like Marín and Communists like Yosa–saw the Conservatives using La

Violencia to erase their few, hard-fought victories. Forced to abandon their farms, they realized that apart, they had little chance of survival. So some chose to join forces, Liberals and Communists, to resist. In 1950, Marín and Yosa were among the 200 men, women, and children who set up camp at a place called El Davis.

Marín was not among the political leaders at El Davis, though he remained in command of the men he had brought or acquired since fleeing Génova. Ghosts in the hills, they collected fallen branches to avoid making noise chopping wood and cooked only at night, to hide the smoke of their fires. Children were taught to be silent. At one meeting, they chose a name for themselves: the "Revolutionary Army of National Liberation." One participant later commented that the name seemed larger than the group itself. It was during his first months at El Davis that Marín earned the first of two new names—Tirofijo (Sure Shot). Among the men most experienced with guns, he trained newcomers and became known as a marksman who never wasted a round. Colombia is a country of nicknames. They go from the obvious, like Skinny (Flaco) or Blackie (Negro), to the threatening, like Poison (Veneno), or the simply odd, like Featherpuller (Arrancaplumas, a name given to men who like to pass the time talking while they pluck feathers from a chicken).

For the United States, El Davis was further proof that the Soviet virus had found a host. But it was a motley bunch that provoked such anxiety. They were farmers, most illiterate, chronically low on food and medicine. They squabbled as much among themselves as with the *pájaros* and police. The Revolutionary Army of National Liberation was like a shabby tarp thrown over a wreck of backgrounds and beliefs. What jutted out were old rivalries and resentments and a shared will to survive, not Marxist unity. At El Davis, the Liberals grumbled at the Communists' efforts to collectivize. Communist commissars even told farmers to harvest only when issued orders (and, some grumbled, await instructions before getting drunk). For their part, the Communists viewed the Liberals as undisciplined. What, after all, were the Liberals fighting for?

For his part, Marín found himself impressed by the Communists. At first, he was drawn by their military skill. Unlike the Liberals, they always set up an advance and rear guard, trained, and had ranks. They enforced discipline by punishing those who broke the rules. As he later told an interviewer, he began to listen to what they were saying. For the first time, Marín heard political issues discussed without Liberal *doctores* shaping debate, providing answers, and pointing to the solution (which favored them and left men like him out in the cold). Around El Davis, Colombia was massacre and terror. Why? Marín hated the Conservatives and attacked them and killed them. He could ambush and steal weapons. Why? If once he had feared that the Conservatives would kill until no Liberal was left, would he do the same, roam the hills until every Conservative was a pile of bones?

The Communists seemed to have answers. Those answers came from men like him, their hands thickened by hard work and gun stocks. Isauro Yosa, for instance. He said that he knew not only why La Violencia had erupted but also how to stop it. The answer was revolution. There were deep inequalities, historic processes, the pure science of Marxism to combat the oligarchy backed by Yankee imperialists. The poor man always pays, Isauro Yosa told Pedro Marín. Marín had no evidence to prove him wrong.

Other Liberals were not swayed. At a Liberal meeting, Gerardo Loaiza, Marín's chieftain, announced that he was breaking the alliance with the Communists. He didn't stop there. He would now order his men to attack their former allies. The government had offered to pay Loaiza and his men for every Communist they killed or delivered to the authorities. The decision outraged Marín. With his fellow Liberals listening, he spoke in favor of the alliance with the Communists. It allowed them to fight their common enemy, the Conservatives. Were they not still the enemy? These, after all, were the men who had betrayed them, pursued them into the hills, allowed Lamparilla and Blue Bird and the other *pájaros* to kill their families and burn their homes. How could Loaiza speak of helping them?

The argument became so heated that men pulled out their pistols as the chill of night seeped into their bones. But no shots were fired. The Liberals split. Marín took some, Loaiza took others. As Marín later admitted, his passionate speech before the men he had considered up until that moment his brothers did not distinguish him as a master tactician. In one night, he had made three enemies where there once had been two. Now, he had to fight not only the Conservatives but also his

former Liberal allies. And then there were the Communists themselves, who made no distinction between "common" Liberals, like
Marín, and what became known as the "clean" Liberals, "cleansed" of
the Communist stain.

Fighting took a new and desperate turn. Once, two Communists
who managed to seize a Liberal farmhouse sat down to eat the pot of
beans still simmering on the fire. They were soon twisted and vomit-
soaked on the ground. The Liberals had laced the pot with poison before fleeing. One day, Marín found himself in combat with a
Communist detachment. He captured fifty men. The Communists
were marched to his camp, believing themselves on the path to Sure
Shot's personal firing squad. Instead, they got a speech. Marín described it years later for a journalist:

> We told them that they were mistaken, that we were not their enemies;
> we explained to them what was happening within the groups of Liberal
> guerrillas, my break with the Loaiza family precisely because they were
> anticommunist and that I had been opposed to that and preferred to
> leave with my people and set up a separate guerrilla group with our
> own leaders. I wanted them to understand who their real enemy was.
> We gave them food, we gave them clothing, we returned to them the
> weapons we had taken from them and we told them that they should
> explain all of this to their leaders. They responded very positively.

The Communists were impressed. Marín decided to rejoin them at
El Davis. For the first time, he became a leader there. He answered any
lingering doubts about his loyalties by killing Liberal snipers nearby.

It was then that Marín began to read, the first time in his life that he
dedicated much time to books. He looked beyond the history that he
had lived in Génova to what the Communists said were the grand
forces shaping the world and blackening the hearts of the Liberals and
Conservatives. Central to this evil, in their view, was the United States.
Its aim was to swallow whole countries like Colombia and put them at
the service of capitalism. Colombia would be enslaved to Yankee business, already planting outposts like United Fruit on Colombia's
Caribbean coast. In one teaching session, Communist Party activists
who had come to El Davis told the story of a Communist trade union-

ist who had died after suffering torture at the hands of the authorities. The man had been seized for his role in organizing a protest against Colombia's decision to accede to an American request and send soldiers to Korea as part of a United Nations delegation. Colombia was the only Latin American country to provide troops, financed largely by the United States. When the class ended, the instructors proposed that Marín take the slain man's name as his war name. This is common practice in Colombia, though it fools no one. Rather than hide an identity, it is a sign of transformation, of having left behind civilian life to become a warrior. At first, Marín balked. It seemed too great an honor. The man, Manuel Marulanda Vélez, was like a Communist saint. Finally, he accepted, though for his own reasons. "As long as I could get rid of this nickname of Sure Shot—absolutely no one failed to call me Sure Shot—so my fondest wish was to escape this nickname, and that was why I accepted the name of Manuel."

ooooo

IF HISTORY IS A SKEIN, HERE IS WHERE TWO THREADS—THE AMERICAN fear of communism and Marín's choice of a path out of La Violencia—met. It could have gone a hundred other ways. Marín could have been killed by the Conservatives. He could have been killed by the Liberals. He could have bowed to tradition and hunted the Communists, saving their heads in a bag to collect the reward. Instead, he chose them and their decision to understand La Violencia as the product of wider forces in the world. One might disagree with his choice. One might find fault with their analysis. Other Colombians who faced the same questions did not conclude that violence, albeit tailored to a more powerful logic, was the answer.

Yet I find this a heartening detail, a glimmer in an otherwise lightless realm. It is often said that Colombia fosters a "culture of violence," a cycle of massacre and countermassacre and counter-countermassacre that can never be stopped. No man is more Colombian or more closely identified with this culture than Marín. Yet he did not give in to mindless violence. He felt compelled to find some logic in it. If his culture was simply one of brutality, he would have stayed with Loaiza, loyal to the blood tie of the Liberal Party and its vendetta. He did not.

In his decision, I perceive a sign that this supposed culture of violence is not inevitable in Colombia. As a man and as a Colombian, Marín chose to try to understand what was happening to his country, to pull his gaze above the bodies and the blood to see a reason for it all. Using tools at his grasp, Pedro Marín began a new life.

The Communists, of course, did not counsel peace. Their ultimate goal was to overthrow the government and replace it with a Soviet-style regime. I am not making the case that Marín was right or that if things had gone differently, such a system would have served Colombia well. Of all the peoples in the world, the Colombians—independent to a fault, self-absorbed, hot for deals, and embedded in their traditions—are among the least likely to accept the kinds of restrictions, sacrifices, and conformity demanded by Communism. Of course, the means that Communists proposed to achieve this objective were abhorrent. By then, Marín had more than proved himself as a man able to carry them out.

Yet glimmering in the violence that surrounded Marín at this critical juncture were the beginnings of a plan to turn it toward something different. In later interviews, Marín never claimed to have had a moment of inspiration. It was a gradual process that began with his enforced captivity in the shack belonging to his Uncle Manuel and the admiration he felt for the Communists' military skill. He emerged with something that wasn't just a desire to kill more Conservatives. Instead of making the flower vase or the monkey cut, he made an idea.

ooooo

THE COLOMBIAN ARMY DEPOSED GÓMEZ IN 1953, THE ACT THAT blemishes Colombia's record as Latin America's most stable democracy. Finally, the violence was too much even for the *doctores* and the generals. General Gustavo Rojas Pinilla seized the president's chair, fresh from a term in Washington at the Interamerican Defense Board. General Rojas promised to stop the bloodbath and impose order. To the rebels, he offered an amnesty. The government would overlook atrocities (including those by the police and military) in exchange for a disarmament and the rebels' return to normal life. For its part, the government would send supplies and cash and would build roads to serve the markets that would sell their harvests. Those who refused the amnesty would be exterminated.

Communists were included in the amnesty. But even as General Rojas offered it, he appealed to the United States for the weaponry and military advice he said he needed to wipe them out. He outlawed the Communist Party, prompting Philip Bonsal, the U.S. ambassador, to praise him for embracing "the program of the United States to persecute subversives and approve anticommunist legislation."

Prior to World War II, the Colombian army had looked to Europe for military assistance. But as concern mounted about the Communist advance in Latin America, the United States courted the Colombians aggressively. At the time, influential advisers were telling President Dwight D. Eisenhower that the Soviets were winning the Cold War. In places like Colombia, they were doing it, the explanation went, by using unconventional techniques, among them peasant guerrillas like those holed up at El Davis. Colombia had signed its first military aid agreement with the United States in 1952. General Rojas expanded the relationship by sending his officers to study military and intelligence theory in the United States and with American soldiers in the Panama Canal Zone (humiliating, it should be noted, since it meant the Colombians had to swallow yet again the disgrace of having failed in 1903 to prevent the United States from stealing what once had been a Colombian province). General Rojas received twenty-five fighter jets and sixteen light bombers from the United States, to secure "collective hemisphere defense." It was understood that in Colombia, the threat to the hemisphere lay with the rebels who followed the Communists and Marín and his fellow "common" Liberals. In 1954, the first Colombian soldiers completed U.S. Army Ranger School at Fort Benning, Georgia. One year later, graduates started the country's own Ranger unit, named the Lanceros, the first counterguerrilla training center in Latin America. Among other things, Americans began to instruct Colombian pilots in how to handle and use napalm, to apply "discreetly," in Ambassador Bonsal's words, to Communist settlements in the central Andes.

There, however, the battle remained fiercest between the traditional enemies who had fought La Violencia. Still considering himself a Liberal, Marín was skeptical of the amnesty offer. As another rebel commented, General Rojas's promise seemed like "the same pig with a new leash." To others, however, the point of El Davis seemed less compelling once they saw that their former allies were turning in their weapons in exchange for cash and jobs from the government. Many Liberals chafed under the Communists' rules. Not everyone believed their talk of revolution. Tempered by war, El Davis crumbled under the promise of peace.

Just before "clean" Liberals attacked and destroyed El Davis, Marín managed to slip away with twenty-six others, including his brother, sister, wife, and father. Once again, he proved himself an alchemist of survival, conjuring life out of a set of seemingly insurmountable odds. Yet this time, he had many more enemies–Conservatives and Liberals, lapsed Communists, the police, and a newly revitalized army–than friends. Marín felt the isolation acutely. "This meant for us a life that was completely disconnected with what was going on in the country; it was as if we were deep in a cave made up only of our own thoughts."

ooooo

GENERAL ROJAS'S AMNESTY WAS UNSUCCESSFUL. ALTHOUGH HE HAD promised to bring peace through order, he was unable to control the *pájaros* or make real progress against the insecurity that reigned across Colombia. Much of the new violence was provoked by banditry as killers from all sides took advantage of the moment to grab what they could.

Marín established several new camps, then finally settled near Colombia's Nevado del Huila volcano, in a place called Marquetalia. The remaining rebels met there in 1956. For a time, they lived in relative peace. A massive national strike and the opposition of Colombia's elites prevented General Rojas from anointing himself president for life. Instead, in 1958, a five-member military junta negotiated an agreement that divided power between the Liberals and Conservatives. The National Front, as the agreement was called, meant that the parties would alternate control of the presidency. Meanwhile, the army was tasked with what came to be known as "public order"–getting rid of the remaining rebels and bandits in the hills.

Before La Violencia, the army had viewed the conflict as, at best, an annoyance. At worst, it complicated the army's ability to do its duty, defend Colombia's borders against rival nations. Like other countries in the region, Colombia has traditionally perceived its neighbors as the most serious threat. The Colombians hate the Venezuelans just as the Peruvians hate the Ecuadorans and Chileans and the Chileans hate the Peruvians (and everyone hates the Argentines). The army left internal matters to the police. But that force had been corrupted by the Conservatives and was itself a major instigator of violence.

President Alberto Lleras Camargo, the Liberal who was the first National Front president, placed the police under army control. For the first time, an army general was given the job of defending "public order." As long as the generals did not meddle in politics, the civilians would give them free rein to run the war, a pact that endures to the present day. To my knowledge, no one ever made it official with a *documento* or *propuesta* or *plan*. But that is the way with many decisions of real substance in Colombia. "If I attempted to command even a small cavalry unit, the first thing I would do is have a discussion with the officers and troops, explore their opinions, ponder them, and attempt to get everyone to agree to a plan, and even try to divine the point of view and feelings of the horses," President Lleras said to his military commanders in his first speech to them in 1958. It was the closest he ever came to describing the pact. "I would not succeed in getting my unit to advance even one mile."

Fernando Landazábal Reyes, at the time a young officer destined to become a general and future defense minister, later wrote that Colombia's elected leaders "tacitly relieved civilian authorities from the primordial task of maintaining [public order]." For its part, the military understood that to meddle in politics meant a quick and usually shameful retirement. There were serious drawbacks to the arrangement. In his aptly titled book *The Equilibrium of Power*, Landazábal noted that it allowed civilians to claim responsibility for successes while "the military took the blame for any defeats." Yet Landazábal and many other officers supported the arrangement. They believed that it ensured the survival of Colombia's democracy against a Communist threat that would have thrust other nations into military dictatorships.

In 1958, Marín helped draft a list of demands to be presented to Colombia's new government as part of a negotiated surrender. His demands were straightforward. In return for disarming, the rebels wanted the Communist Party to regain its legal status. They wanted certain democratic freedoms restored, among them the right to organize unions and peasant associations. They wanted more government investment in schools, roads, health clinics, and bridges. They wanted land seized by *pájaros* to be returned to its rightful owners. In the grand scheme of things, it wasn't much. The Liberal rebels had negotiated a similar deal (though, as would become notorious, the government did not deliver on many promises). More than anything, what was at stake was recognition, respect. With increasing frequency, the government was calling Marín a delinquent, a bandit, and a thief, ignoring the reasons that had driven him to war. Marín was making a bid to have the rebel struggle recognized and compensated, at least a little bit.

Marín let some fighters return home. Briefly, he worked as a highway inspector, his last legal job. His faith in the National Front was shallow. To him, it looked like a mechanism to return the *doctores* to power and pretend that La Violencia had never happened. He believed that the *doctores* did not think they owed anything to him or to the thousands who had fought with him. More likely, they were sick of the rabble, Gaitán's leavings. The bloodshed had shamed them before the world. In their "delighted chats between enemies," they had apparently agreed to forget the whole thing. That meant it was time to get rid of men like Marín. They wanted him to disappear.

Other Colombians were as skeptical of Marín as he was of them. Some felt that La Violencia had not gone far enough, among them Álvaro Gómez Hurtado, the son of the acid-tongued Laureano Gómez (who had first called the Liberals a basilisco of communism). A senator, Gómez had inherited his father's obsessions and fervor. From his podium, he charged that President Lleras and the Liberals tolerated "the most aberrant behavior, for instance allowing there to be areas in the very heart of the country where armed groups do not permit the entry of Colombian authorities." These were "independent republics," he claimed, that challenged the existence of the Colombian state.

Pushed to take a hard line, President Lleras made a single counteroffer to Marín, non-negotiable. He would parley on one condition: No Communists were allowed at the table. At the same time, Lleras appealed to the Americans for help. Colombia's conflict, he said, was a key front in the Cold War. As long as the superpowers remained at a standoff, the Communists were using rebels like Marín to "stir up trouble." American military aid, he argued, was essential to winning this fight.

In hindsight, it all seems so regrettably scripted. Colombia's story could fit into two distinct and contradictory narratives: Either Colombia was an important Cold War theater of war or it was a tragic flaw in the American analysis, fruit of what Walter Lippmann had called the "human propensity" to make facts fit an established worldview. Perhaps a simpler story is also possible. Marín's crime may not have been political at all. In the end, he was guilty of being loyal and surviving the consequences. He had conjured a miraculous survival out of certain death, like an alchemist turning straw into gold. He had gone into the depths of La Violencia and come out whole. He refused to betray the people who had sheltered him and taught him how to fight. Loyalty was impossible for either the Liberals or Conservatives, schooled in double cross, to forgive.

War took an angry and confused youth and made him into a crafty man. Marín no longer heeded the Liberal *doctores*. On principle, he had broken with Loaiza, his chieftain. Then Loaiza had tried to kill him. The men he trusted most–among them, Charro Negro, his representative to the National Front–were Communists. From his point of view, the government was trying to get him to betray his most valuable allies, tempt him with promises that would prove as fatal as a pot of poisoned beans.

In 1960, Liberal gunmen murdered Charro Negro, in a plot Marín believed involved the government. With him went the last shred of Marín's credulity. To this day, Marín mentions Charro Negro in interviews. In all that he has suffered and lost, this is the life he holds on to, the vial that hangs around his neck on an invisible chain. Behind Charro is a crowd that Marín alone remembers. But the loss of this one proved to him beyond doubt that the *doctores* and their American friends were not to be trusted. It is an old loss, perhaps, but not for that reason any less instructive.

There would be no deal. Marín ordered his men to fortify Marquetalia. And he waited.

ooooo

WITH GENERAL ROJAS GONE, THE AMERICANS NEEDED A NEW ALLY
in the Colombian army. They found one in General Alberto Ruiz
Novoa. As a colonel, Ruiz had commanded the battalion of Colombian soldiers in Korea. Assigned to the U.S. army's Thirty-first Infantry,
Ruiz could not have had a more experienced guide to the military demands of the Cold War. The Thirty-first Infantry had been formed in
the Philippines and tempered in Siberia after World War I, then earning the nickname the "Polar Bears." In Korea in 1950, the Thirty-first
Infantry lost both its commander and deputy commander to a Chinese
attack in one of the "hot" battles of the Cold War. In two years in Korea, the Polar Bears lost 131 men (the Colombians also fought several
times and suffered casualties). In the 1960s, the Polar Bears went on to
fight in Vietnam's Plain of Reeds and Cambodia before being absorbed
into other units.

After Ruiz's return from Korea, the National Front tapped him to join
the army leadership. General Ruiz began to tackle the challenge of the
"independent republics." To defeat them, he proposed winning people
away from Marín with the promise of prosperity. First of all, he proposed that Colombia invest in areas where La Violencia had been worst.
Political rivalry may have played its part in the conflict, but poverty and
frustration also fed rebellion, he believed. "So long as these issues were
not addressed in an appropriate manner, the action alone of the security forces would have no success," he once wrote me when I asked
about his first months on the job. "The social and economic situation
demanded improvements in [the] living standard of the population."

At the same time, General Ruiz knew that he lacked the troops and
money to win the war against Marín. The army was being asked to
guarantee security over an area the size of France and Spain combined.
Its topography went from the oxygen-thin heights to leagues of jungle.
General Ruiz's second proposal was to pair investment with a campaign to recruit civilians to fight with the army, to become its eyes and
ears and, most important, the muscle that soldiers could call on when
it came time to rustle Marín out of his secret spots. Civilians knew the

rebels' supply routes and often the faces of the rebels themselves. More effectively than recruits, civilians could force the rebels out of their "independent republics." This strategy would "drain the sea," General Ruiz told me, a deliberate paraphrase of Mao Tse-tung and the metaphor he used to describe the civilian population in *On Protracted War.*

In our correspondence, General Ruiz used the term "self-defense groups," *autodefensas,* to describe the men the army began to train. They were "a very select group of peasants" who kept in "permanent contact with the military units assigned to the regional jurisdictions, which would also assist them. They would also do intelligence work and this is a critical element in guerrilla warfare." Ultimately, these self-defense groups were meant to isolate Marín (whom he identified as a rebel and a bandit with equal fervor) from the people. "With these activities, we were trying to identify and locate the bandits with the goal of protecting the civilian population."

General Ruiz's strategy was not entirely new to Colombia. During La Violencia, some ranchers and army officers had created "self-defense groups" (they called them "guerrillas of peace") to combat the Liberals and Communists who stole cattle and horses and extorted money from local farmers. "Major Lister," the Communist who became one of Marín's tutors at El Davis, also called the farmers who fought landowners "self-defense" groups. General Ruiz's innovation was to link the "self-defense" groups to the army through government spending in roads, schools, and health care. Tied together as a cohesive strategy, he called his proposal "Plan Lazo." In Spanish, *lazo* means a tie or a bond. In English, it could be translated as "Plan Unite." Ruiz believes that the *doctores* in charge were so impressed that they promoted him again, to the position of army commander and later war minister.

Although General Ruiz downplays the link, it is clear that Plan Lazo also drew heavily on American ideas that emerged from a seismic shift in the way war was waged across the globe, most visibly in places where the United States feared that the Communists had gained a foothold. In 1959, the United States sent the first of many military advisory teams (made up of Philippines and Korea veterans) to Colombia to assess the war and the methods used by its army. The three-volume U.S. report advocated an extensive network of advisers and direct U.S. involvement in counter-rebel actions there. By 1961,

U.S. military hardware designed to vanquish the "independent republics" included helicopters, vehicles, communications equipment, and small arms. Within a year, the Colombians flew their first air assault on an "independent republic" using an American helicopter piloted by a Colombian with a U.S. air force instructor at his side.

Hardware was only the most visible contribution. The Americans believed that it was critical to change the way that the Colombian generals perceived the rebel challenge and to develop strategies to defeat it. In February 1962, the U.S. army sent another team to Colombia, this time headed by Brigadier General William P. Yarborough. As the head of the army's Special Warfare Center at Fort Bragg, North Carolina, Yarborough was a lead practitioner of the arts of the Cold War. Earlier, Ruiz had met him at Fort Bragg and was struck by how much the American already knew about Colombia, even though most of his time had been spent on Vietnam. "[Yarborough] was very interested in our experiences with guerrilla war, which he had become familiar with through reports from the military attachés," General Ruiz wrote me. "The problems of guerrilla wars like the one in Vietnam, as everyone now recognizes, is that it is impossible to win these wars without the support of the civilian population, a factor that the South Vietnamese and Americans were unable to achieve in Vietnam."

Yarborough's report on Colombia was grim. The army had poor coordination between brigades, no real planning system, and bad communications. Troops were stationary, not mobile, and unable to pursue rebels effectively. Colombia should implement better training, Yarborough concluded, and improve intelligence gathering and operations planning. He stressed the central role of "civic actions," some carried out with food donated by the Americans (including for the soldiers themselves, whom Yarborough described as poorly fed and poorly paid).

But there were deeper problems that could not be fixed with supplies. Yarborough believed that the generals lacked the political power to make necessary changes, not because they weren't willing but due to the propensity of Colombia's civilian leaders "to ignore their national responsibilities and to seek personal aggrandizement." For Yarborough, Colombia's only hope lay with the direct intervention of the United States. Only if Americans took what he called "positive measures" could the Communist threat be eliminated. "Even complete implementation of the recommendations made in the basic report will not bring decisive or lasting results," he wrote in a secret supplement. The Americans needed to create what he described as a "clandestine" force able to perform "counter-agent and counter-propaganda functions and as necessary execute paramilitary, sabotage and/or terrorist activities against known communist proponents. It should be backed by the United States." This combined civilian and military force should respond to U.S. command, not Colombian, he noted. "This would permit passing to the offensive in all fields of endeavor rather than depending on the Colombians to find their own solution."

Yarborough's conclusions marked an important development in strategy since the end of World War II. During the latter half of the war, the Allies had supported partisans in places like Italy and France as adjuncts to troops, able to disrupt the enemy from behind established lines and support elements of an overall, coordinated attack. Yarborough's proposed force would also coordinate with troops; yet there were no battle lines, since the war was within and among Colombia's people. He wanted this force to take independent action and hit rebels where and when they least expected it: not in battle, but at rest, through their neighbors, their habits, and their stomachs.

Yarborough also recommended that within this clandestine force, the Americans create "hunter-killer" units to collect intelligence and execute suspected rebels or their supporters. In Vietnam, the hunter-killer units were part of the CIA's Phoenix Program, launched in 1967. Vietnamese operatives were supposed to target civilian members of the National Liberation Front, thus hampering its ability to fight. In its first four years, Phoenix Program operatives killed over 20,000 people, many of whom, its critics claimed, were civilians wrongly accused of rebel activity. In Colombia, these units faced a similar issue. How were they to identify the enemy? During La Violencia, it hadn't mattered what a person did to support one or another group. All that mattered was that the person belong to a certain political party or live in the town that the party controlled or an area said to be under that party's influence. It didn't even matter whether the person was a woman (in Colombia at the time, rural women were rarely considered political) or even a child. Guilt transcended will or action; it was suspended like smoke in the air.

In the end, the question of determining the difference between the enemy and the innocent went unanswered. Imperceptibly to some and all too gruesomely to others, La Violencia transformed from a clash between political parties to a campaign against subversives and their suspected supporters within the society at large. Instead of being guilty because they were Liberal or Conservative, people became guilty because they lived in or near an "independent republic" or had thoughts that could be said to be influenced by the Communists.

General Ruiz's Plan Lazo was a "hearts-and-minds" strategy that had at its core a military-civilian force and covert hunter-killer units able to strike at rebels and their perceived supporters. Over the next three decades, the hearts-and minds component of the army's strategy would wax and wane in importance. But just as they had during La Violencia, civilians would continue to dominate the casualty lists of the conflict. That, at least, remained the same.

ooooo

WAS MARÍN A COMMUNIST WHEN GENERAL YARBOROUGH FILED HIS report in 1962? Were the people at Marquetalia committed to Soviet or Maoist revolution? If so, were the measures taken—the recruitment of civilians, the napalm, the hunter-killer units—the best way to beat them? Fighting the communist threat had become the foundation of U.S.-Colombia relations. Was that justified? What was really happening at Marquetalia?

There were Communists at Marquetalia, without doubt. Luis Morantes Jaimes, better known as "Jacobo Arenas," was a trade unionist and Communist Party leader who arrived at Marín's camp in 1960 and rarely left Marín's side again until Morantes's death in 1990. Morantes carried in on mule back a basic library of Communist literature, some of it seized by the army and presented later as proof of Marín's suspicious alliance. Communist Party members like Alape trekked to the heights to see Marín for themselves, a guerrilla star in gestation. Although he had not joined the party yet, Marín was clearly comfortable with Communist rhetoric and willing to risk his life rather than betray the Communists beside him.

Yet non-Communists in the "independent republics" still far out-numbered the Communists. There were disaffected Liberals, families fleeing persecution, farmers left penniless, hangers-on, army deserters, and a few real *bandoleros*, and thieves and cheats fleeing the law. In the light of kerosene lamps, the rebels could not even decide on a name for themselves. For a while, they called themselves the "Southern Block." Then the "Agrarian Movement of Marquetalia." At the time, they had no manifestos or grand objectives beyond survival.

Even the Americans, in their secret intelligence surveys, estimated that there were no more than 2,000 armed Communists in all of Colombia. That included newcomers like Alape, inspired by Castro's victory and fresh from Havana. In fact, Marín pitied them. Once, he said to Alape that most of these newly converted guerrillas had perished within weeks of their return to Colombia. As late as 1964, Marín claimed only forty-two fighters. Not all of them were armed.

Certainly, Colombia's leaders phrased the threat as Communist-inspired. But it was cunning strategy to lash appeals for money to Cold War fears then the order of the day in Washington. One U.S. embassy analyst wrote in a cable in 1955 that the Colombians realized "that the problems involved are much more complex than the relatively facile explanation of Communist agitation would indicate." At most, the analyst concluded, "Communist efforts at provocation exist, and are made easy by the state of fear, disorganization, and atmosphere of vengeance brought about by banditry and the remains of the politically motivated fighting of past years."

Even among the Communists, there were sharp divisions. At Marquetalia, some ridiculed the notion proposed by new converts like Alape that revolution could ignite with the insertion of a few guerrillas into a capitalist country in turmoil. Championed by the Argentine-born Ernesto "Che" Guevara, who had fought with Castro, what became known as the "*foco*," or focus theory, held that it was possible for a few committed fighters to topple a government using bold attacks against the symbols of power. Their nationality or experience mattered less than their resolve. With his brutal practical joke on Alape, Marín had demonstrated how thin that resolve could be for novices to Colombia-style combat.

The argument that Colombia faced a serious Communist threat was dubious at best. Marín treated General Ruiz's "self-defense" groups and the hunter-killer units as just another variation on an old tactic, *pájaros* with a new name. They were the same Conservatives he despised and the "clean" Liberals Marín had once led. When they crept up the trails to ambush him, he was ready, dispatching them with an efficiency born of long experience.

The soldiers, however, were a different matter. During La Violencia, Marín had rarely faced them. They moved differently, thought differently. Marín told Alape that he noticed that as the months went by, the soldiers' skills improved, perhaps, he surmised, a sign of American training. Marín sent small teams against the army's supply columns. He field-tested new tactics, like the creation of his own hunter-killer unit, trained in a "Lancero school" for guerrillas. He called it the "Mobile" and equipped it to move fast and strike hard. It was classic guerrilla warfare, something Che Guevara might have counseled. Except Guevara had never been pushed to the wall like Marín. By 1964, Marín was beginning his fifteenth year at war. Most of his allies and many family members and friends were dead. The only people he trusted were the ones willing to give up as much as he had.

President Guillermo León Valencia, a Conservative, took office in 1962. One of his pledges was to exterminate the "independent republics." In 1964, Plan Lazo culminated with an attack on Marquetalia, considered at the time the strongest and most dangerous of the "independent republics." It began with the "hearts-and-minds" overture, an invasion of doctors, dentists, canned goods, and promises for future assistance. Overhead, airplanes did reconnaissance and dropped leaflets promising to solve the region's problems in exchange for help fighting the rebels.

Marín was contemptuous. For him, it was fraud, beans and a sack of rice for a people facing starvation. Later, Marín said that if the government had spent even a fraction of the money it used equipping soldiers to help needy farmers and build roads and schools, it might well have avoided decades of trouble with the FARC. "The government lacked the brains to think it through."

Years later, the officer who led the army's attack, Lieutenant Colonel José Joaquín Matallana, told Alape that he miscalculated the depth of local support for Marín and the level of his skill on the ground. Like General Ruiz, Matallana had served in Korea and was among the army's most skilled and thoughtful officers. Only a few Páez Indians, who had rejected the rebels' attempts to absorb their villages, were willing to guide the soldiers. Pressed to react, Marín innovated, always his strength. He used the tools at hand, his "Mobile" and his own intimate knowledge of the terrain. He knew that he could not defend Marquetalia. Instead, he transformed his followers into a force with no fixed camp, whose main weapon was movement. In the past, he had always defended land–Génova, El Davis, Marquetalia. Now, land was a liability. It gave the army a better target. "Today we are here, tomorrow we are not," he said to Alape. "This was the tactical and strategic idea that at first we tested with the small core of forty-two men, precisely to avoid being destroyed, because the government and the top military commanders were able to annihilate any organization that did not use the tactic of mobile guerrillas."

The army's attack began on May 27, 1964. Led by Colombia's Sixth Brigade, the military used all of its helicopters, Lanceros trained by the United States, fighter planes, and thousands of soldiers (the exact numbers are a matter of dispute between Marín and the officers who took part in the operation). During the assault, U.S. advisers monitored developments from a nearby army base.

The assault lasted a month. Colombians had never before seen so many and so much launched against so few of their fellow Colombians. Personalities from around the world protested, among them French intellectual Jean-Paul Sartre, who had also protested French counterinsurgency operations in Algeria. As Lieutenant Colonel Matallana later recalled, one of the biggest obstacles was not the rebels, but the land itself. "It is a jungle usually covered with cloud, an ancient forest that had immense trees that have fallen within the same jungle and have created an almost impenetrable knot, with huge vines and vegetation that is extremely difficult to penetrate." In a daring move, he flew his helicopter to a clearing at Marín's camp and ordered his guard to cut down trees to allow other helicopters to follow. General Ruiz declared victory. "[Colombia] was completely pacified and the guerrillas were exterminated. In 1965, not a single policeman was killed by guerrillas in the entire country."

But Marín himself was nowhere to be found. The former highway inspector and salesman had managed to create a kind of Ho Chi Minh trail across the spine of the Andes that united Marquetalia with the other "independent republics" and the southern jungle that would over the next two decades become the FARC's vastly expanded "independent republic." Like its Vietnamese counterpart, the trail was not a single trunk, but a complex network of old and new trails, used to this day, that allow rebels to move undetected. Behind them, they laid mines and traps as simple as a line of string tied to the pin of a grenade stolen from a soldier. Jacobo Arenas later told a journalist that the rebels lost only two people during the assault on Marquetalia. As they retreated, they were so weighed down by the weapons they had seized from soldiers that they had difficulty walking. Regrouped weeks later, Marín made his political preference official. He would be a Communist. The rebels set up a political and military wing. They adopted a new goal, "thinking big"–in Arenas's words, "create the Southern Block and seize power for the people." For Marín, Marquetalia marked the beginning of a new period and was "the symbol of the guerrilla struggle from 1964 until now." In 1966, the rebels adopted the name FARC.

"What were the consequences [of the attack on Marquetalia]?" the soldier Matallana later asked. His conclusion was stark: The army helped give birth to something that had not existed up to that point– "the mobile guerrillas today called the FARC."

General Ruiz's celebration was short-lived. In January 1965, he refused to mobilize troops to halt a labor strike. The *doctores* forced him into retirement. Privately, President Valencia accused General Ruiz of failing to honor the pact with civilians. Although General Ruiz's disciples went on to lead Colombia's military, few shared the depth of his conviction that insurgencies could not be defeated with military might alone. Over the years, the lesson became, like Ruiz himself, a footnote in the telling of a history that has yet to be fully understood.

ooooo

LA VIOLENCIA WAS FINISHED. THE NEXT WAR WAS ALREADY UNDERWAY. On the surface, Colombia seemed at peace. In their suits and ties, the civilians took the places of honor on the dais. The military brass sat to the side and behind, subordinate. In reality, the pact held firm.

The generals had full authority to proceed as they thought necessary against the guerrillas. The civilians awaited results, to embrace if positive and to lay firmly at the feet of the generals if not.

Elsewhere in Latin America, relationships between civilians and the military were disastrous. The 1960s and 1970s were decades of military coups in Brazil, Peru, Chile, Argentina, and Ecuador. There, U.S.-inspired hunter-killer units morphed into death squads. In comparison, Colombia was a vision of harmony. Liberals and Conservatives and their generals were like debutantes at a dance, whirling to the same tune.

Although General Ruiz had claimed victory at Marquetalia, neither the generals nor the *doctores* really believed that "public order" was assured. It showed in their actions. President Guillermo Valencia legalized "self-defense" groups in 1965. He also introduced "state of siege" legislation that authorized troops to arrest and even court martial civilians deemed guilty of vague and generalized crimes, such as "altering the peaceful development of social activity." The wording gave the army latitude to arrest people who organized a strike, took part in a march, or simply voiced criticism of the military. Colombia was governed under a state of siege for most of the next twenty-five years. The definition of who was a subversive and could be arrested (or executed illegally) expanded even as the threat of real revolution was declared dead.

Repression bred resentment and more rebellion. For the young and contentious, the only avenue for dissent appeared to be taking up weapons. Guerrilla groups proliferated, producing a torrent of acronyms that makes reading the history of the time feel like assault by capital letter. There was the ELN, EPL, the ADO, PRT, MIR, PCML, Jega, ERP, the ORP, the PLA, the FUAR, the MOEC, the M-19, and the Quintin Lame (an all-indigenous group).

Like the FARC, the National Liberation Army (Ejército de Liberación Nacional, or ELN) chose to do battle in the countryside, announcing itself in 1965 by seizing for several hours the small town of Simacota. Fabio Vásquez, the ELN's charismatic first commander, had first considered taking up arms not for revolution but to avenge his father's murder by *pájaros* during La Violencia. Former Liberal guerrillas were among the first fighters to join the ELN.

But there were fundamental differences between the ELN and the FARC. Several ELN founders had studied and trained in Cuba, finally fulfilling the Americans' fear that Castro's plan to dominate Latin America was bearing fruit in Colombia. The *elenos*, as they became known, studied Che Guevara's *Guerrilla Warfare*, published in 1961. When I interviewed an ELN commander in a Medellín prison in 1996, he proudly showed me their code of conduct, which was based on a Cuban model.

Other ELN recruits were drawn from a surprising source: the Catholic Church. After Simacota, four priests joined the ELN: Colombian Camilo Torres and, after him, three Spaniards. The son of a Bogotá doctor, Torres was already a figure of some renown in Colombia. A sociology professor at the National University, the country's largest center of higher education and a magnet for poor students, Torres had publicly protested the attack on Marquetalia and afterward attempted to join the FARC. Marín was suspicious and rejected his appeals, perhaps due to the Catholic Church's historic support for the Conservative Party and their *pájaros* during La Violencia. Torres found the ELN more receptive. At first, his job was to stay at the university and set up a political wing that would promote the ELN's ideas in public debate. Quickly, however, the group's leaders realized that the task implied virtual suicide. The new authority granted to the security forces by President Valencia meant that anyone could be arrested, tortured, and locked away in jail. Instead, Torres was ordered to join an ELN unit. The ELN provoked national scandal when it released a statement by Father Torres explaining his reasons for taking up weapons. One daily headlined its story "Camilo Torres, Bandit Chief."

In later years, Colombians faulted the ELN for sending Torres into the hills. His talent as a speaker and political thinker was wasted when he was made into just one more guerrilla. The repercussions of the decision almost tore the ELN apart, part of a murky history of accusations, desertions, executions, and periodic purges fomented by the mercurial Vásquez (eventually, the ELN deposed Vásquez and sent him to an early retirement in Cuba, where he lives to this day). But at the time Torres vanished, many accepted the decision as natural, unavoidable. Even Che Guevara had given up his career as a doctor and his government post to go to Angola and then Bolivia. "At that moment, no one could even contemplate the idea that a combatant would not immerse himself in the basic reality of guerrilla life, since war was what we faced and for that reason it was necessary to prepare," Nicolás Rodríguez Bautista, an ELN commander known as "Gabino," once told journalist Carlos Medina.

Some Catholic activists on the left, among them Dorothy Day, saw Torres as a modern-day Christ and assumed, wrongly, that he "would never bear arms, nor would [he] take life." For Day, Torres was a champion of the poor even as he made his first, fumbling efforts to shoot a rifle. Torres went on his first armed action in early 1966. The guerrillas ambushed an army truck. Torres had been instructed to stay back until the shooting stopped, then collect weapons taken from the dead soldiers. He moved too quickly. A wounded soldier shot him, then shot and killed the three guerrillas who tried to recover Torres's body. Torres was thirty-seven and had been a guerrilla less than a year.

The three Spaniards lasted longer. Manuel Pérez, Domingo Laín, and José Antonio Jiménez were "worker priests" who had practiced their faith by laboring in factories or brickyards by day and praying and ministering to the poor at night. They were captivated by the seeming romance of Torres's example of devotion paired with armed action. Like him, they became foot soldiers. They endured excruciating marches and meager food as if it were a private Calvary, their blood, sweat, and tears sanctifying their decision to take up arms for the poor.

Jiménez was the first of the three to perish. One day, he stopped walking and said that he felt ill. Then he threw up and died. In his biography of Pérez, who later became the ELN's leader, writer Walter J. Broderick surmised that Jiménez was felled by snakebite.

In 1973, the army came close to eliminating the ELN near the town of Anorí. Dozens of guerrillas died in the fighting, among them the Spanish priest Domingo Laín. Like Torres, he was shot while trying to grab a soldier's weapon. Others, disoriented and few in number, searched out their remaining comrades in the jungle. It took the ELN over a decade to regain the numbers lost in 1973. At one point, the priest Manuel Pérez said that they were down to forty fighters.

The ELN's rocky start underscores yet again how fragile the Communist threat was in Colombia. The explosion of revolutionary acronyms was deceptive. None of these groups posed any real threat to Colombia's government or to the United States. And around Colombia, similar movements were failing dramatically–to the south, Luis de la Puente's in Peru and to the east, Douglas Bravo's in Venezuela. In 1967, Che Guevara met his end after being abandoned by Bolivia's Communist Party and delivered to the Bolivian army and its CIA advisers by peasants who wanted nothing to do with the starving, filthy men who drew soldiers after them like flies to raw meat. Certainly, the Colombian guerrillas were a nuisance. They robbed banks, extorted ranchers, and demanded supplies from businesses. But as late as 1981, Colombia's Defense Ministry estimated that, all together, there were no more than 1,800 guerrillas in Colombia. That's 1,800 against 30 million. The odds seemed all in the government's favor.

ooooo

ONE OF GENERAL RUIZ'S DISCIPLES, GENERAL ÁLVARO VALENCIA Tovar, took command of the army in 1974 and was the last army chief to wholeheartedly embrace the "sociological" focus of Plan Lazo. Like his mentor, he had served in Korea. He fought the FARC at Marquetalia and the ELN at Anorí. Although a decade had passed since Marquetalia, the *doctores* had done little to address the poverty that some of the generals saw at the root of unrest. Colombia's statistics were startling. Most of the land remained in the hands of less than 5 percent of the population. Less than 5 percent of the population received half the nation's income. Fewer than 10 percent of Colombians started high school. The rates of infant and maternal mortality, preventable disease, and the other indicators of health remained despairingly high.

But General Valencia was forced to resign after only five months. His retirement marked the end of an era. As flawed as it may have been in execution, winning the allegiance of Colombians by building a state that provided economic security, education, and health care was an idea with merit. Ruiz and his associates were men whose vision was essentially democratic, particularly in comparison to their colleagues in neighboring countries. Several went on to become amateur historians and political analysts; one, General Valencia, even wrote novels.

The man who replaced Valencia, General Luis Camacho Leyva,

was strikingly different. Camacho was not known for battlefield prowess or democratic sensibility. Like the conquistador Jiménez de Quesada, he was a *doctor*, specifically, a lawyer. He had risen in the ranks through intrigue and palace plots. For him, the enemy was dissent in all its forms, only the most extreme of which was communism. Where General Camacho saw dissent rooted, he struck. He began what students of the period call the "hard war" approach.

After taking command of the army, General Camacho proposed modifying Colombia's constitution to include what he called the "crime of having an opinion" *(delito de opinión)* and authorized the military to "prejudge" civilians whom it believed had dangerous thoughts. For him, ideas were as dangerous, perhaps more so, than bullets. "Academics and intellectuals became the preferred targets of the military," noted Francisco Leal, a sociologist who has studied the Colombian military. After General Camacho launched a smear campaign designed to link writer Gabriel García Márquez to support for guerrillas, the novelist moved to Mexico. Once, after ordering the arrest of an elderly poet, General Camacho commented, "Here, the poets are worthless."

For General Camacho, thought stirred a restive population, the children of farmers and laborers moving to the cities for jobs and education. These were not necessarily Colombia's poorest families, but they were the ones with ambition, plans, and expectations. They drove a political wedge between the Liberals and Conservatives, who neither understood nor controlled them. Decades earlier, party affiliation had been a birthright, handed down with family photographs. By the 1970s, it was becoming a relic, to be discarded like last season's shirt.

When I once remarked on this shift to Alfredo, a Colombian colleague, he playfully identified his family as an example of what I meant. To me, he appeared to be the classic intellectual: John Lennon glasses, the author of several books, an encyclopedic knowledge of Cuban music from the 1930s. But his grandparents had been in some of the worst of La Violencia and had moved his parents from the farm to the town. Alfredo made the final transition to Bogotá and was the first in his family to finish college. When I asked if he was a Liberal or a Conservative, he flicked his hand in the air, a gesture that meant not only no, but also how could I possibly hold him in such low regard as to imagine him trapped in such an antiquated and corrupt system.

General Camacho got his promotion just when Josué took the same step, with his move to Bogotá and the decision to complete a university degree. Josué broke with family tradition and enrolled in law school. Then his path was further complicated by the political ferment he found on Bogotá's streets. "I took advantage of my time and dedicated it to reading more than I had ever read in my entire life. I became a mouse in the library. For six months, I would shut myself into a cubicle and read until 3 or 4 o'clock in the morning. One of my brothers, who was my real guide during this period, studied in the Free University; he had a lot of books about politics and the law and these were what interested me the most."

Josué experienced the shift that took place within the armed forces firsthand. While walking one day, he fell in with protesters on their way to the city center. "I joined the march out of curiosity, to learn about why they were marching and what had inspired them. And I began to pick up the slogans because I couldn't help but get caught up in the emotion that such a large demonstration produced, the largest I had ever seen in my life. But the march ended in fighting, I inhaled tear gas and one policeman began to choke me. The students burned a trolley bus and the police began a determined hunt for students. As I fled among the crowd, the neighbors along the route of the march began to open their doors so that the students could race in and hide. I ran into one just as the police were going to arrest me and they paused; but just as they were about to enter the house, they decided to chase some other guys who continued to run."

A national strike was called for September 14, 1977, to protest worsening economic conditions and the army's repression of dissent. At the same time, the strike confirmed General Camacho's belief that guerrillas parlayed small numbers into a more powerful force by manipulating and infiltrating the unions, student organizations, community groups, nongovernmental organizations, and academics who led the strike. Certainly, guerrillas tried to place their people in key positions to further their political goals. Once, an unusually forthright union activist had identified for me the affiliations of the leaders of one union, all elected, in his words, "at bullet point" and under pressure from guerrillas. At the same time, the organizations that led the strike were not entirely run by guerrillas. Overwhelmingly, they represented legitimate political leaders and demands, among them an end to the creaky National Front and the election of people capable of addressing the problems that had festered since La Violencia ended. Strikers froze traffic in Bogotá. Twelve people died as a result of clashes between police and protesters.

For General Camacho, there were no shades of gray: All was subversion. Guerrillas didn't need thousands of fighters in the countryside. They had millions in the cities, in suits and ties. They were what he called the *"brazo desarmado,"* the unarmed wing, of the guerrillas.

Liberal Julio César Turbay won the presidency in 1978. In General Camacho, Turbay found an ideal partner. Turbay (no relation to the ill-fated Gabriel, who after his loss in 1946 moved to France and died eighteen months later) had no interest in dealing with security questions. He signed a presidential decree, called the Security Statute, that gave the security forces broad authority to arrest and punish protest, including peaceful marches. Even as General Camacho publicly exhorted Colombians to "arm themselves any way you can" to fight the guerrillas—words that guerrillas gleefully embraced as license to kill police and soldiers—he approved new tactics to combat suspected guerrillas in the cities, where he believed the crucial battles would be fought.

What worked in the countryside, like the rocketing of villages, could not be transferred to an urban environment. Still in the toolbox left by the Americans was the concept of hunter-killer units. In Colombia, a shadowy group calling itself the American Anticommunist Alliance, or Triple A, claimed responsibility for "disappearing" strike leaders and planting bombs in public places, to cause panic that could be linked to protests. Three former army intelligence agents who later fled Colombia told journalists that Triple A was created by the army's intelligence battalion. Their charges were never fully investigated. For the first time, Colombia began to appear regularly in the reports of human rights groups. People began to vanish off the street or from their homes. Between 1970 and 1978, Colombia registered a total of thirty-three "disappearances," the unacknowledged arrest by the authorities of civilians that could end with that person's murder. In 1979 alone, there were thirty-two "disappearances."

The security forces rounded up and tortured not only accused guerrillas and their direct supporters but anyone who criticized the government. "The idea was to attack popular organizations and supposedly in that way hurt the guerrillas," noted sociologist Alejandro Reyes. "Of course, this only made things worse, since joining guerrilla groups became the only way to protest."

For his part, President Turbay reacted with incomprehension. Anyone who was not guilty had nothing to fear, he said. If only people would let the security forces clean out the bad elements, all would be well. "The only person tortured in Colombia," he once complained to reporters, "is the president of the republic."

General Camacho hated guerrillas. But he hated some more than others. The FARC annoyed him. Yet they kept mostly to the hills. For its part, the ELN was moribund.

The group that really needled him and provoked furious tirades and hundreds of searches and arrests was the M-19. Its full name was the April 19 Movement (Movimiento 19 de Abril, or M-19), taken from the date of a 1970 presidential election that its members believed had been stolen by the Conservatives. Improbably, one of the M-19's heroes was General Rojas, the anti-Communist who had led the coup d'état during La Violencia. A political movement he launched in the 1970s became the first to credibly challenge the two-party system. Many of the youths who gained their first experience in politics by following General Rojas later took up arms for the M-19.

Unlike the FARC, the M-19 did not hide in the mountains and jungles, but in Colombia's cities and slums. Some, among them the group's founder, Jaime Bateman Cayón, had begun their guerrilla careers in the FARC. Bateman's memories of growing up in the shadow of United Fruit Company factories fed his rebellion. Colombians could not swim in company pools or shop in company stores, even as they harvested the fruit and packed it for shipment. But the FARC was too set in its ways for the vivacious Bateman, whose Afro, unusual height, and stamina for dancing made him a legend among young Colombians. The FARC expelled Bateman after he tried to convince Marín to move from the bush into the cities, where guerrillas would have more impact.

Other M-19 guerrillas came from universities or unions, and many had families with deep roots in the system they wanted to overthrow. Carlos Pizarro Leongómez, for instance, was the son of a navy admiral, the grandson of an army colonel, and the nephew of generals. His mother, Margot, once told me that the first time he was arrested, she tried to use her military connections to get past the prison guards to see him. A dignified, resolute woman, she has a cap of white hair earned with dozens of visits to Colombia's jails. Along with Carlos, Margot's daughter, Nina, also belonged to the M-19. Another son, Hernando, belonged to the FARC. At one point, Margot was visiting all three children in prison, while she cared for her three grandchildren left temporarily orphaned. When she attempted to see Carlos, the guards rebuffed her. Her husband prohibited further attempts and later died without having seen his son again. "My husband told me never to ask for anything for my children. I never claimed that they were innocent, but that did nothing to change my love for them," Margot said.

The M-19 announced itself not with bullets or bombs but with an advertising campaign that teased Colombia for weeks before the group made its appearance. "The M-19 is coming." "Listless . . . sluggish? Wait for the M-19." On January 17, 1974, M-19 guerrillas slipped into a Bogotá museum and stole the sword of Simón Bolívar, then announced that the M-19 was taking up Bolívar's fight against "the exploiters of the people." To many Colombians, the M-19 was fresh and exciting, creative. The Eme, as the group was known, made the FARC look like a sad and shameful relic of Colombia's past. The Emes were inspired by the Summer of Love and rock and roll; they weren't the *doctores*, but their rebellious sons and daughters. They were convinced that they could cut the country loose from its rotten past with fabulous actions and, of course, the immediate and unconditional love of the people whom they believed supported them. Bateman even rejected the FARC's stale vocabulary, as dated as photographs of La Violencia. "We are not a movement of the masses or a political party, we are armed propagandists and that is the end of it," he once told a journalist.

Vera Grabe, an early member, was recruited—and seduced—by Bateman, who had a wife and a series of other, sometimes simultaneous lovers. Daughter of German immigrants, she was typical of many recruits: college educated, cosmopolitan, drawn in by the M-19's romance and intrigue. In her memoirs, it is hard to disentangle the political from the amorous assault.

[Bateman] captivated me. There were no slogans or demands, but rather trust and a freshness. Confidence in the people, which showed a confidence in himself and what [the M-19] was doing. What surprised me–and many others–was that in this group, not only was everything more informal, but it was also more real. There was room for doubt. It wasn't an alley with no exit. It did not mean that one had to break with whatever one had previously thought or done, but just the reverse, to give everything and be with every one.

The M-19 was the FARC's opposite. Its adherents had learned to think before they learned to fight. Like Marín, those in the FARC had learned to fight before they learned to think.

ooooo

OUT OF THE SPOTLIGHT, THE FARC WAITED. AS THE EXPULSION OF Bateman showed, Marin was not interested in expanding his appeal beyond disaffected peasants or slum dwellers. He occupied rural areas few Colombians cared about or even visited. The *ruana* Marín draped over his shoulder was a badge of humble origin and persistence that spoke powerfully to peasants, not university students. In some rural areas, joining the FARC (and to a similar extent, the ELN) became as settled a career track as law or teaching. A few, like Guillermo Saénz Vargas, known as "Alfonso Cano," joined after completing university degrees, drawn out of an intellectual commitment to revolution.

But most were more like Jorge Briceño Suarez, known as "Mono Jojoy," currently the thirty-something commander of the FARC forces in southern Colombia. The nickname comes from Briceño's fair complexion (called *mono* in Colombia) and a monkey common in the jungle; it fits his cunning and gleefully destructive style. Mono Jojoy is among the FARC's most effective field commanders and is considered a likely successor to the now seventy-something Marín. He wears a black beret that evokes Che Guevara, though his significant belly, pushing insistently at the camouflage he favors, speaks of more sybaritic pleasures. The Toyota Prado 4x4 Mono Jojoy drives (the deluxe edition retails for $50,000 in the United States, though it is very likely that Mono Jojoy's car was either stolen or part of an extortion payment) once drew criticism from "Alfonso Cano," who preaches the austerity he practices as a fellow member of the General Secretariat, the FARC governing body. Mono Jojoy was unrepentant. Once, he told journalists that he joined the guerrillas because he had a talent for war, like being good at math. "I was nothing when I was a civilian. I was created by weapons," he said.

By millennium's end, the powerful logic that had rescued Marín from the senselessness of La Violencia had become an end in itself, as stuck in place as the trigger of a rusted gun. The same qualities that allowed him to survive treachery—an animal caution and a loyalty only to those closest to him—prevented Marín from examining the cost of this war to Colombia and his increasingly remote chance of ever seizing power. Instead, Marín, a frugal man, gathered what he had and made war his business. For the young men and women who continue to join him, war is now a culture and their reason for being—war as an end in itself, a profession and an identity and a lens through which to view the world. One analyst once labeled the FARC "autistic," and the description contains a bitter truth. Around Marín are men like Mono Jojoy, who views power through the muzzle of a gun as a birthright and an inevitability, like age but with none of its burdens.

What is left to be arranged, then, are the mechanics of survival. How does Marín pay and feed his fighters? How can he keep them dressed and mobile, trained and eager? Money was something Marín needed to sustain the FARC even as popular support among Colombians dwindled. One source of cash was kidnapping.

Kidnapping in Colombia dates to at least the 1960s, when criminals used it to collect ransoms. The guerrillas embraced the technique a decade later and in the 1980s transformed it into big business. ELN leader Gerardo Bermúdez Sánchez, known as "Francisco Galán," once told me that guerrillas began kidnapping as a response to General Camacho's technique of "disappearing" people. But kidnap victims now far outnumber the "disappeared." Still suffering the debacle at Anorí in 1973, ten years later the ELN kidnapped a German engineer and two Colombian employees of the German multinational Mannesmann. They got $1 million for him and used it to recover and expand by a factor of five in just one year.

Currently, guerrillas take an average of 1,500 people per year, putting Colombia first on the list of countries where kidnapping is rampant. "Mono Jojoy" has defended kidnapping by describing hostages as members of the hated "oligarchy" and therefore deserving of their fate. The ransom is a "tax" those in the middle class must pay, just as they pay the government. But the truth is that most of the guerrillas' victims are average Colombians. After all, the really rich have bodyguards and security walls and bulletproof cars. In *Confesiones de un secuestrado*, a chronicle of his captivity in the late 1990s, a Colombian bank executive described his first meeting with the FARC commander responsible for determining the amount of his ransom. The executive had just completed an exhausting forced march to the guerrillas' mountain camp, where he could tell that dozens of other Colombians had been imprisoned or still waited for their freedom in the huts that passed for shelter:

FARC   What assets do you have, you old son of a bitch?

EXECUTIVE   A 1993 Subaru pickup truck that I am still paying off.

FARC   I am not asking you what you owe, just what you have. Everyone says the same thing, they have nothing, only debts. Tell the truth to me or I'll send you to be hung by your balls! And be careful not to forget anything, remember that your family and everything that you own can be blown up by a bomb.

EXECUTIVE   I have a house with a mortgage.

FARC   What is it worth? What else do you have? Cattle? Land? Be careful, because here liars have stayed for more than seven years until they finally remember what they possess. I will order a relative of yours hooded and brought here to confront you and then of course you will have to tell the truth.

EXECUTIVE   Bring him–I responded–I have nothing more.

FARC   How much in the bank?

EXECUTIVE   Overdrawn–I said.

FARC   Get lost, you son of a bitch, before I bust that face!

In the late 1990s, Marín told his commanders that they were responsible for their own finances and could not depend on the leadership for cash, so some converted their troops into kidnapping specialists. Guerrillas began *"pescas milagrosas,"* miraculous fishing trips, by mounting roadblocks on heavily traveled roads and taking any traveler who appeared solvent. In 2000, the FARC announced a new "revolutionary law": Law 002 (Law 001 dated from the 1960s and related to land reform). Law 002 required everyone with assets of more than $1 million to pay the FARC the equivalent of 10 percent of their worth, effective immediately. The consequence for not paying was a kidnapping. To underscore the law's existence, guerrillas took a three-year-old boy from his Bogotá home and kept him for nineteen months.

Kidnapping has served its narrow purpose, but it has also damaged the FARC's credibility as a group purporting to fight for most Colombians. Another tactic that has further eroded any popular support they may elicit is their use of gas cylinder bombs. This bomb is confected out of a propane tank, nails, dynamite, and a launching tube. Guerrillas fill the propane tank with a mixture of gunpowder, metal shards, and propane. Through a hole in a metal tube, they thread a slow wick connected to sticks of dynamite. On top of the dynamite they pack dirt. Then, guerrillas load the propane cylinder on top of the dirt, which acts as a cushion. When the dynamite explodes, it propels the dirt and the propane tank into the air. The tubes are installed on the beds of pickup trucks, which can approach a target surreptitiously, then scurry away after the tank is launched.

The invention, also called a "barracks buster," was developed by the Irish Republican Army (IRA) to attack the British in Northern Ireland. The weapon is cheap and easy to assemble. But it cannot be aimed reliably. The aim is influenced by a dozen variables: the angle of the tube, the elevation of the pickup truck, the wind, the amount of dynamite in the charge, the amount of material in the tank, the expertise of the guerrillas. That means that in attacks, a number of the cylinders always land on homes, stores, and offices. "It takes us at least three shots to get the aim right," one guerrilla told journalists in May 2002, by way of explaining why the FARC had launched a gas cylinder bomb into a church where refugees were housed in Bellavista, Antioquia. A single cylinder killed 119 people, over forty of them children.

Attacks like these made the headlines and outraged Colombians and outsiders alike. Just as disturbing to me were the everyday incidents that rarely received more than cursory mention in Colombia's press. These more mundane acts suggested to me that not only was Marín uninterested in gaining support. By his seventh decade, he had authorized a deliberate campaign meant to maximize terror. It was as if he had once again become the angry man in his Uncle Manuel's shack, with no purpose but revenge. With increasing frequency, Marín's forces matched and occasionally even outdid the macabre theatrics that had once marked La Violencia.

In 1995, for instance, guerrillas planned to ambush a bus transporting twenty-four banana workers loyal to a political group they considered a rival. As I later learned from investigators, the guerrillas missed the bus they had meant to stop. Rather than plan the action for another day, they simply caught the next bus. The passengers were not the people they sought and they knew it. Nevertheless, the guerrillas forced the men to lie face down on the ground, then executed them one by one. Some were beheaded. Later, news photographers took the shot the FARC seemed to have designed just for the cameras: dead men lined in a row that paralleled the bus, a Colombian *chiva*, incongruously festive with its bright primary colors and open sides meant to catch the rare, refreshing breeze. A guerrilla later explained to a local reporter that they meant to send a message to anyone who challenged their control. Challenges would not be tolerated. The fact that the dead did not belong to the rival political group mattered not at all. What mattered was the power of the message sent by the bodies laid out in the road.

In my interviews with them, guerrillas would promise to stop abuses and issue orders that would protect the innocent. Afterward, I would see news or hear reports that showed that nothing had changed. Also, guerrillas would try to woo me with what they described as their *fariana*, or FARC, culture, to show that they were not just waging a war but building an alternative world. They had songs, poetry, art, festival days (like the anniversary of Marquetalia), and a kind of guerrilla chic of camouflage and gun holsters and the knee-high rubber boots necessary to navigate Colombia's muddy trails. Marín was the distant, revered founder. But it was Mono Jojoy who epitomized their aspiration, a jolly, vicious, fun-loving murderer who drives a flashy vehicle with his pistol on his hip, girls on the running boards, and a rum bottle at the ready. There are some who believe that it is he, and not Marín, who is really in control and sets the new tone of an army now seeking a new reason for being. Once, a guerrilla gave me little wallet calendars decorated with photographs of beautiful boy and girl guerrillas bathing in sparkling streams, grouped around campfires, and dancing and grinning contentedly into the camera lens with their arms draped around each other's shoulders. It was summer camp with sex included, the guns the only real clue that they were not on holiday.

I took away a different message, not the one that these guerrillas intended. It was reflected in the joke a humanitarian aid worker once told me as we toured the latest refugee camp created by Colombia's fighting. Mono Jojoy is preparing for Christmas, so he approaches the nearest church to make his gift request. In Colombia, children leave requests for presents with the Virgin Mary, who then delivers them to the Baby Jesus. In his note, Mono Jojoy describes his behavior as excellent. He asks for a bicycle. But the Virgin Mary glares. Mono Jojoy has to start over. "I have been trying to be good," he writes, "and I want a bicycle." The Virgin continues to glare. He revises his note again and again, each time revealing more of the true nature of his behavior. Nothing works on her. Finally, Mono Jojoy tosses off a sentence and throws it at the Virgin Mary's feet. "Unless you give me a bicycle," the note says, "you'll never see the Baby Jesus again."

THE HIPPOPOTAMUS

THERE IS A CYCLE TO VIOLENCE IN COLOMBIA JUST AS THERE IS A cycle to the lives of most of the people who live there. Not only the good die—so do the bad or indifferent. People are also maimed and scared and vengeful and unrepentant. Killers kill again. Things are always bad around Christmas and in August, peaking before an election, after a big soccer game, on weekends, when there are parties. When there are not parties. But there are always parties.

For many years, I believed it necessary to my work to drink and dance as much as my Colombian colleagues. That meant a lot. My ears would ring from the salsa blared in a string of dark and mildewed bars. I danced every night in cigarette smoke and the fumes of rum and *aguardiente,* which tastes of licorice and is as sweet and potent as liquid sugar. After my visits to Colombia, I would be so hung over that it would take me days to recover a firm grasp on the horizon. I would like to say that I eventually learned my lesson and practiced moderation. The truth was that I swore off the grief and the rum that was a kind of supercocktail. The sad stories embraced me by day and at night a salsa beat shook me from my ankles to my ears. My dreams were pursuit and Piel Roja cigarettes, dry-mouthed hunts where I watched, in colors as lurid as polyester dancing shirts, my personal dramatizations of what had been described to me. There was never enough coffee in the mornings to fully shake the night's alcohol-soaked edge. So I embraced my inabilities. I pledged the secret society of Colombians who prefer jazz and lemonade. It's easy to spot us, the flightless birds who grip the edge of the dance floor.

I don't linger. My nightly ritual is the news, which wastes no time on health and consumer stories (thankfully, Colombia has resisted the temptation of jokey meteorologists). Perhaps they have too much else to talk about. There are yesterday's massacres and the day's fresh tragedies, delivered in the rushed style drilled into the models employed as anchors. These men and women don't pretend to be reporters. They are professionally pretty. With twenty minutes worth of script, they cover atrocity, corruption, needless suffering, sports scores, and beauty pageant results.

Colombians are crazy for beauty pageants and have hundreds of competitions for titles like Miss Coffee, Miss Banana, Miss Petroleum and Miss Flower. The first Miss Colombia pageant was held in Cartagena to welcome U.S. president Franklin D. Roosevelt in 1934. Since television was introduced to the country, it has fixed its gimlet eye every November on the beauties gathered in Cartagena to vie for the crown. The Miss Colombia competition is more popular there than the Academy Awards are in the United States and draws half of the available television viewership on the competition's final day.

Colombian woman can be spectacular. During the Miss Colombia pageant, the loveliest among them parade on beaches, beside pools, and in restaurants. The country's largest network sends dozens of its staff to cover the three-week-long competition. Each day is tightly scripted and there is rarely unplanned scandal. But the coverage is not soft. The reporters review each contestant's anatomy with a chef's eye for prime cuts. Camera angles focus on breasts, hips, calves, and bellies, not necessarily to admire but to examine in detail. For hours, veteran reporters and former contestants discuss evidence of cellulite, a too-short torso, a too-long nose, or less-than-perky breasts. Plastic surgery is considered successful, a disaster, or insufficient, but never cheating. Done well, it is lauded as a way to slip the bonds of genetics and bad behavior and embrace beauty.

I don't remember seeing a talent competition. American talk-show host David Letterman once caused an outcry in Colombia after he joked on camera that a Miss Colombia had won the Miss Universe talent segment by swallowing fifty bags of heroin (he later invited the reigning Miss Colombia to his show and apologized). Most contestants are white, but not all are from wealthy or even middle-class families. In 2001, an Afro-Colombian won for the first time. A beauty plucked from a slum is hampered mainly by the costs associated with preparing to compete: plastic surgery, hair and makeup artists, personal trainers, gowns, instruction in walking, diction, and what to say. What ultimately matters is the final package, bone and tissue and hair shafts tinted and gelled into artificial nonchalance, not the effort expended to achieve it or where the contestant hails from.

Once, a beauty pageant even helped avert a coup. In 1999, the defense minister resigned, prompting Colombia's highest-ranking generals to threaten a walkout to express their support for him. The dispute was over the civilians' support for peace negotiations with guerrillas, a topic guaranteed to anger the brass. Cooler heads strategized that the evening's broadcast of the Miss Universe pageant–Miss Colombia was favored to reach the top ten–would help distract attention while measures were taken to ease tension. It worked. In the morning, the top generals remained at their desks. (Miss Botswana won.)

The Miss Colombia pageant coincides with Colombia's pre Christmas massacre season. Unlike their American counterparts, Colombian journalists often file graphic images of carnage. For a news viewer like me, the effect on a night's broadcast is striking. During pageant week, the newscast fills with talk of bodies. Sometimes, the broadcasts feel less like news than a macabre kind of performance art, as images compete to reveal the fragility of the human body or its beauty and the endless ways it can be molded, whittled, or twisted. There are whole bodies and also body parts, bodies dressed well or incompletely, bodies in water, body parts in water, bodies in the grass, bodies face down or face up. There are bodies from a distance. There are bodies close up. They are beautiful or gruesome or vacantly peaceful. Of course, the two types of bodies look nothing alike. But an occasional Colombian television viewer like me can't help but be impressed by the fascination for variations on the human form, either as a way to express hatred or to celebrate the female form.

Cartagena looks beautiful. I have never been there. I see what pageant organizers select of the salt-bitten stone walls and bright ocean vistas. These shots are a relief in comparison to the dank and close takes of the latest massacre site. Cartagena is yellow sun, blue sky, the white of the sand. Massacres are shadows and the color green or brown, from the grasses and leaves and beaten dirt at makeshift morgues. Sometimes, massacres seem as scripted as the pageants, as if all journalists sent to such events are told to film and narrate them in a certain way. People kneel in grief. Journalists in vests with the word *"PRENSA"* (press) bustle about, finding the best angles to relay the carnage. Authorities dither and stare. Various coverings are used to hide the bodies, but something always sneaks out. It could be a hand or a shoe, a distinctive cut of hair, a hat. It always seems to be the case that the faces, when they are visible, are calm, perhaps mildly surprised, yet resigned to this final display of their earthly form.

To most Americans reading the news about Colombia, massacres appear as normal as sunsets. It is true, massacres have come to be a frequent occurrence. Yet I can identify certain peaks and valleys in the year. The calmest time is in early January, when many Colombians take advantage of Southern Hemisphere summer by going on vacation. It may well be that this is a false ebb and coincides mainly with the vacations so many journalists take. And November, as I said, always seems particularly bad, as if everyone bent on a little killing wanted to get it out of the way before the holiday parties begin in earnest.

But again, there are always parties. Sometimes, in the prickly quiet of my hotel, I hear them in the distance, the throb of music and the voices fading in as songs end. This is long after I sleep, when the busses have stopped running and the crowds of the day are gone. Parties sound alike no matter where you are. To my knowledge, none of the news anchors I am familiar with was a Miss Colombia. I imagine them as runner-ups in smaller contests for Miss Pensilvania or Miss Mango. I could write something here about the poetics of beautiful women dishing the day's horrors, something evocative or insightful–beauty and death, life and tragedy, grace and pathos. But I confess that I like seeing those pleasing faces before I close my eyes. I like hearing their clipped and careful diction making sense of the senseless. They soothe.

ooooo

THE STATE OF ANTIOQUIA LEADS COLOMBIA IN BOTH MISS COLOMBIAS and massacres. Among Colombia's most populous states, Antioquia is roughly the country's throat and lungs, sucking in the Caribbean at the

Gulf of Urabá, then opening wide to breathe in the humid and lush Magdalena River Valley as it cuts its way through the Andes. Slightly west, the smaller Cauca River cuts its own rocky way through the Western Range, which curls like a finger at Panama.

Although it gets much of its wealth from the rivers and jungle, Antioquia is in essence a mountain state. Its difficult terrain and abundant natural wealth have fostered a people known for their tenacity and hard work. The *paisas*–as people from Antioquia are known–are considered canny, avaricious, out for a fast peso. Many *turcos* settled here, so there are Abads, Turbays, Cafarzuzas (a mangling of Kafarsouseh), and Ferises in the markets and banks, especially along the Caribbean coast. One joke has a *paisa* discovering a magic lantern in his yard. After he rubs it, a genie appears and offers three wishes. The only catch is that the man's neighbor will receive the double of each wish. So the *paisa* asks for a beautiful blond, a fortune, and a fright that leaves him half dead.

Unusual in Latin America and much of the rest of Colombia, Antioquia encouraged small-scale farms, not rich and absentee landowners. A robust and politically engaged middle class was the result. In the early 1900s, textile mills drew farmers to the capital, Medellín, and the backwater became a factory city and financial center, playing New York to Bogotá's Washington. With a population of over 2 million, Medellín is now Colombia's second-largest city. Among Colombians, Medellín has a reputation for business success and the arts. It is home to one of Colombia's leading universities, the University of Antioquia, one of its most powerful business consortiums, the Sindicato Antioqueño, and some of its most thoughtful politicians and most interesting artists (such as the painter and sculptor Fernando Botero). Its temperate climate makes it a refuge from the steaming lowlands and frigid heights. In Medellín's government plaza, a sculpture celebrates the *paisas* who colonized the difficult terrain. Human figures are lifted on the sharp edge of a three-story-tall machete pointing into the sky. Called "Monument to the Race," it is a Colombian Vooertrekker monument, communicating both pride in *paisa* identity and a threat to anyone who stands in the way.

Medellín's reputation outside Colombia is quite different. In 1992, the first time I visited, my stomach clutched as the wheels of the

Avianca jet from Bogotá touched its tarmac. This was, after all, Medellín, the world's murder capital. At the time, the city's homicide rate was roughly 260 murder victims per 100,000 residents. Detroit—considered among the most violent American cities, though substantially smaller than Medellín—had a rate of 60 per 100,000. Medellín was also home of the Medellín Cartel, the drug trafficking network that dominated the trade in the 1980s.

In part, the violence brought me to Medellín. I hoped to find out why children were drawn into it and what might be done to keep them out of danger. I was also appalled by it. How could people, I wondered, live a seemingly normal life—work, shopping, parties, school—in the midst of so much bloodshed? As I left the Avianca jet, I entertained fantasies of bullets zinging into the terminal, screams erupting to the screeching of the baggage claim carts. Of course, nothing of the sort occurred. My seat mate was an executive, dressed in a crisp suit appropriate for a day's worth of meetings and an evening flight back to Bogotá. On the long drive into the city, the trees were the vivid green of a child's drawing. Picturesque houses—white, with red banisters across a second-floor balcony, highlighted with brilliant pink and purple bougainvillea—nestled in the small hollows. At the time, they seemed incongruous, given the city's reputation for violence, pasted in from some crazed tour brochure hawking tourist gloss in the midst of danger. Slender men and women walked the road's shoulder. Their gracefulness as cars and trucks sped past, so close that the air wakes ruffled hair and pressed polyester shirts and skirts to bodies, seemed at the time to me almost as exotic as the sight of a Kazakh horseman.

Around a curve, the panorama of Medellín opened as suddenly as a fall in a dream. Who would build a city there, I thought, wedged into such a narrow, steep valley? Its skyscrapers were breathtaking, gleaming white spires against the magnificent lift of the Andes. Along Medellín's shopping avenues, I later discovered, you could buy designer labels—just the labels, mind you, carefully trimmed—to whipstitch into your shirts and pants. In the poorest neighborhoods, young men had new motorcycles and women swept their shacks with hands laden with gold-colored rings.

That night, I met some colleagues for a drink on the roof of the ho-

tel where I was staying. As Pablo and Vicky, Medellín natives, chatted,
a breeze ruffled the cocktail napkins. The city cupped us like a rhine-
stone bowl. Night deepened, and its sides melted into the stars above.
The sides were the *comunas*, or slums, where most of the killings took
place. Yet at a distance, with the grime obscured and the want invisible, they seemed adornment, a tasteful setting for the power and glam-
our of Medellín's skyscrapers. Violating the norm in Latin America,
the rich live low and the poor live high, with a stunning view of the
opulence of the flats. Although *comuna* can be translated as "com-
mune," what residents share generally goes no further than desperation. That desperation did not lead most *comuna* residents staring
down at the pools and the Ferraris and the designer clothing to hate
the rich. They wanted to be rich. The steeper the street, the more desperate the want. Medellín was a well of desire. With a gun and a motorcycle, virtually anyone could get rich. The trick in Medellín was not
getting money, but staying alive. Money was everywhere, in quantities
that were quite literally impossible to comprehend.

Vicky was a lawyer and represented victims of violence. Pablo
worked for an organization that proposed ways to stop violence. Two
of Vicky's colleagues had been shot on a central Medellín street, assassins unknown. Pablo worked in the *comunas*, where what he called a
war between the police and youth gangs was then at its peak. The city
was under a kind of military siege, as the authorities backed by the
United States scoured the streets for drug trafficker Pablo Escobar, who
had left his prison (essentially a luxury retreat) and was on the run.

Most of the dead were young men. Some took part in the violence
as hired killers or gang members. Others were young men guilty only
of being young, whom the police hunted as representatives of a poisoned generation. At night, it was virtually impossible to move in the
city because of the dozens of police roadblocks. Police fell on house after house in their search for the fugitive Escobar. Sometimes, the dead
were unrecognizable, their faces burned with acid and their fingers,
feet, and teeth removed.

Yet on top of that hotel, sipping cool drinks, we were not surrounded by war journalists or disaster aid professionals or missions of
church people who had come out of the goodness of their hearts to
one of the world's trouble spots. There was laughter and low talk, a

beautiful dress, lovers secreted in a dark corner of the poolside dining area. I remember the marvelous sparkling bowl that surrounded us, the whisper of the breeze. Of course, we did talk about what had brought me to the city. In my journal, I wrote that night: "Everyone is waiting for the surrender of Pablo Escobar, but a tension prevails as he hunts and is hunted. When I arrived, the town was full of the news that his main bodyguard had surrendered. A day later, after being released, two of his bodyguards were shot right here in Medellín. The bodies had more than fifty bullet holes apiece."

ooooo

PABLO ESCOBAR WAS BORN NEAR MEDELLÍN. AFTER HE BECAME THE world's most infamous drug trafficker—and among the richest men on the planet—he peddled a myth of a poor upbringing, part of a sophisticated, brutal campaign to win sympathy and a permanent place in Colombian politics. But it wasn't true. Escobar wasn't raised in a *comuna*, but was part of Medellín's middle class. Like many Colombian fathers, his, a farmer, was usually absent. His mother, Hermilda, was a teacher. She raised the family of seven pretty much on her own.

Hermilda gave her children a classic Colombian upbringing of strict and spirit-haunted Catholicism, an emphasis on school, and a hunger for status, if only through a better quality of shirt, a late-model car, or a fancier house. Obeying the law was preferable, but definitely optional if circumstances required. The example had been set by Escobar's maternal grandfather. He had raised Hermilda on the profits of a Colombian home brew known as *tapetusa*. To smuggle it past the authorities, he used empty coffins and hollowed eggs. As a girl, Hermilda had once been tricked into letting police into the house to search for the *tapetusa* stash. They arrested her father. But after making a deal with police, he was released and was soon smuggling more than ever.

In his memoirs, Escobar's eldest brother, Roberto, recalled how his mother taught school during the day and at night cleaned the house, shopped, cooked, sewed all of their clothes, and did the wash, providing them with "simple, but very clean clothes." Yet a thread of larceny and desire runs through even this familiar tale. Once, Roberto wrote, Pablo was sent home from school because he had gone without shoes.

Hermilda's paycheck as a teacher always arrived late. So she shoplifted a pair of shoes from a local merchant. She inadvertently brought home two different sizes, however. Crushed, she confessed to a priest, who counseled her to return the shoes. Understanding her motivation, the merchant found her the correct size and sold them on credit.

The lesson was simple but was repeated often in Escobar's childhood–having little money was no excuse for looking poor. The authorities agreed. In Medellín, appearance is half the battle. To remedy this lamentable situation, the authorities would cut deals, even with God.

Escobar followed in his grandfather's footsteps by smuggling ciga rettes, liquor, clothing, and household appliances picked up at the *paisa* port of Turbo on Colombia's Caribbean coast. In the 1970s, Colombia was awash in marijuana. The trade brought in so many American dollars that the government authorized the Bank of the Republic, a kind of Federal Reserve, to begin exchanging them for Colombian pesos, no questions asked.

It was a friend Roberto called "Cockroach" (Cucaracho) who told the Escobars about a better business–cocaine. At the time, the *coca* bushes used to manufacture cocaine were concentrated in Peru's Upper Huallaga Valley and Bolivia's Chapare region. The bush looks like a dwarf Yaupon holly. It flourishes on the slopes of the forests that mark the transition from mountain to jungle. In Peru, farmers grew and harvested it themselves, ripping the leaves from the branches with a single pull from trunk to tip. After a day's worth of work, their hands and the hands of their wives and children and the boys hired to help out would be green from the alkaloid sap that contains cocaine. Yet even if a harvester licked the sap, there would be no cocaine rush. To activate, the alkaloid must be paired with a catalyst, like a crumb of limestone or ash. In Peru, highland dwellers call this the *llipta,* inserted into the mouth with the dried leaves. For centuries, highlanders have used the leaves in religious ceremonies and as a way to dull fatigue and hunger. *Coca* is chewed like tobacco, then spit out when the chaw is through.

The Escobars were after more than leaves. For decades, farmers had been able to process leaves for their alkaloid content and produce a powder that could be further refined for export to the United States. Once the leaves are gathered in sacks, the farmers take them to crude "kitchens" in the forest. In vats made of wood and black plastic, *cocineros,* or cooks, stir them into a series of chemical stews. Men stir the leaves like rustic vintners crush grapes, tramping them with their bare feet. After each stage, the effluent is poured off and the sediment is further refined.

On his first trip, what Escobar bought was the raw cocaine, called *pasta básica,* or *base,* as dense as a cake of brown sugar. It was easier to haul than appliances or the fragrant bales of marijuana. What's more, it promised fabulous profits. Escobar bought a truck in Peru and fashioned a cargo area under the mud flaps. As a test, he drove a kilo of raw cocaine grown and refined in Peru across three borders into Colombia. He was not caught or even questioned. Within a couple of months, he was bringing across twenty kilos per trip and had to buy larger vehicles with more room.

Roberto said that he and Pablo further refined the *pasta básica* in Roberto's Medellín house, using old refrigerators they refashioned into rudimentary ovens to leach out the brown impurities and crystallize finished white cocaine. Commercial-grade cocaine hydrochloride is a white salt that is between 65 to 75 percent pure. The deadly crack is manufactured entirely in the United States; dealers take the cocaine powder and cook it with baking soda and water, a process that extracts the hydrochloride molecule. The rock residue crackles when it is lit, giving the drug its name. The vapor that users inhale through a cigarette or pipe is a full and highly addictive dose of pure cocaine. Using more volatile chemicals, the process known as freebasing produces a similar, pure cocaine.

Pablo and Roberto would wrap the cocaine in blocks, mark it with their "brand," and pack it into suitcases with false bottoms. Couriers known as "mules" hauled it to the United States on commercial flights. The profits in dollars would return in those same suitcases, $60,000 per kilo. Roberto's dreams of becoming a professional bicycle racer were soon overshadowed by his new talents for refining and wholesaling cocaine.

In 1976, Roberto recalled, Pablo was arrested and charged with possession of raw cocaine hidden in the spare tire of a truck. Moved to a prison, he fled when he thought the Colombian army was about to seize him. Until 1987, Colombian civilians could be prosecuted by the military, a legacy left by General Camacho. That day, Roberto said, Hermilda got a telephone call from the prison warden. He explained to her that Escobar's escape made his legal situation worse. "Immediately, my mother called Pablo and she personally took him back to the prison. Pablo and I always did what our mother ordered us to do."

From his cell, Escobar finessed and bribed his way out. The case was dismissed for lack of evidence. Then Escobar turned his attention to killing the men he believed had turned him in. As his mother had in the incident of the mismatched shoes, Escobar made a deal with the authorities and got what he wanted. The killing part was his innovation on what was by then a distinctive family style.

Even other traffickers were afraid of him. In an interview with the Public Broadcasting series *Frontline,* fellow trafficker Jorge Ochoa said that Escobar's violent streak surprised him. "Frankly, he intimidated us, and many other people in Medellín, Cali, and Bogotá. He intimidated everyone. It wasn't just us, but the rest of Colombia and all of the United States. . . . He thought that whatever he wanted is the way it should be done, and he didn't ask anyone for an opinion. He didn't take anyone into account to do this or that."

By 1981, Escobar had killed and threatened his way to the top. He was king, El Patrón, the Boss. Before him, people had killed in Colombia for a cause, for loyalty, out of anger, for vengeance, to protect what they thought was theirs. Escobar was an innovator. He killed for all that and more: for money.

ooooo

AT FIRST, ROBERTO SAID, IT HARDLY EVEN FELT LIKE CRIME. IT TOOK a lot of work to navigate the treacherous Andean roads, then cook the cocaine. Anyway, it was the *gringos,* the Americans, getting high, not Colombians. For himself, Escobar preferred marijuana. The Ochoas drank scotch and fine wines. The fact that El Patrón was sticking it to the *gringos* was an extra, like the lemon twist on a cocktail. It made the profits seem like free money. Colombian police and judges looked the other way. Or they were in on it. Smuggling has a long and illustrious history in Medellín, and what was being smuggled—*tapetusa* or cocaine or crates of Marlboros and Old Milwaukee beer—didn't much matter.

Smugglers were local heroes, engines of economic power and lots of fun, to boot.

One of the hardest partyers was Carlos Lehder Rivas, who had pioneered the first cocaine flights into the United States. A short, darkly handsome man, Lehder had moods that swung sharply from visionary euphoria to homicidal rage (fueled, in part, by the product he liberally sampled). At one point, Lehder converted an entire Bahamian island into a shipment center. Only one in every 100 cocaine flights was detected by U.S. authorities. At five flights a week, a normal rate, that meant a gross profit of $200 million a month, over $2 billion a year. By 1982, cocaine earned Colombia more than coffee and made up an estimated 30 percent of its total exports.

One of Escobar's shipment centers was especially ingenious. On a ranch in Colombia's eastern plains, Escobar ordered a landing strip built behind the main house. He found some Medellín families to move there and built them houses, each equipped with wooden wheels. As Roberto explained, "When the airplanes loaded with raw cocaine arrived from Peru, over the radio they would give a warning, and the workers would push the rolling houses to the side, leaving the landing strip clear for the pilots to see. It was a rapid operation. Each family had the obligation to move its rolling house in three minutes."

Roberto estimated that it took the U.S. Drug Enforcement Administration (DEA) between three to five years to discover each innovation in the way they shipped cocaine north. By then, the traffickers would have moved on to something new. Single flights gave way to flotillas of Air Commanders, which were replaced by 727 jets bought from defunct Eastern Airlines, capable of carrying 10,000 kilos of cocaine on a single trip. The cocaine was hidden in fish powder, freezers, bales that would sink in shallow waters and beep their position to specially equipped boats, liquid rubber, wine, and remote control submarines built by Russians laid off from shipyards in Severodvinsk and St. Petersburg after the collapse of the Soviet Union.

Escobar began to hang out with a new crowd. He aspired to join Medellín's elites, the *paisas* Hermilda had taught him to admire. They had made their fortunes in land and cattle and manufacturing, some with no more scruples, he felt, than he and the street thugs who had taken over the cocaine business. When he chose to, Escobar could be quite polite and charming. He especially admired the Ochoas, who had originally dabbled in cocaine only to earn extra money to breed show cattle and Paso Fino horses. Roberto Escobar, an avid bicyclist, even bought himself a Paso Fino stallion named Terremoto de Manizales (Manizales Earthquake) for $2 million.

At first, Medellín's leading families looked down on the capos. Despite their pedigree, the Ochoas were snubbed at the country clubs and top restaurants. Juan David Ochoa later told one interviewer that the cocaine business began to sour for them not because of the threat of jail time, but when "the kids weren't being accepted into the [private] schools—when we started to do badly in the social sense."

Others, however, were eager to party on the riches that seemed to shower the city like rain. The family of my friend Teresa was among them. They were neither rich nor poor. Before his retirement, her father had worked at an office and was proud of the gleaming glass buildings and fashionable shops and sleek automobiles that narco-wealth brought Medellín. It made Teresa's family feel like true world citizens, like the America they saw on television sitcoms and in Hollywood movies. In their eyes, local elites were not so clean. They had earned their place in society through the old pursuits of ranching and textiles that had, in some cases, the still pungent scent of the trickery practiced under the veil of La Violencia. Their exclusive clubs, pleasing country retreats, and sense of entitlement grated on *paisa* families like Teresa's. So when the narcos threw open their doors and tossed invitations like Mardi Gras coins, Teresa's family grabbed what was within reach.

Escobar bought a ranch in 1979 called Nápoles, a sprawling, seventeen-mile spread on the Magdalena River. Named by the conquistador Jiménez de Quesada, the Magdalena creates a physical gulf between Bogotá and Medellín. On the property, Escobar built seventeen lakes, a bull ring, a hospital, a mansion, and the Mamarosa airport and heliport. At its peak, Mamarosa employed over 200 people and hosted twelve flights a day, south and north, picking up raw cocaine in Peru and Bolivia, bringing it north to Colombian laboratories, then making the final leg to the United States. Sometimes, there were so many dollars entering Nápoles on the return flights that it was impossible to count them. Instead, Escobar had the dollars baled and weighed, then calculated their value.

At Nápoles, Escobar once hosted a birthday party for Manuela, his daughter. My friend Teresa was invited. She and a dozen other little girls gathered at Medellín's airport to take the short helicopter ride. "There were clowns and animals and balloons and cake," Teresa remembered, "and everyone was so nice. It was only later that I realized why she had such a big birthday party. At the time, such things seemed almost normal."

Teresa remembered seeing animals but couldn't describe a single one. That's just one measure of how easily Medellín fell into a kind of stupor with cocaine wealth. Teresa's memories of that party are as hallucinatory as the dream sequence in *The Nutcracker,* with dancing sugarplums and giant mice. At the time, Escobar reportedly kept 2,000 African zebras, antelopes, buffalo, and hippopotamuses at Nápoles.

The animals grazing through the drone of airplanes and helicopters served multiple purposes. They burnished Escobar's image as a man who gave back to the community. Colombians could visit the ranch to see them, a popular attraction for parents looking for a day's outing for the children. They fed Escobar's outsized ego, since the Ochoas also kept exotic animals. Legend has it that for a time, Escobar used the feces to coat packets of cocaine and fool drug-sniffing dogs. For many years, the Colombians couldn't—or wouldn't—charge Escobar with drug smuggling. But a fearless—or clueless—customs inspector did try to charge him with illegally importing the animals. Even that didn't stick.

Years later, after Escobar was dead and the ranch abandoned, the Colombian government seized it and resettled there hundreds of families displaced by war. The authorities removed the Cessna that had once adorned the formal entry gate (Escobar claimed it had flown his first kilos north). The authorities left the rest—the pool covered in algae, the bull ring carpeted with weeds, the cobwebs and mold the only remaining decor in the main house. In a garage sit the remains of Escobar's collection of vintage automobiles, charred and twisted relics of his battle with the Cali Cartel (in 1993, the rival cartel helped place bombs in the warehouse where the vehicles were stored). Most of the animals were relocated to zoos in Bogotá and Cali. But the hippopotamus, a Medellín taxi driver once told me, had escaped. He said that the locals told him that the beast had made a home along the Magdalena's banks, where the muddy deltas and fallen bananas and papayas became its solitary Africa. The taxi driver did not claim to have seen the hippo. Nor had anyone I later questioned about it. Occasionally, though, people said that farmers would find a fence crushed as if by tremendous force. Night splashes were heard. Bellowings. Paths to the water were trampled. There were curious leavings in the water.

But few who dared peer into the workings of Escobar's empire later prospered. People preferred not to inquire. That evidence, those noises, could be something quite different, the driver said to me. Escobar also dumped his victims there, like pieces of a human puzzle tossed into the Magdalena's current.

"Who knows," he said, shrugging, "what you might find in the weeds?"

ooooo

MERE RICHES DID NOT SATISFY ESCOBAR. AFTER PARLAYING RUTHlessness into a place among the world's wealthiest human beings, money no longer seemed to thrill him. What Escobar craved was status, respect, recognition. He wanted a seat at Colombia's large table. It ended up being the most lasting of Hermilda's lessons. Escobar was too lazy and corrupt to earn it. But he had the cash to buy it. If that didn't work, he had dynamite and guns.

Like his parents, Pablo Escobar belonged to the Liberal Party. He bought a seat as a substitute Medellín city council member in 1978. Four years later, he arranged to be the substitute congressman for Envigado, the Medellín suburb where Hermilda had once taught elementary school. Substitutes have the same privileges as the elected officeholder and in their absence can vote and take part in debate.

At the same time, Escobar began making large donations to the *comunas*. He built soccer fields, housing, and roads. As Roberto wrote in his memoirs, Pablo had an especially close relationship with the Catholic Church, since he had donated millions to church-sponsored charities. Among the church leaders he spoke to most frequently was Monsignor Darío Castrillón, at the time the bishop of Pereira, a coffee-growing center not far from Josué's home in Pensilvania. Now a cardinal who is a leading candidate to be elected the first Latin American pope, Castrillón once said that he accepted Escobar's money to prevent its use in "illegal activities."

At about the same time, Escobar's honeymoon with law enforcement ended. The crack explosion in the United States and increasing concern about the link between drug trafficking and crime prompted a change in the attitude of the Americans. On the urging of the United States, Washington and Bogotá ratified an extradition treaty in 1981. For the first time, the Americans had the ability to bring traffickers like Escobar to the United States for trial and imprisonment. In 1986, President Ronald Reagan signed Directive No. 221, which declared drugs a national security threat. Funding for the treatment of drug addicts in the United States began the decline that continues to this day. Instead, what began to be called "the war on drugs" was focused on the source countries, among them Peru (where the *coca* was grown) and Colombia (where criminal syndicates like the one controlled by Escobar refined, packaged, and sent cocaine north).

To drum up the political support necessary to fund the new war, the Americans needed a good enemy. Escobar and his cartoonish cronies could have been cast by Hollywood. With his fortune, Carlos Lehder mounted a political party with Nazi sympathies that had as its main proposal the legalization of drugs. In his home state of Quindío, he paid the city fathers to erect a statue of John Lennon. Lehder was the first to be extradited to the United States and is currently serving a fifty-five-year sentence. Another associate was Gonzalo Rodríguez Gacha, a rough, profane man who got his start in the emerald trade. Rodríguez lacked Escobar's ambition. He was content to make piles of money (some of which is still rumored to be buried beneath his former houses across Colombia). In 1984, Colombian National Police and the DEA raided the cartel's largest laboratory, Tranquilandia. The DEA had found it by placing tiny transmitters in barrels of ether that the Ochoas bought in the United States and shipped to Colombia for use in refining cocaine. At Tranquilandia, the police found 13.8 metric tons of cocaine, worth at least $34 million. It was the most cocaine they had ever seen in one place.

The Medellín Cartel took its own lesson from the raid on Tranquilandia. The U.S. war on drugs was getting serious. It was the first bust that really hurt. They fought back. Months later, killers paid by the cartel murdered Justice Minister Rodrigo Lara Bonilla in Bogotá. Lara had committed two sins that Escobar could not forgive. Lara supported extradition. And for the first time in public, he had linked Escobar to trafficking. It was during a speech on the floor of Colombia's Congress in 1983. Although this was a *secreto a gritos*, a "screamed secret" in Colombian parlance, it had earned the thirty-five-year-old minister Escobar's fury.

Lara was the first government minister murdered while in office in Colombian history. The killers used a new tactic: the *parrillero*. The *parrillero* is the passenger who rides behind the driver of a motorcycle. When armed, the passenger can shoot, then escape on a high-speed bike. Lara was killed with a MAC-10, a submachine gun capable of plastering a car with .45 caliber slugs at thirteen rounds per second. As the gun catalogs explain, "burst fire is the only good tactic at close range. At blank range, going full auto allows the spread to pound your target to death."

Two decades later, *parrillero* killings are commonplace. Whenever violence gets particularly outrageous in a Colombian city, the mayor will ban motorcycles carrying *parrilleros*, producing an immediate, though temporary dip in the murder rate.

The Ochoas and other cartel associates denied planning Lara's murder, which they attributed solely to Escobar. Nevertheless, the crackdown that followed forced Escobar, Rodríguez, and the Ochoas to Panama for several months. But after a falling-out with General Manuel Noriega, they shifted to Nicaragua. It was soon after this move that the DEA took the famous photograph of Pablo Escobar personally loading an airplane that was headed north, part of a bucket brigade that included uniformed Sandinista soldiers.

But the Colombians pined for their homes and, as important, the safety of Colombia. They returned. Escobar vowed never to be forced out again. He was ready to wage war. Top on his hit list was anyone who supported extradition or tried to put the cartel leaders in jail for their crimes. The victims are well known in Colombia. Guillermo Cano, the editor of *El Espectador* and a critic of traffickers, was shot as he drove to work in 1986. Carlos Mauro Hoyos, who led a govern-

ment investigative agency, was shot the following year. With them are
thousands of other Colombians, among them bystanders killed by the
dozens of bombs Escobar ordered detonated in Medellín and Bogotá.

Judge Consuelo Sánchez investigated the Cano murder and found
that the evidence pointed directly at Escobar. During her inquiry, she
received a death threat signed "The Extraditables," the name used by
the Medellín Cartel. At the time, judges did the preliminary investigation of a crime, a task performed in the United States by the police and
district attorney. The threat informed her that issuing a warrant for Escobar's arrest would mean "commit[ting] an error that would stain
your life and would plague you until your dying day. You are perfectly
aware that we are capable of executing [you] any place on the planet.
... [B]e aware that if you call Mr. Pablo Escobar to trial, you will be
without forbears or descendants in your genealogical tree." The threat
went on to name numerous government employees already murdered
on Escobar's orders.

Sánchez was thirty-three, among the youngest judges in Colombia.
The government housed her on a military base and drove her around
in an armored car. She signed the warrant but paid dearly for it. "I was
doing the right thing, I knew, but I knew that I might pay with my life
for it," she told me over coffee in a Washington, D.C., Starbucks in
2001. Sánchez is a moon-faced, eager woman who still dresses in the
prim suits favored by female judges in Colombia. Once the warrant
was made public, the Colombian government flew her out of Colombia, to the only place they considered safe–the United States. There, a
local newspaper learned that she had taken the post of Colombian
consul in Detroit and published a story. Her neighbors asked her to
leave the apartment complex where she lived, fearful of Escobar's
transnational reach.

Sánchez was transferred to Washington, D.C., though she still did
not feel safe. The Medellín Cartel had long arms and did not pardon.
One gunman reputedly paid by the Ochoas murdered former cartel pilot turned DEA informant Barry Seal in Baton Rouge, Louisiana, in
1986. The following year, a gunman went all the way to Budapest,
Hungary, to shoot Lara's successor, former justice minister Enrique
Parejo González. Parejo had been sent to Colombia's embassy there
for his safety. He miraculously survived. Another justice minister, En-

rique Low Murtra, was sent to Sweden for the same reason. When he returned to Colombia and retired, a cartel gunman found him leaving the classroom where he was teaching in 1991 and killed him. In 1992, a baby-faced gunman was paid a reputed $1,500 to kill Manuel de Dios Unanue, a Cuban-born journalist who wrote for New York's Spanish-language press. Unanue had apparently infuriated a member of the Cali Cartel, José Santacruz Londoño, by publishing stories and photographs linking him to drug trafficking. To Americans, Santacruz was perhaps best known because he built above Cali a residence that was modeled on the White House. The seventeen-year-old assassin ambushed Unanue as he sat at a Queens bar.

Although her decision robbed her of her country and family, Judge Sánchez told me that she never regretted signing the warrant. "It was what I had to do, as a judge and as a Colombian." Still, Sánchez told me, she has nightmares about an attack. This is the image that stops her breath: a slip of a boy. A boy wearing a gold chain with a cross. A boy in fresh and costly sneakers. A boy turning toward her with eyes flat as nickels. A boy like thousands of others, a boy with a thousand faces. A boy who could come a thousand times for her, and another thousand, until she was dead. During the 1980s, the image of killer boys, the preferred *parrillero*, struck panic into the hearts of Colombians engaged in politics, journalism, and human rights work. But to the boys themselves, it was candy, as delectable to them as the image of the crowned Miss Colombia was to many of the girls. The *sicarios*, or killers, that Medellín is famous for are mostly boys from families that witnessed the horrors of La Violencia and fled to the city to save their children's lives. Instead of eluding violence, however, these families saw it woven even more firmly into the world that surrounded their surviving children and grandchildren.

Guerrillas were the first to see the potential of the boys. Guerrillas set up training camps among the shacks and gave the boys weapons, then invited the best among them to join their ranks. But some of the boys had other ideas. They formed gangs and began to rob. For Pablo Escobar, the boys were a natural resource, like the creek water needed to turn *coca* leaves into cocaine. The *comunas* became a proving ground for the thugs Escobar needed to protect his interests and confront the authorities.

The boys are known by their nicknames, more attached to their faces than any baptismal words a priest spoke. Birthmark, Beer Gut, Green Eyes, Popeye, Beauty, Bad Face, Sausage, Bullfrog, Earring, Missile, Little Bear, Grime. The younger the better, as far as Escobar was concerned. Colombian law does not allow children to be prosecuted or punished as adults, and any child convicted of a serious crime is assigned to juvenile rehabilitation facilities that are reliably overcrowded and lax on security. Often, killer children are quickly released—"rehabilitated"—or simply let go to ease overcrowding.

Among Escobar's most valuable killers was La Quica (Wince), whose real name was Dan Denys Muñoz Mosquera. His presence at Escobar's side baffled some, who wondered what such a young and beautiful boy was doing with the sometimes slovenly Escobar. The answer was that La Quica not only killed on command but did it with a savagery that delighted his boss. At trial, one former Escobar pilot testified about having seen La Quica at Escobar's side at Nápoles. Escobar showed the pilot a Polaroid snapshot of three informers. "There were three dead men. They'd all been skinned alive. Their testicles had been cut off, and their throats had been cut. I asked Escobar, 'What kind of person would do this to another human being?' Escobar looked at Mr. Mosquera. Mr. Mosquera looked back at him and smiled, and that was the end of it."

In 1991, La Quica made the mistake of traveling to the United States. He was arrested while calling his mother in Colombia from a pay phone in Queens. Currently, he is serving five life sentences at the supermaximum prison in Florence, Colorado, convicted, among other things, of the 1989 assassination of presidential candidate (and almost certain winner) Luis Carlos Galán; the bombing that same year of an Avianca jetliner on a Bogotá-Cali run with 108 passengers and crew aboard (the debris killed another three people on the ground); and the detonation, also in 1989, of a 500-kilo truck bomb that destroyed the headquarters building of the Administrative Security Department (Departamento Administrativo de Seguridad, or DAS) in 1989, Colombia's FBI, killing sixty-three and wounding over 600. The target of the attack, DAS chief general Gabriel Maza Márquez, survived, but his secretary died after being decapitated by flying glass.

Galán's murder was especially devastating. A handsome, agile politician, Galán seemed the right man for the moment, equipped with the political skills needed to handle Colombia's fractious populace as well as the United States, which considered him a promising (and pro-extradition) replacement for the increasingly senile Virgilio Barco. But, as is the pattern in Colombia, Galán's talent was his downfall. Escobar saw him as a dangerous opponent. It was better to be rid of him.

Like Palestinian suicide bombers, many killer boys accepted death as a natural part of their lives. But they did not look forward to heaven. What their jobs guaranteed was a brief, exciting life and perhaps a measure of fame. Sometimes, they earned enough to buy their mothers a house in a *comuna*. No one's life is guaranteed, the boys say, in a phrase as close to a prayer as many get: *Nadie tiene la vida comprada.*

I once accompanied a Catholic nun to a Medellín *comuna* to visit Albeiro, the head of a gang that fed boys into Escobar's organization. The *comuna* was not the poorest I'd seen. Worse was Moravia, built on a trash heap. The methane gas seeping from the tons of garbage that supported the shacks and paths caused one of my colleagues to swoon like a sapling felled with an ax stroke. Albeiro's neighborhood was tidy, and the house itself had been recently painted in pastels that softened the afternoon glare. Sister Teresa was visiting on a Sunday, and most of the men were already well oiled with *aguardiente* and beer. They sat in the bars and were bathed in the lime-green glare of televised soccer matches.

Albeiro was sober. Rare among Colombian men, he did not follow soccer. He lived with his mother and his girlfriend, who looked barely fourteen. Her hip-length black hair and round face lent a sweetness to the bare walls and cheap furniture. Albeiro had survived many gun battles with rivals and police. Once, a rival's bullet had severed his spine, leaving him a paraplegic. He continued to run his gang, though now hid his pistol between his thigh and the seat of the wheelchair. Sister Teresa told me that Albeiro had agreed to take part in a citywide effort to negotiate a peace among gangs, including the one that had crippled him and left him for dead. She had worked on the agreement for more than a year. It was holding, Albeiro informed her, as we settled in to talk.

With us was Edwin, one of Albeiro's boys. Albeiro did not trust the agreement enough to forgo bodyguards, and several more boys lounged on the sidewalk that Albeiro's mother kept swept. Their gangly bodies appeared deformed by the bulges at their waists, pistols that I assumed were the latest in Medellín gunware. In retrospect, I realized we had passed several layers of security to reach Albeiro's house. What had seemed like a short trip had actually been a crossing of borders, each patrolled by young men invisible to me but as obvious to locals as white tigers. My permission to enter had been Sister Teresa.

Albeiro's mother—he had bought her the house and the sofa set with chair and glass coffee table—offered soda. As a rule, killer boys adore their mothers and despise their fathers, who are usually absent or estranged. Albeiro supported his mother and younger siblings on the money earned from robbery and the occasional contracts for murders that his gang signed. In return, he got absolute loyalty. When he was killed, as he fully expected to be, his mother would be the one to collect his body from the morgue, arrange the funeral, and keep the niche where his body lay as neat as she kept his house.

Albeiro and Sister Teresa talked about how to move him in and out of the neighborhood that his gang controlled so that he could attend meetings meant to strengthen the peace pact. Crossing a street that bordered the neighborhood was a potential death sentence for him. A *parrillero* could pull next to the car, and there he would be, paralyzed, unable even to duck. In 1986, the average age of murder victims in Medellín was between thirty-five and forty-five. Within two years, it had dropped more than a decade, to young men between twenty and twenty-five, largely reflecting the number of killer boys shot down in the war between Escobar and the authorities.

There was no malice or even curiosity in Albeiro's occasional glance. Yet the mere brush of his eyes left me cold. He had the most disturbing eyes I had ever seen. They seemed completely devoid of emotion. They were the eyes of a killer, of course. But they were also the eyes of someone who had been killed. His gaze was blank as a concrete wall. Before my visit to his house, I had never believed writers who described people with dead eyes. To me, it was an exaggeration, at best a metaphor for what was essentially a spiritual void. I was wrong. Albeiro seemed to live in a world of paper-cutout people, except for his mother and the pretty girlfriend who fussed around his chair and carried his gaze around the room as if she were the last person left alive on earth. I took their picture. It was the only time during the afternoon that Albeiro smiled.

Escobar paid a reward to every killer who took down a police officer. He circulated their home addresses and even the license plate numbers of their cars. When I met with former gang members in the *comunas*, they could give me the make, color, and license plate numbers of all of the police vehicles that they claimed were hunting them, like sharks patrolling the liquid shadows of the streets. Of course, the boys hunted, too. Police could no longer even enter some *comunas*. Others had to, since their homes and families were there.

That was the case of Jairo Alberto Flórez, a police officer who lived in a neighborhood known as Villatina. In 1992, boys gunned him down in front of his house, one of the hundreds of police officers who died that year in Medellín. His colleagues wanted revenge. On November 15, 1992, a dozen police surrounded seven boys standing on a Villatina street corner. Nearby was Johanna, an eight-year-old girl with a cast on her broken leg. According to witnesses, the dozen police agents first demanded that the boys show them their identification cards. Then, they forced them to lie face down on the sidewalk. They executed them one by one. When one police officer aimed at Johanna, another tried to stop him. But witnesses told Vicky, my human rights colleague, that he replied, "Why should we leave alive this band of sons of bitches if they are the ones killing us?" He fired, killing her.

As it turned out, the boys belonged to a local church group that had just attended mass. They were not in a gang. Johanna was unlucky, unable to run because of the cast. A boy she was with survived, only to die two years later of a heart attack that his parents were convinced resulted from grief.

One of Albeiro's boys lived around the corner. He invited us to his house. Edwin was all angles and energy, a jaunty cap on his head and his eyes alive to the street and the passers-by he examined to ensure that they were not coming to kill Albeiro. Inside, he sprawled on a chair like any teenage boy. Edwin told the story of how other gangs were attempting to infiltrate the neighborhood to kill them. I soon lost track of the intrigue, filled as it was with other boys' nicknames, old disputes, and the street slang that made his talk like an intricate dialect. Proudly, Edwin lifted up his shirt to display a startlingly pink scar left from a bullet wound that had ravaged his gut but miraculously let him live.

"Medellín's doctors are the best in the world for gunshots," Edwin said. He seemed proud until someone pointed out that the wound had been caused when the gun that he had been carrying misfired.

At that moment, shots rang out. Edwin crouched, then ran out the door. Through the window, I saw other people running–but they were running to the shots, not away. A Colombian policeman had once re- marked to me that this was common in Colombia. Colombians run to- ward the sound of gunfire, making it difficult for police who may be near the scene to find a shooter. Within a minute, the boy returned, shrugging. Just a bar fight, he said. Peace could still be said to hold over the *comuna*.

ooooo

DESPITE HIS FORTUNE, ESCOBAR REMAINED HIS MOTHER'S SON. HIS comfort food was rice and scrambled egg, with a side of fried banana. He was as devoted to his own family as she had been to hers. He rarely touched cocaine (though he enjoyed showing visitors that his ciga- rettes contained marijuana). And he cut deals, with the authorities and with God. In 1991, he negotiated his surrender with then president César Gaviria Trujillo, the campaign manager for Galán who became the Liberal Party candidate after Galán's murder. A bureaucrat, Gaviria was outmatched by Escobar's cunning, learned from Hermilda: negoti- ate with your accusers and best them at the game. Bishop Castrillón was the last to arrive at Escobar's hideout before he surrendered. Like everything else about the deal, the bishop had been selected for a rea- son. Escobar had long contributed to his charities. An added bonus was that Castrillón had married President Gaviria to his wife, Ana Milena. In exchange for his surrender, Gaviria allowed Escobar to build his own facility above Envigado, a Medellín suburb where he had gone to high school, run his first scams, and acquired his first killer boys.

The ranch-style structure topped a hill known as the Cathedral. The property itself had been a farm, with a stock of trees to the back and a habit of shrouding itself in mist in the mornings and afternoons. These were qualities, Roberto Escobar noted, that made it ideal if Escobar needed to leave the facility ("escape" being a laughably inappropriate word to apply to his luxury retreat) or defend it from attack. Several years later, it came to light that the Cali Cartel had indeed planned to kill Escobar by dropping a bomb on the Cathedral from a helicopter. The cartel purchased three MK-82 bombs from corrupt Salvadoran army officers and flew them to Colombia for that purpose. The MK-82 was used extensively by the U.S.-backed Salvadoran army against guerrillas and later by U.S. troops in both Operation Desert Storm in Iraq and Operation Allied Force in Serbia. Escobar learned of the plan and ordered an anti-aircraft gun to be installed to shoot down any suspicious aircraft.

Escobar calculated that his agreement to stay in the Cathedral would ease tension and allow his business dealings to return to normal. He remained able to mobilize his forces to protect his interests, in particular from the Cali Cartel. He had easy access to all of the people he needed to see, brought via what he and his crew called the "Tunnel." It was actually the trucks that came and went from the building, carrying business associates, beauty queens, killer boys, soccer stars, musicians, and whores, among others.

Conditions inside the Cathedral were luxurious, as befitted a man used to comfort. His suite was equipped with a bar, wide-screen television, and a hot tub, as well as an arsenal of weapons and state-of-the-art communications equipment. By the time I was sitting on the hotel roof with Vicky and Pablo, the Cathedral had become Medellín's newest tourist attraction. From the hotel roof, they pointed toward it, a white splotch in the thickening haze of late afternoon.

If Escobar had completed his term in the Cathedral, he would have rinsed his record as clean as one of Hermilda's hand-laundered sheets. But his penchant for violence without limits was his undoing. It was the part of her son Hermilda was unable to change.

While in the Cathedral, Escobar heard a rumor that Kiko Moncada, a cartel associate, had met with representatives of Cali Cartel leaders Miguel and Gilberto Rodríguez Orejuela. About the same time, Fernando Galeano, known as "El Negro," apparently refused to give Escobar a bigger cut of a $20-million cache he had piled in a nearby apartment. It was so poorly stored that the bills were rotting in damp clumps. Escobar smelled a conspiracy. Galeano was summoned to the Cathedral via the Tunnel on July 3, 1992. Escobar sent men into the city to capture Moncada and bring him back. Escobar was in no mood to bargain. Later, Galeano's family, escorted by government investigators, appeared at the Cathedral's gates to plead for the men's lives. It was in vain. Over the next several days, Escobar's men hunted down and killed one additional brother per family, as well as over a dozen other traffickers. El Negro's surviving brother finally negotiated only the return of the men's bodies. Escobar shipped them out via the Tunnel. In a way, the families were lucky. Later, the authorities dug up a dismembered and burned body that Escobar had ordered buried under the Cathedral's soccer field.

The families threatened scandal. Not only was Escobar trafficking from his supposed jail, but he was using it as an execution chamber. President Gaviria ordered Escobar moved to a real prison. Escobar refused. In the end, Escobar stuck with Hermilda's script, insisting on the terms of the deal he had cut. He shouldn't be blamed, he reasoned, if they were unhappy with their bargain. With Roberto Escobar, Popeye, Grime, and Little Angel, Escobar walked out of the Cathedral through the grove of trees. Roberto's son spread false information to the press about the Tunnel, prompting the authorities to fruitlessly dig up the grounds in search of the escape route. "The only thing they will find is the money buried in the ground," Pablo noted, "$10 million. Finding it drove them crazy and I don't think they ever did." That is, if there was anything, really, to find.

Once Escobar was out, the Americans threw themselves into the hunt, at one point sending so many spy and cargo planes to Medellín that a special team had to be sent south to direct air traffic. Although my *paisa* friends couldn't name or even recognize these machines if they saw them on the ground, they claimed that in the wee hours of the night they could hear them, making restless circles over the valley. The Americans wanted to smoke Escobar out, "even capture his dreams," one friend said to me. After the discos closed and the street vendors shut up their stands and before the morning buses choked the avenues, I imagined I could hear them, too.

Some in Colombia still admire Escobar for his flamboyance and skill at outwitting the government. But his tale was ultimately cautionary. A Colombian John Gotti, Escobar proved that crime and fame do not mix. Like elsewhere in the world, the most successful criminals in Colombia do not announce themselves like cartoon villains but are the ordinary faces that circulate in human society without arousing suspicion.

Escobar did leave an unmistakable legacy, though, as big in its way as the phantom hippopotamus that still roams Colombian legend. He made extreme violence a Colombian dialect, as recognizable as the grilled corn cake called an *arepa*. Colombians are convinced that anything–absolutely anything–is possible, from uncountable wealth and killing former friends in a luxury prison to skinning men alive while their eyes can still take in the separation of their tissues. It is violence without limit, making deals with God and talking the old fool into ceding more than planned. It is creating a world where no law but gravity holds true.

CHAPTER FIVE

A PERFECT CIRCLE

COLOMBIAN WRITER ANTONIO CABALLERO ONCE WROTE THAT HIS fellow citizens reduce all disputes to a question of words. As an example, he cited two articles published in Colombia's leading newspapers. In one, historian Antonio Panesso Robledo argued that it was incorrect to use the phrase "detained and disappeared" to refer to people seized by the Colombian authorities, then killed without their arrest recorded or acknowledged, effectively disappearing them from the world. Outside Colombia, "disappeared" has precisely this meaning and is a legal term of art incorporated into international treaties.

Panesso protested. The verb "to disappear," he argued, is intransitive. Therefore, it cannot be used as an adjective. In other words, you cannot say "a disappeared person." Such a thing did not—could not—exist.

Using similar logic, Rafael Nieto Loayza, a jurist, argued that the word "war" should never be applied to the conflict in Colombia. In order to have a war, he wrote, it is necessary to have parties that are legitimate and acknowledged as "belligerents." Since no one has awarded the Colombian guerrillas the status of belligerents—one imagines he had in mind some sort of official certificate issued by the U.N. Security Council—Colombia is not at war. Similar logic is used to defend, for instance, the American decision to deny suspected Al Qaeda members status as prisoners of war since they pledge no country and use terror to fight, not tanks or armies. Yet I find that in Colombia, these semantic games are everywhere. They are like chess matches in a leafy park, pleasing to the players and entirely separate from the grind of everyday life or death.

The love of the game crosses generations and political ties. For instance, Colombian guerrillas claim that they never kidnap. What they do, they say, is "retain." People "fall" into retention, like a pothole in the road. Once they fall, guerrillas "tax" them. When families pay, the "retainees" are released.

Pablo Escobar was a genius at this game. For his skill, some Colombians celebrated him as a trickster bandit who took from the rich (the Americans), stuck it to the powerful (the *doctores*), and strategized his way out of the consequences (the *paisa* grand master), at least for a while (one of the Rodríguez brothers, himself adept at manipulating the government, is nicknamed the Chessmaster). "A while" is a lifetime in Colombia. The admiration for Escobar had nothing to do with the product he peddled. Colombians, for the most part, shun cocaine and heroin as a vice. Yet many find the image of the all-powerful Americans sucking up Colombian cocaine darkly pleasing. It shows that the *gringos* have a weakness. They are not invincible. They are not perfect.

Even as Escobar led his pursuers on a chase, few Colombians doubted that his end would be bloody. That's part of the story. It's expected. The wolf eats the grandmother (at least in Colombia), the violent meet their own justice *(ajusticiados)*, there are no second acts. While he lived, however, neither the American nor the Colombian authorities could hide the delicious fact that Escobar had screwed them all. And he did it while eating fried banana on rice, with his singsong accent, while adoring his children and draping his wife in gold and diamonds and screwing the young girls he went through like the sneakers he favored, hundreds of pairs that were exactly alike, white and soft enough to allow him to pad around without making a sound.

ooooo

AT FIRST, THE FARC TREATED ESCOBAR'S BUSINESS LIKE ANY OTHER. By the time he bought Nápoles, trafficking was a profitable enterprise in the Middle Magdalena. The FARC knew export-import. After all, Colombia's best bananas were always packed and shipped to Europe, like gold bars tucked in Styrofoam. The guerrillas charged a "war tax" on each crate. They began charging a "war tax" on cocaine. To them, it was just another product. During the FARC's Sixth Conference in

1982, guerrillas established a per-gram fee on coke laboratories. Already, the FARC's Southern Block had a deal with Gonzalo Rodríguez Gacha, Escobar's associate, to protect drug laboratories in exchange for cash and his agreement to pay farmers a higher rate for their *base*. Where there was money to be had, all could benefit. There was enough money to satisfy even the greediest appetite. The huge expanse of Colombia suited for cocaine—thinly populated, ignored by the state, shockingly poor—was precisely the region the FARC had dominated for decades.

Merchants trucked food and drink to the narco-ranches. Lawyers filed bids for new purchases and more apartment buildings and fancier hotels to launder the profits. There were cars and motorcycles, boats and all-terrain vehicles to fuel and repair. Cooks prepared delicacies for the parties with guests flown in from Bogotá and Medellín. On it all, the FARC skimmed its percentage, its collectors as well known as the fruit seller with the best *chirimoya* or the lottery man with the hottest streak of wins. The FARC's collection methods could also be ingenious. One Colombian businessman explained to me that he paid the guerrillas in ways that were immune from detection. "For instance, a manager will 'hire' a FARC guerrilla, paying a regular salary and benefits to an employee who never shows up. Or shipments of goods like boots and clothes will be 'lost' in transit, actually delivered to the FARC."

Even after paying a ransom, some kidnap victims would be forced to continue to pay or to manage FARC funds, in effect becoming a guerrilla broker. These individuals would have no criminal record and seemed to be operating legally, making it virtually impossible for the authorities to detect guerrilla transactions. For this businessman, guerrilla demands drained his profits and took a daily toll on his health. If he told the authorities, the FARC would kill him. Or his family. If he didn't, eventual financial ruin was his only escape. Finally, he decided to sell his business, accepted a diplomatic post that paid him half his salary, and left Colombia a happy man.

In Colombia, I would occasionally find myself in a "narco-hotel" built to launder cocaine cash. Usually, these were concrete slabs in the middle of a town whose annual agricultural profits would likely be absorbed by the cost of maintaining the pool/sauna/exercise room/

massage parlor. In each room would be a stocked minibar, a basket of shampoo, lotions, and shoe shine cloths, and an air conditioner blasting dust over a king-size bed. During the day and well into the night, I would collect tales of atrocity. Once, a woman told me that a gunmen had pulled her husband and their two daughters off a public bus, then shot him at the side of the road. All night, the girls watched over his body. The next morning, the police took the girls to the nearest hospital, where their mother found them being treated for dehydration. One of the girls, she told me, still suffered from a "view paralysis"–her eyes immobile, as if still locked on her father's body. Afterwards, I returned to my narco-hotel, where the staff seemed always to be lounging in the lounge. With so few guests, there wasn't much to do. I curled onto a corner of the bed and covered myself with blankets to ward off the air conditioner's worst (dial-less, its frayed cord plastered into the wall). To drown out my thoughts, I watched satellite TV–*telenovelas* from Venezuela, variety shows from Mexico, and *MacGyver*, always *MacGyver*, from a Florida superstation.

In his book on the Middle Magdalena region, journalist Carlos Medina Gallego interviewed ranchers and community leaders about their relationship with the FARC before Escobar and his colleagues began to buy up the valley. For over a decade, the FARC had skimmed off cattle or money or supplies. Most residents gave the guerrillas what they asked for, out of sympathy or simply because the FARC backed their requests with guns. There was never a choice. But by the end of the 1970s, the amounts guerrillas demanded increased along with the penalties for refusing. The FARC had begun a growth spurt. The money it made from extortion was channeled into new units sent to places like the Middle Magdalena, where there was cocaine wealth. Marín assigned what he called the Eleventh Front to the region around Nápoles and put it under the command of a guerrilla known as "Ramón." Truthfully, it was the FARC's tenth unit. With it, guerrillas began a tradition, now pronounced, of inflating their apparent strength by skipping numbers to identify fronts (their highest numbered front is currently in the sixties).

If a family refused to pay, "Ramón" would kidnap a family member for ransom. In other cases, he simply ordered the head of the household killed, "*ajusticiado.*" His behavior was in marked contrast to that of other commanders, who had not seemed so greedy (eventually, Ramón deserted with a sack of cash stolen from his dues to Marín). As a former mayor told Medina, "These men and this commander completely changed [the FARC's] behavior, different from the [guerrillas] before them; they came to abuse, to demand, to ask for too much, to kidnap without a second thought, without anything. [Ramón] is the one responsible for losing the support of the peasants."

To combat the Eleventh Front, the Colombian army sent more troops. But soldiers managed to do little more than antagonize the locals. In light of today's daily news from Colombia, the abuses seem tame: frequent roadblocks and searches, limits on supplies taken to ranches (to prevent guerrillas from using farmers to obtain food), an occasional forced disappearance. One army officer assigned to the region at the time explained to me that his unit "never had intelligence that would allow us to act and when we would get it, it would be too late, we would arrive too late or simply not go, to avoid setbacks that might damage the careers of the commanders, who thought more about their careers than the lives of the local residents."

Instead of making people feel more secure, the army taught a dangerous lesson. No one was going to look out for the security of the locals. Both the FARC and the army abused them. If people wanted protection, they would have to provide it for themselves. "The army's operations intensified along with the population's frustration, since they felt increasingly unprotected," Medina found. "The guerrillas had a minimal ability to defend the peasant population against potential army operations, which were gradually undermining the guerrillas' base of support. People were facing real difficulties."

ooooo

THE FARC SAW COCAINE AS JUST ONE MORE TAXABLE BUSINESS. BUT the M-19 guerrillas smelled opportunity. They were city people, world travelers who had partied in New York and L.A., where the white powder was everywhere. They knew a fortune was entering Colombia. For them, the question became how to get their hands on the bonanza and use it to topple the government. The answer must have seemed simplicity itself. The M-19 had neither the ability nor the patience to collect "taxes." It had no forces in the areas where *coca* was grown or refined. Nor did it have a Ramón to instill fear in the locals who refused to pay their monthly percentage. Instead, Jaime Bateman, the M-19's leader, chose to strike at the heart of the matter: the traffickers themselves. He decided to kidnap traffickers and their family members for what he expected would be fabulous ransoms.

Kidnapping had worked before. In 1975, M-19 members had seized an American, Sears executive Donald Cooper, and successfully collected a $1 million ransom. With it, they invested in businesses that provided them with the steady income they needed to mount their most audacious action yet: the theft, in 1978, of over 7,000 weapons from an army warehouse in Bogotá. To do it, they dug a 246-foot tunnel from a house next to the army base to the building where the weapons were kept, nicknamed the Blue Whale. Bateman believed that the ransom paid for a drug trafficker would net them at least as much. This time, they would invest in the M-19's grand plan to move from the cities into the countryside. Only by fomenting an uprising, Bateman believed, would the M-19 triumph. The group was trapped in the cities, marginal, waging war mainly through advertising campaigns. With cocaine cash, Bateman gambled that he would be able to make the M-19 a formidable force that would eclipse the FARC.

Already, M-19 guerrillas were training in Cuba in preparation for what they called an "invasion" of Colombia. They needed weapons, radios, uniforms, food, and supplies. Writer Alfredo Molano, who knew Bateman, told me that the M-19 leader did not hesitate before ordering the kidnapping of traffickers. It had a "double advantage," Molano said. "The traffickers were rich and illegal, or at least they couldn't appeal to the law for help." For Bateman, otherwise a genius at gauging the Colombian mood, it was a surprising and fatal miscalculation.

The M-19 put the plan into action in 1979. The first target was Carlos Lehder, the flamboyant Colombian pilot who had flown the first large quantities of cocaine into the United States. M-19 guerrillas grabbed him, but Lehder was wily. He escaped his abductors even as a thug sent by Escobar to rescue him closed in on the M-19's hiding place. The guerrillas chose easier targets next: not the traffickers, but their children. On October 6, 1981, guerrillas with links to several

Bogotá universities grabbed the three children of Carlos Jader Álvarez, a trafficker with routes that connected Colombia to Miami. The children—a five-year-old, a six-year-old, and a seven-year-old—were taken out of the family car as the chauffeur drove them to school in the capital.

At first, things went smoothly for the guerrillas. They stashed the children in a safe house in the city and delivered the $5-million-dollar ransom demand. Álvarez agreed to pay. But a disagreement on the amount and terms arose. Even as he parleyed, Álvarez put into motion other plans to recover his children that were traditionally associated with the world of trafficking: bribes, threats, torture, and murder. The M-19 miscalculated the power of his rage as well as his firm ties to the authorities. With the help of the police, Álvarez located the safe house. Witnesses reported that men driving a Mercedes Benz—Álvarez's car and a model prized by the cocaine lords—snatched university students suspected of belonging to or helping the M-19 from their houses and streets. In a panic, the guerrillas moved the children to the mountains near Bogotá. As the crow flies, their location was not far from the wealthy neighborhood where the children had been seized. But following the dirt track and trails necessary to get there by land made it an arduous trip. The children were kept in a shack guarded by locals, who fed them and kept them clothed. The locals also clipped the children's hair and fingernails to send to their father as proof they were alive.

At the time, Álvarez had other, serious problems. In Miami, the DEA had set up an elaborate sting, with Álvarez as the main target. Journalist David McClintick, who wrote a book about Operation Swordfish, described how the DEA agents recorded Álvarez's mounting panic as he pressed his dealers to take more cocaine and sell it faster, to gather cash for the ransom (or to pay his people to find and kill the guerrillas who had taken the children).

Five weeks after guerrillas grabbed the Álvarez children, the M-19 kidnapped Martha Nieves Ochoa, the sister of Juan David Ochoa. She had been on her way to classes at the University of Antioquia in Medellín when guerrillas shoved her into a car.

For Escobar and his associates, Ochoa's kidnapping was the final straw. Escobar called an emergency meeting at Nápoles. Later reports indicated that 233 people pledged their support, even Escobar's rivals in the Cali Cartel. There is no record of who named the group (or if Álvarez attended), but it was likely Escobar himself, nothing if not direct in his manner of speech. The group was called MAS–Death to Kidnappers (Muerte a Secuestradores, or MAS).

Escobar later told journalist Germán Castro Caycedo that the traffickers were

> alarmed because if there wasn't an immediate and powerful reaction, [the guerrillas] were going to continue screwing our own families–what I mean is, we had to make a clean break–and in a matter of two hours we gathered on the table 200 million pesos ($500,000). At the time, this was everything we had. This was all the money. And they also put at our service about a hundred cars and motorcycles and airplanes and people. And even a submarine, do you believe that? And we paid law enforcement 80 million pesos for the information they had at this moment about [M-19] members and the next day–and this was long overdue–they began to fall. [My people] took them to certain houses, to certain ranches and people from law enforcement went there and hung them up and began to bust them up. I mean bust them up, understand?

In December 1981–with the Álvarez children and Martha Nieves Ochoa missing–MAS announced itself by sending small airplanes to drop leaflets over the country's main sports stadiums during soccer games. Dozens of M-19 guerrillas, their associates, and probably innocent people were captured by police, then delivered to MAS to torture and kill. Their techniques were the same as those used by General Camacho on captured guerrillas and political prisoners. Particularly after the M-19's theft of the army weapons in the Blue Whale operation, General Camacho's fury knew no bounds: electric shocks on open wounds, the submarine (where the torturer holds a captive's head under filthy water again and again), beatings, hanging by the arms behind the back, the amputation of fingers, toes, ears, hands and arms, threats against spouses and children. The traffickers also contributed macabre innovations. Once, MAS operatives doused the daughter of an M-19 commander with gasoline and threatened to set her afire.

It's impossible to know exact numbers, but dozens died before the M-19 agreed to free Ochoa on February 16, 1982. The dispute wasn't settled by her release, however. Sometime the following April, the guerrillas apparently blindfolded the three Álvarez children, then shot them one by one in the head (an act they denied, unconvincingly). The murders may have been payback for the MAS onslaught, but they only further goaded the traffickers. Álvarez hunted, caught, tortured, and killed the people he believed had helped the M-19 grab and hide his children, among them ten college students (only three of whom were eventually found guilty in absentia of renting the Bogotá safe house). Before killing them, Álvarez had them call home to say good-bye and confess their alleged crime. In September, a guerrilla captured by Álvarez with the help of the police finally led them to the spot where the children were buried, two in one sack and the eldest in another.

The M-19 membership halved, in part because so many were killed or scared away by MAS. The M-19 had misjudged how rough things would get. They were like adolescents on a joyride, ignorant of consequences. That attitude was visible in almost everything they did. After stealing the weapons from the Blue Whale, for instance, some guerrillas hid them in the homes of their parents and friends, ensuring that the people dearest to them would be dragged into the army's barracks and made to confess under torture to crimes they knew nothing about. One early member, Vera Grabe, wrote in her memoirs that the group believed that weapons alone could solve Colombia's problems: "The only thing that was really important [to the leadership] was what was accomplished 'packing heat.'"

A meeting was arranged between M-19 commander Iván Marino Ospina and Escobar. Ospina gave the capo a Soviet submachine gun as a token of the M-19's pledge never to kidnap traffickers or their families again. The Ochoa family claimed that no ransom was ever paid, though such statements are often viewed in Colombia as the verbal covering over every million-dollar ransom delivery successfully made.

Álvarez never escaped the misfortune that dogged him since the day his children were kidnapped. Another son committed suicide. In 1985, he was among the first Colombians extradited to the United

States to face drug trafficking charges stemming from Operation Swordfish. A federal judge sentenced him to forty-five years. After serving thirteen, however, Álvarez was returned to Colombia and rearrested, this time to face charges of colluding with police in the forced disappearance of the ten students. During a court hearing in 2001, Álvarez turned his back on the family members of the students, his face, a reporter noted, "still disfigured by the pain he has suffered" since finding his children buried on that abandoned slope.

ooooo

COLOMBIA'S HISTORY TURNED ON THE FATE OF THE ÁLVAREZ CHILDREN and Martha Nieves Ochoa. MAS cared only about the traffickers and their families. But the example it set was intoxicating to the Colombian army and to many residents of the Middle Magdalena Valley. There, Ramón's demands on behalf of the FARC had forced businesses to close. Ranchers could not live on their properties for fear of being kidnapped or killed. Only traffickers were willing to buy land, since they moved in a cloud of bodyguards and could afford the equipment necessary to sleep safely at night.

In Puerto Boyacá, a new mayor decided to act. Army captain Óscar Echandía had been ordered by Bogotá to take over the mayor's office, after squabbles among town council members and threats by the FARC deadlocked municipal business. The appointment of military officers as mayors was a frequent tactic used to fill seats left vacant or made irrelevant by violence. The alternative was leaving the office empty, a tacit admission of defeat. In 1982–at the time MAS was attacking guerrillas to force the release of family members–Captain Echandía invited local landowners, political leaders, and representatives of the Latin American division of Texaco, called the Texas Petroleum Company, to a meeting.

"It was necessary to create an armed group, a kind of guerrilla insurgency, and war is very expensive, it's necessary to equip [fighters] with weapons, with clothing, with hammocks, feed them, clothe them, and pay them," one of the meeting participants later told journalist Carlos Medina. Captain Echandía proposed collecting donations that he would use to hire and equip men to fight the FARC. "This is very expensive, so here it was decided that every rancher would 'collaborate' ... depending on how many head of cattle he had."

It was Plan Lazo, with a twist. The army was in charge and would use locals to fight and collect intelligence to guide army attacks, just as General Ruiz had envisioned. Soon, people began calling them "para-militaries," because of their relationship to the army. The army equipped them and also provided them with the information they used to select targets. Once, Captain Echandía drove one of the assassins who killed a local mayor to the hospital after the man was wounded in the attack. He even paid the man's bill out of an army account.

The twist was that some of the locals who contributed money and men did not make their money from legal business, but from drugs. Escobar and Rodríguez used land and livestock like beautiful jewels—a way to invest their fortunes, adorn their alibis, and act as a huge money-laundering machine. This was the beginning of a huge counter land reform in Colombia, as traffickers bought thousands of acres from medium-size and small farmers, concentrating it in the hands of a few super-rich. The purchase of land and their new status as "ranchers" al-lowed traffickers to become what in Colombia is called *"gente de bien,"* good people. In this phrase, "good" does not mean moral but rather one of us, someone who is reasonable and can be dealt with—"people like us" versus "people like them."

Trouble between the traffickers and the FARC was inevitable. At its core, the FARC remained a movement of peasants and ideological purists who hated everything the traffickers represented but coveted the power of their money. For their part, the traffickers cared nothing about the FARC's decades-old claims against Colombia's elites, like stinking rags compared to their designer wear. They wanted to co-opt the powerful or, in Escobar's case, to join them and have a place at the table of government to ensure that the business would prosper. The FARC wanted to smash the table; Escobar wanted to buy it. One for-mer army major explained to me the army's logic in creating an al-liance that included traffickers:

> The leaders of ancient Rome and many other contemporary empires al-lied with their less powerful enemies (considering Pablo Escobar and Gonzalo Rodríguez Gacha as less threatening than the guerrillas) to for-

tify themselves, and once the principal enemy is defeated the smaller ones are no problem. This means less of a drain on the army and quicker results. The other point is that organizations like drug traffickers and, at the beginning, "self-defense" groups, could use dirty war tactics against the guerrillas because at the end of the day they do not obey any of the country's laws or international laws. So this can be a way to make up for the government's limitations or inefficiencies, since these forces can carry out a war without quarter. . . . In the end, what I believe happened was that the guerrilla threat was magnified by the ineptitude of politicians and military officers, and for that reason they strengthened these irregular forces.

For many, the equation was simple. "The one who bares the most teeth wins," one local rancher once told me.

In a deposition he later gave to Colombian investigators, Captain Echandía said that locals in one village caught and killed Ramon's couriers, the men who collected the month's "taxes." The next target was a rancher accused of handling the FARC's finances. The men who killed him were local thugs who called themselves "Los Gordos," the Fat Guys. To pay them, Captain Echandía took a special collection. The work, he said, was a "great effort at disinfecting the region against the FARC." Early on, several murders were carried out by men on bicycles, since the paramilitaries couldn't afford a motorcycle. Bodies were left where they fell or were dumped in the Magdalena River, their abdomens opened so that they would sink to the bottom before appearing, weeks later, in the shore reeds.

Among the first to die were Communists or people whose politics closely mirrored those of the FARC. Soon, however, the menu of targets expanded to include anyone who failed to support the army, criticized the government, organized a protest, wrote something intelligent in the newspaper, or revealed a paramilitary secret on the radio. These individuals belonged, using General Camacho's logic, to the "unarmed wing" of the guerrillas. Many were reported as "subversives" killed in action by the army, though they had been executed by paramilitaries. Sometimes, soldiers would truck bodies back to the base and dress them in camouflage to show to the press, in that way boosting their monthly tallies for guerrillas killed in action. The fact that the bullet

holes in the bodies didn't correspond to the bullet holes in the uniforms (and the uniforms were oddly fresh, even as the skin beneath
flaked with dried blood) often escaped the photographers. The numbers were so impressive to the generals in Bogotá that they gave Captain Echandía a special award.

By 1983, the paramilitaries were linked to 240 killings. Investigators
also recorded a curious new development. At some point, the two
phenomena–MAS and Echandía's paramilitaries–had merged, at least
in terms of the name that people used to identify them. Colombia's
Inspector General, the official who investigates reports of abuses by
government employees, announced that he had a list containing the
names of 163 members of MAS. Fifty-nine of them were active-duty
members of the security forces, among them Captain Echandía. In
public, Captain Echandía rejected the name MAS. He preferred "*autodefensas*," self-defense groups, the name adopted during Plan Lazo.
This force was legitimate, he claimed, and foiled a guerrilla onslaught.
The generals backed him, praising the "civilians" who fought the Communists. In turn, they accused the Inspector General of instigating a
"dirty war," using guerrilla propaganda to damage the army's image.
Military tribunals speedily acquitted all fifty-nine officers.

Despite Echandía's protests, the acronym MAS began to appear
everywhere in the valley: spray painted on walls, written on placards
left on bodies, typed on death threats slipped under doors, whispered
in telephone conversations. With characteristic flair, Colombians
played with the word MAS: Masetos, Masacre, mas-ery (for misery),
más de lo mismo, more of the same. In some towns, they thought up
more creative names: Los Tiznados (Blackened Faces), Los Magnífi-
cos, Los Cenizos (Ashes), La Mano Negra (Black Hand), Los Perros
(Dogs), KanKill (an insecticide), Serpiente Negra (Black Snake). One
group called itself Los Apóstoles (Apostles) and was run by the local
priest. In sermons, he would denounce the pernicious Communist
stain. Before each attack, he would bless the fighters just as some
priests had done for *pájaros* during La Violencia.

Deep down, all were MAS. In this way, it was not a typical death
squad or even a particularly well-organized force. It was disperse, the
creature of local differences, as much an idea as a fixed structure. One
investigator once termed it "a state of mind," available to anyone who

decided that death was the only possible answer to the problems that plagued Colombia.

ooooo

SOMETIME IN THE LATE 1970S, A HIGH SCHOOL STUDENT NAMED Diego Viáfara joined the M-19. Like many young Colombians, Viáfara was fascinated with its panache. His background was classic M-19: a solid middle-class family, devoutly Catholic, an excellent student. He was assigned to a cell run by a local school teacher, Rosemberg Pabón. Pabón had been given the odd name (spelled with an "m") by his parents to honor the sacrifice of Ethel and Julius Rosenberg. Later, Pabón went on to lead the fifteen M-19 guerrillas who seized the Dominican Embassy in 1980. Guerrillas held hostage over fifty people, among them fourteen ambassadors, including U.S. ambassador Diego Asencio. They released the hostages after sixty-one days in exchange for a $1-million ransom and safe passage to Cuba.

Viáfara's first assignment was to join forces with the FARC and offer medical services in the Middle Magdalena Valley, part of Bateman's grand plan to build the alliances necessary to move the M-19 out of the cities. But Bateman's timing almost killed the young doctor. The town where he was supposed to make contact with the FARC was Puerto Boyacá. When he arrived, his M-19 contact had already fled MAS. And MAS knew exactly who Viáfara was and why he had come. Viáfara ended up begging the local priest for sanctuary. The priest told him that his only option was surrender. MAS escorted Viáfara to the army base, where he was offered a deal: join MAS or die. In late 1983, Viáfara became the official MAS doctor.

Years later, Viáfara surrendered to the authorities and became one of the government's best informants on how MAS operated. To support his medical work, MAS bought Viáfara a pharmacy in Puerto Boyacá. The pharmacy bore the name of the legal association that paramilitaries used as a public face in the region, the Association of Middle Magdalena Ranchers and Farmers (Asociación de Campesinos y Ganaderos del Magdalena Medio). With the association's support, Viáfara led health brigades to villages that MAS recruited to be part of its antiguerrilla campaign. Occasionally, Pablo Escobar, Fabio Ochoa,

and Gonzalo Rodríguez would join him to take credit for their generous donations. They appeared in the videos that Viáfara shot to record
his work. The traffickers lent the association their bulldozers and
graders, bought to maintain the landing strips where cocaine flights
came and went. Rodríguez even offered to underwrite a special team
of economists, lawyers, doctors, dentists, and engineers to draft an
economic development plan for the region.

MAS grew so fast that by late 1984, there was a financial crisis. The
contributions did not cover the expanding demand for weapons, communications equipment, and vehicles. That year, Viáfara noted in his
diary, the paramilitaries accidentally seized a truck loaded with cocaine. An emergency summit with the Medellín Cartel ensued. The
paramilitaries returned the shipment in exchange for a new Toyota
four-door pickup truck. Traffickers agreed to increase their payments
in exchange for MAS's help with security for cocaine shipments and
the traffickers' ranches.

For the Colombian army, the emerging alliance between paramilitaries and drug traffickers was not a problem, but a boon. The basilisco
of communism remained the most serious threat they perceived, not
trafficking. Eduardo Pizarro, a historian who has studied the Colombian military (and the brother of Carlos Pizarro), described what he
called the generals' "hypothesis of war" as "impervious to change." For
the first time since Marquetalia, MAS made it possible for the army to
claim headway against the FARC. As lists of reported guerrilla casualties grew, officers were promoted. MAS paid cash bonuses to the officers it worked with and hired officers when they retired. Generals
were awarded new medals and the thanks and praise of the *doctores*.
The relationship became so close that the army and MAS began calling each other *primos,* cousins.

Even veteran FARC members began to reconsider their allegiances.
Guerrillas who deserted were well paid for their valuable experience
and information. They turned over lists of the people who had helped
them, the location of their stores and farms, the names of their children and wives. For fighters, MAS was a full-time job. Recruits went
through a thirty- to sixty-day orientation. At the end, they got a uniform, a hammock and rope to tie it off, a mess kit, and a daily ration
that included the obligatory block of brown sugar, known as *panela,*

that Colombians use to sweeten coffee and water. Their salary was based on rank, just like the army. A new recruit started at roughly $50 per month, all expenses paid. Commanders got as much as $300 per month, a fortune compared to their counterparts in the Colombian army. Their families were allowed to buy on credit in the association's stores. When fighters were sent further away, their families received a bonus of food and other essentials.

In 1986, Colombia's chief prosecutor spoke about the relationship between MAS and the army with a directness unusual for public officials in Colombia:

> MAS was an authentic paramilitary movement. Attempts to cover up this truth have failed. The military was extending its custom of seeking support among private individuals to carry out counterinsurgency operations, thus fulfilling an area of action denied to them. This was simply a practice of officials who could not put up with temptations to expand their capacity of action by taking advantage of private individuals who were first used as "guides" and "informants," as general collaborators and auxiliaries. But the [army officials] ended up using these individuals as an armed front, as hired killers who could do unofficially what was not permitted officially.

Paramilitaries did not just kill suspected guerrillas. With the help of police, they also began to punish street crime and the unpleasant signs of poverty and social decay that appeared in towns and villages. At night, their Toyota SUVs hunted *"desechables,"* "disposable" people, a term used in Colombia to refer to the homeless, street kids, prostitutes, and drug addicts. Sometimes, MAS gunmen shot them where they lay. If they wanted to set an example, they would set the person's clothes on fire and then shoot them. If the victim had smoked *bazuco,* the poisonous residue left from the purification of cocaine, traces left on a shirt or blanket would send up an especially brilliant flame.

ooooo

IN THE YEAR 1986, JOSUÉ RETURNED TO PENSILVANIA TO PRACTICE law. By then, MAS had reached out of the valley and into the heart of his hometown. "A paramilitary group went down the Magdalena, killing local leaders and activists associated with the left in each of the towns they visited," Josué told me. "Most of the paramilitaries had been born in the village of San Daniel, which is an hour away from Pensilvania. They would return there for their vacations, two or three months of the year, and then they would start again their terror trips. The army and traffickers would give them the lists of people they had to kill."

The traffickers' new influence in Pensilvania shocked him. One newly rich local hosted lavish block parties featuring roast pig, music, and free liquor. "In the space of what seemed a day, Pensilvania began a radical change. From a peaceful town that seemed like a seminary for young priests, where the only notable noise was the daily pealing of the bell to mass, it became like a brothel. The trafficker brought in prostitutes from the capital; he opened bars and dozens of drunks would wake up in the streets every morning. With his money, the trafficker also brought in his assassins."

By that time, Josué had broken with his father's Conservative Party. To him, it seemed antique, like a horse and buggy in the age of all-terrain vehicles. The problems facing Colombia were so serious that Josué thought neither the Liberals nor the Conservatives could solve them. They fought over the spoils, not ideas. Each political dynasty—the Lópezes, the Pastranas, the Llerases, the Gómezes—had their newspapers or senatorial seats, foundations or boards that they used to circulate in and out of power. But they only seemed to look out for their supporters, not Colombia.

Josué was far from contemptuous of all of his father's *"coreligionarios,"* as fellow party members were often called. After narrowly winning the presidency in 1982, Conservative Belisario Betancur Cuartas broke with the past and many of his own party members by calling for peace negotiations with guerrillas. Betancur's own upbringing made him an especially credible broker. One of twenty-three children born to poor farmers, the handsome, white-haired Betancur could face Marín across a table and match every tale of hardship and struggle. As a youth, Betancur had fervently supported Laureano Gómez, the leader of the Conservatives' right wing. But age had mellowed his political views. From the presidential palace, he described peace like something as basic as breathable air: "We need peace because we are weary of violence, tired of it, saturated with it."

Marín reciprocated by ordering the release of all of the FARC's hostages. For a time, hope soared. In 1984, the government and FARC agreed to establish a new political party for guerrillas willing to lay down their weapons and stand for election. The new party, called the Patriotic Union, also included members of the Communist Party as well as Colombians searching for a new way to take part in politics. For Marín, the Patriotic Union was a way to test Betancur and the men who stood behind him, whom he had spent his life fighting. As was his custom, he moved cautiously. Marín approved of talks and eventually signed a cease-fire. Meanwhile, the FARC added "Ejército del Pueblo" (People's Army) to its name and declared an important shift in its strategy: "The FARC will no longer wait for the enemy in order to ambush them, but instead will pursue them in order to locate, attack and eliminate them." Marín was shape-shifting again, from classic guerrilla to the commander of an army ready to test itself against trained Colombian troops.

By then, the FARC guerrillas had uniforms, guns, mortars, grenades, and even their own ranks and soldiers' code of conduct. They also intensified recruitment drives, and by some estimates succeeded in doubling their fighting force during Betancur's term of office. This was no contradiction; for Marín, the Patriotic Union was but one facet of his overall plan. During the same conference that had resulted in the decision to tax *coca*, Jacobo Arenas described the Patriotic Union as part of the effort to combine "all forms of mass struggle" to win power. Using that logic, the leadership presented the Patriotic Union not as a surrender to their enemies but as a new front in the war. The per-gram fee on cocaine was meant to boost revenue at this critical juncture.

Josué knew all of this history and also understood the risks inherent in joining a political party so closely tied to the guerrillas and their plans. Yet he saw in the Patriotic Union a hope that was new. He was not alone. Thousands of Colombians joined the party with the idea that it would eventually lead to an end of the war. They were not following guerrilla orders; quite the opposite, their presence meant that the guerrillas were not the only ones determining what the party's platform would be or who would stand for election.

Immediately, this provoked fights within the fledgling Patriotic Union Party. Some members boasted that guerrillas "guaranteed" their safety and future plans by remaining armed. Others rebelled against the FARC and worked to make the Patriotic Union an independent force, thus earning the guerrillas' ire. Within Colombia's largest labor federation, the Unified Workers' Central, the fighting was intense. Pro-guerrilla factions argued that any deals between workers and the government had to be channeled through the FARC at the negotiating table. They called on the leadership to purge members who disagreed. Some were threatened not by MAS, but by the FARC.

The FARC wanted party members, but silent and obedient ones. Josué was many things; silent was not one of them. "It seemed to me to be a valid alternative to broaden Colombia's democracy. I thought that the men and women who had taken up weapons to rebel against the system should have an opportunity to fight for their ideas legally."

I admired his decision and, most of all, his optimism. In retrospect, though, it seemed either painfully naive or suicidal. Didn't Josué grasp the implications? To the army and MAS, the Patriotic Union was nothing more than a Trojan horse meant to hide fighters. Even as Betancur's representatives hammered out details with the FARC at the negotiation table, MAS and the Colombian army were systematically eliminating anyone who "smelled of guerrillas," in MAS's words. They took the easiest targets—Colombians who had joined the Patriotic Union. A person would have to be crazy to join a political party under those circumstances, I often thought to myself. Properly speaking, Josué wasn't risking his life. Joining the Patriotic Union was like sending an embossed invitation to MAS to schedule your murder. The only "risk" was that Josué might survive the first shooting, as he did.

By 1986, the FARC guerrillas who had run for public office as Patriotic Union members had already returned to the hills, convinced that they were safer armed and attacking army patrols than in a suit on the campaign trail. A psychologist named Estela whom I once interviewed told me that many of her patients were doctors, lawyers, and managers, middle-class Colombians like Josué, who had joined the Patriotic Union with the same sense of optimism. But they were less able than Josué to manage the threats and fear that inevitably followed. Some had panic attacks and nightmares severe enough to make leav-

ing the house each morning a daily ordeal. Six of her patients had
come to her after being diagnosed as mentally ill by other psychia-
trists. One element of the diagnosis was their membership in the Patriotic Union party. The doctors considered it a symptom, like hearing
voices. "One psychiatrist treated a Patriotic Union member who was in
the hospital recovering from a botched assassination attempt like a
criminal. The doctor said to him, 'How could you join them, you
come from a good family!' I tell people that they don't have to accept
this kind of psychiatric help. But they prefer to hide their political affiliation, out of fear that they may not receive medical care."

Working-class Colombians who joined the Patriotic Union treated
these symptoms with lemon balm tea and prayers to folk saints. But
those cures didn't work for middle-class Colombians, Estela explained
to me. Nothing did. They had to learn to live with it, like a physical
disability. After speaking with Estela, I had to wonder if being crazy
was not a metaphor, but an actual prerequisite for membership in the
Patriotic Union. Perhaps that was what it took, the kind of crazy, illog-
ical hope. When Mahatma Gandhi removed his lawyer's cravat and
donned khaddar cloth, he looked like a crazy beggar. Nelson Mandela
spent his prime locked in a cell, believing against all evidence that
change was possible. Even in the United States, the civil rights movement went from spark to flame with acts of courage described as crazy
at the time.

Josué recruited his friends. They had meetings and poetry readings.
To them, it was no suicide pact, but fresh air in a long-locked room.
"Quien nada debe, nada teme," the saying goes: Those who are not
guilty have no need to fear. Josué had a pure heart. It was his only defense. Guerrillas may have meant the Patriotic Union to be war by
other means. But Josué and thousands like him—many more, in fact,
than fought for the guerrillas—believed otherwise.

ooooo

SOON AFTER JOSUÉ'S RETURN TO PENSILVANIA, THE FARC SET AN
ambush outside town. Their target was Amado, Josué's childhood
friend and a new recruit to MAS. Several of Amado's men were killed,
but he escaped. Amado suspected Josué's involvement. After all, he

was the new Patriotic Union leader in Pensilvania. For Amado, his childhood playmate was not a democrat, but a guerrilla in lawyer's clothes. "Although the monkey dresses in silk," another Colombian saying goes, "it's still a monkey."

Amado wanted revenge. His first move was to visit the local police commander, who gave his blessing to the murder plan. As a first step, the police searched the home of Josué's father, where Josué lived. "I told my father he should do nothing to stop it," Josué said. "To the contrary, I wanted them to do it as soon as possible so that they would see that we were hiding nothing, that we had no connection whatsoever to any subversive organization. My father knew that, of course, because he was familiar with all of my work and knew all of my friends. We never conspired, either in thought or deed, we wagered our hearts fully on the promise of democracy precisely to overcome war. . . . And I told my father not to intervene to try and defend me. Since he was my father, they would never believe that he was objective."

Not long afterward, two of Amado's men, also childhood friends, told Josué that Amado planned to murder him. The police had agreed to look the other way. If Josué paid them, the men said, they would turn on Amado and kill him instead. Josué declined the offer. It would have compromised his ideals, turned him into the monster Amado thought he was. In any case, he told me, he reasoned that somehow Amado would change his mind or some miracle would prevent the assassin from shooting or that he would survive it, somehow. Josué concluded that he was safer in Pensilvania than if he were to flee somewhere else, vulnerable to an ambush on the road.

He exercised more, to outrun a bullet. He alerted the mayor, although he already knew that the mayor had told the police chief that he would do nothing to prevent the murder. Josué stopped going out at night. He went only to his office and home again. He imagined the bullet deceived. With the force of his gaze, he saw himself converting the bullet's mortal path into a foundry, melting lead into liquid and then into air, leaving only the faint metallic tang that permeates Colombia's towns. In other words, he took the drunkard's cure. He convinced himself that the rules of Colombian violence did not apply to him.

In Colombia, I have heard this rationale in many guises: how measures can be taken to minimize risk and how you can elude Death as if it were a bill collector with a rusted muffler on its car. I've even been told that it applies to me—that with certain careful arrangements, I can elude death. As I have been told, death is fooled by last-minute changes in itineraries. Or secret hotels and assumed names. By never announcing my arrival or my departure. By staying away from discos. Traveling with others. Traveling alone. Turning right instead of left. Left instead of right. Moving forward. Standing quite still.

At least once that I know of, I almost made the fatal step. I had been traveling with colleagues in the Middle Magdalena Valley. We were gathering testimonies about MAS. I took every precaution. I traveled with local officials who knew the region and its residents. We traveled during the day. We had informed the authorities about our plans, so that they would know that they would be blamed if something happened to us, thus (using Colombian logic) convincing them to cancel any pending plan. Our three *camperos* raced along the dirt roads with the latest salsa blaring, to scare away doubt. We had divided the foreigners between the cars, just in case: two Americans, a Spaniard, an Englishman. Each car, in other words, with a *gringo* amulet inside.

None of the farmers dared speak with us. The paramilitaries in the area had a particularly nasty habit of burning the faces of their victims with acid and dismembering them. Some patrolled in white cars, earning themselves the nickname the "Surgery" (La Cirugía). The rolling, grassy hills seemed to hide a plague that had struck all of the people and even their dogs. We passed a crocodile farm, where some enterprising families were attempting to take advantage of the valley's heat and water to produce a new variety of meat. At one schoolhouse—a thatch roof over poles, open to the breeze—we waited for people who never came. A lone horseman appeared, then vanished.

Like playing with words, reading danger is another favorite Colombian sport. Practice increases your chances of grasping danger's magnitude and intricate folds. But it guarantees nothing. At any moment, a fluke or unexpected event or missed detail can doom the most careful arrangements. In this case, my Colombian colleagues had withheld a crucial piece of information from me.

What I knew was this: Several days earlier, a human rights worker named Wilson Cáceres had vanished at a paramilitary checkpoint. Someone had seen him next to his red-and-white motorcycle, which had been tipped into a roadside canal. His disappearance followed the arrest the previous week of an army major in a distant valley town. The major had been charged with helping paramilitaries carry out a massacre earlier in the year. The paramilitaries were infuriated by the major's arrest. They attributed it to guerrillas disguised as international human rights monitors.

What I didn't know was this: Cáceres had volunteered to tell local families that I was coming to listen to their stories about MAS. Apparently, the paramilitaries tortured and killed him after learning about my visit. For the Surgery, a lot was at stake. Their group had forced the FARC to withdraw from many of the villages. Hundreds of other "suspected subversives" had been killed or had fled, leaving their lands available for new owners who supported MAS. Once again, businesses were reviewing plans for big factories, to produce cloth and soft drinks (not weird crocodile steaks). The local bishop called this "forced development," economic investment at gunpoint. I had arrived at the precise moment when the paramilitaries wanted to phrase a powerful response to human rights workers, who were the only real obstacle to the success of this variety of economic boom. In Colombian terms, I violated the golden rule of risk—*dar papaya*, that is, literally offering a papaya fruit of opportunity to experienced killers. It was one of those things, a dreadful convergence, that can often lead to disaster in Colombia.

Since my efforts to conduct interviews had been so spectacularly unsuccessful, we decided to head back to town. On the road, however, we received a telephone call reporting a massacre in the village of La Cristalina, not far from where we stopped to evaluate the information. As it happened, we were at the crossroads, just the spot to make a right turn that would deliver us to the site within the hour. Since I was the person who had organized the trip, the question was put to me: Should we go?

I got out of the *campero*. Around me was the rush of tall cane. It was late afternoon. The intense heat was gone, like air escaped from a balloon. We had not interviewed a single person. I had wasted an entire day. Perhaps this would salvage it? My eyelashes were heavy with dust. I wanted a beer. My heart pounded. Should we go? It was easy to make the turn. We were close. The drivers were willing. A grieving family was waiting, we were told. I had never seen the aftermath of a massacre. I was not squeamish, but felt morbidly curious. I also hated to waste time. Couldn't this make up for the lost hours? Wasn't this what people like me did?

I said no. We would return to the town. I can't say I could have won the argument if anyone protested, but no one did. We were tired and discouraged. I felt a buzz in my head, like distant machinery. It didn't feel right, that was all. That night, I curled up in my narco-hotel with an episode of *MacGyver*. Days later, I learned that the Surgery had communicated the false report of a massacre on purpose, to entice us into the ambush that apparently awaited us. My caution had saved us, just as, in slightly different circumstances (if they had placed the ambush on the road back to town), it would have killed us. Of course, attacking foreigners was the worst thing the Masetos could have done if they wanted to prove the region safe for investment. But they were canny. I could imagine them betting that the furor over a couple of human rights workers, regardless of the color of their passports, would not have lasted long.

The idea that you can outschedule or outmaneuver death is crap, of course. It's delusion. In the eyes of my children, I see clear as cut crystal my stupid and avoidable death. When I sit at the Miami gate of the flight heading to Colombia, I am sick with guilt and dread. Always. My fellow passengers are that curious mix produced by countries flailing at the edge: the rich returning from shopping sprees, journalists with the latest in survival gear, American businessmen who will be met by bodyguards, Washington politicos, me. I put my Colombia face on. I imagine that it hides the conflict that rages in my brain. Those of us who are safe in our beds and protected by laws and sure of the odds being ultimately in our favor imagine that it is impossible to truly appreciate how it feels to live each day like Josué did, as if it were his last. It is not like having a terminal illness, the announcement of which comes as unexpectedly as an earthquake in the course of life. The kind of death I am talking about is manufactured, in large part by one's own hand. It comes because you go. It is because you speak. It is because, however insanely, you imagine a future that is different from the present, a future that is as tangible as a cut papaya.

The miracle cure is simple and knowable: Stop. Do not take a stand.

Do not speak. Bear the future around you, desperate and destroyed. Colombians do not pay money to see Hollywood's noir thrillers about the future. They live them. All in all, they prefer the quick resolutions of *MacGyver.* For a long time, when I thought about Josué and how he must have felt, I imagined it as a kind of higher consciousness, a confidence in method and purpose that was completely foreign to me. I could never aspire to it. Later, however, I came to see that Josué was not so different from me. He had faith, yes, but it could be shaken. Josué was a man, not a saint. It's not so different, in the end, from how I or others of my race or class or nationality would feel. Until he was shot, I think he believed that death wouldn't happen to him. Like me, he saw it, but he refused to believe in his own death. Winds whittled at neighbors and friends and colleagues. They stopped at a doorstep and grasped someone else. In Colombia, as elsewhere, people say that they don't believe it can happen. They are sure they have arranged things or hidden well or performed the correct incantations and prayers. Or that it just isn't their time. *Nadie muere en la víspera:* No one dies on the eve of their death.

Josué realized that all of this thinking about a miracle change in Amado's heart and outrunning the bullet was irrelevant the moment the slug hit him. He fell, for a million yards. As he fell, he saw the steps that had led to it fanned like a ghostly deck of cards. Would he take them again? He would, he told me. Josué made a choice and he faced it. Death was not the most terrible thing. It was not the thing that scared him. Giving up was. Failing to hope, however insanely. For Josué, it became the only way to live. It was the soil that nurtured hope. It was the only hope.

ooooo

EVEN AS PRESIDENT BETANCUR PROMISED CIVILITY, MAS AND ITS allies in the security forces and civil society practiced the arts of murder and terror. They were committed to blocking peace and they murdered the Colombians committed to it on anything but their own bloody terms. Powerful officers, among them former defense minister General Landazábal, even accused Betancur of derailing a certain military victory over the guerrillas by imposing the cease-fire.

In 1987, MAS held an unusual workshop on the grounds of one of Rodríguez's ranches. With the military's help, foreign mercenaries from Israel and the United Kingdom were flown in to teach recruits how to shoot from moving cars, set up ambushes, and make explosives. The graduates were later linked to some of the most destructive acts of violence in Colombia's history, among them the assassinations of four presidential candidates, including Luis Carlos Galán. One military officer who attended the training later repented and in a letter to me said that the workshop helped create "a monster" that has yet to loose its grip on the country.

For their part, the guerrillas argued among themselves over the point of negotiations and began to train their invective, and guns, on each other. In 1985, authorities made a gruesome discovery near the town of Tacueyó, Cauca. Over 180 bodies of FARC guerrillas were stacked in muddy graves, some still in their uniforms. They had been killed not by the army or MAS but by their comrades in a splinter group. The dead had been accused of being government infiltrators, of *"grupismo,"* a crime that meant failing to think as the commanders demanded. "Thought crime," it seemed, knew no political boundaries in Colombia.

Remarkably, though, the cease-fire between the government and FARC held. Commissions and subcommissions, civic commissions and auxiliary commissions met. Every day, the Colombian newspapers and radio news shows and television broadcasts filled with chatter about what was happening with the peace process, what was not happening with the peace process, who had violated the agreement and who had defended the agreement, who was in charge, and who didn't have the faintest idea of what was going on. Writer Gabriel García Márquez called it the "information war." Guerrillas accused the government of lying. The government accused the guerrillas of continuing to kidnap. "It is no longer clear who is telling the truth. Or if they are lying on purpose or because they simply don't know the truth," García Márquez said.

What was beyond doubt, however, was that the guerrillas kept their weapons, recruited heavily, increased extortion demands, and taxed cocaine. So did MAS, with the security forces' help. The statistics from the time are remarkable. By the time Josué was hospitalized with bullet wounds in 1986, the number of political killings in Colombia had gone from 92 in 1980 to 1,387 in 1986, fruit of the political war as well as the emerging conflict with the Medellín Cartel. By the decade's end, that figure would more than double, leaving Colombia with the highest murder rate in the world. The peace process was like a neatly written play performed in the dead zone between massing armies.

MAS finally crossed an invisible boundary in 1989. The story begins, as many do in Colombia, with a massacre. Two years earlier, the Colombian army passed a juicy bit of intelligence to MAS. According to the army, nineteen Colombians posing as salesmen were bringing weapons and munitions to the FARC from Venezuela. Their route passed through the Middle Magdalena Valley. MAS caught them, took them to a ranch, executed them, and threw their bodies into the Magdalena River. For months, the investigation into the men's disappearance languished. Finally, in January 1989, it reached Judge Mariela Morales Caro. Like Judge Consuelo Sánchez, the first to indict Pablo Escobar, Judge Morales suspected that she had been chosen in part because she was female. Her superiors must have calculated that MAS might spare her life out of gallantry. Or no men were willing to take the case. Judge Morales knew that these had been no ordinary salesmen. For her, it didn't matter. Someone had brutally murdered them. Like many public servants I have met in Colombia, she accepted her role with a kind of detached professionalism. It is astonishing, in such an environment, that anyone retains respect for the law. Remarkably, people like Judge Morales believe that it is their duty to find and punish lawbreakers regardless of the political views of their victims.

I have heard it said in cases like these that the truth is impossible to determine. But Judge Morales knew that it was only a question of diligence. The truth is often glaring in Colombia, the mountain that marks the end of a plain. Judge Morales found a clear connection between the murders, MAS, drug trafficking, and the army. It was an alliance no one had gone to particular pains to hide. Judge Morales believed that she could trace the salesmen's killers to the generals who had been early MAS supporters and may have given the orders that the salesmen be killed. To gather the supporting evidence she needed, Judge Morales assembled a team with another judge, two assistants, nine police evidence specialists, and two drivers to travel to the area where the massacre had taken place and search for and interview witnesses to the salesmen's abduction and murder. The evidence specialists had pistols, the equivalent, it turned out, of carrying feathers into a rattlesnake den.

It was a road trip not that different from the one that had almost led to tragedy for me. But Judge Morales was of infinitely more interest to MAS. Gonzalo Rodríguez, Escobar's associate, also feared that she would discover the cocaine labs that the paramilitaries protected in the region. MAS paid off local police to plead overwork that day, so that no bodyguards would accompany Judge Morales's team.

With guns and weapons provided by the army, MAS dispatched one of its most experienced fighters to end the inquiry. Alonso de Jesús Baquero was over six feet tall. His African heritage had earned him the nickname "El Negro," the Black. His colleagues in MAS also called him "Vladimir," a reference to Lenin and El Negro's previous work as a FARC commander. He had been one of many to switch sides, shrugging off Marín's tired ideology like last year's designer shirt. Baquero studied assassination with the mercenaries brought to Colombia, once staying at "Fantasy Island," part of a Rodríguez ranch in the Middle Magdalena Valley. In one course, British mercenaries taught the students how to freeze a grenade into a block of ice, remove the pin at the proper moment, then place the frozen grenade at a location where the melting of the ice would cause it to detonate. The trick seems little suited to the ferociously hot Colombian lowlands, and I have never seen a report of its use. But it impressed paramilitary doctor Diego Viáfara so much that he described it in his official record of MAS activities. At the time Baquero was assigned to kill Judge Morales, he claimed to have already taken part in five massacres, including the murders of the salesmen, killing over 100 people.

Baquero was violent but also cunning. On the morning of January 18, Judge Morales and her team were interviewing locals in the village of La Rochela, near the place Baquero and his crew had executed the salesmen. Suddenly, the investigators found themselves surrounded by armed men. Once the police technicians had been disarmed, the leader appeared. It was Baquero. He spoke calmly to Judge Morales, presenting himself as a FARC commander who was only interested in helping her with the investigation and ensuring the team's safety.

He offered the investigators information and interviews with local farmers, claiming they could prove the paramilitaries' involvement in the massacre. The false guerrilla warned Judge Morales that a military patrol was near, which was a lie. For her safety, he recommended that the investigators allow their hands to be bound. This was critical, Baquero told them. If the soldiers saw the team, they would assume that the guerrillas had taken them hostage, thus saving her from having to explain what they were doing together.

Judge Morales told her colleagues to comply with every request. They boarded their vehicles. Baquero got in a separate car. They started driving. Then Baquero ordered everyone to stop. While the investigators were still in the cars, the paramilitaries opened fire. "I told my men, 'Don't spare the ammunition,' [and] afterwards toss grenades into the cars," Baquero later admitted. The paramilitaries emptied their clips, but they forgot about the grenades. They spray painted the vehicles with FARC propaganda, to make it seem like a guerrilla attack.

No one was fooled. One of the drivers, Arturo Salgado, survived. Salgado fell beneath a colleague who was killed. The dead man was so fat that the paramilitaries refused to lift him to check for Salgado's vital signs. Within minutes, a vehicle that happened to be carrying reporters from the local newspaper came by and shot pictures of the macabre scene. Along with Salgado's story of what really happened, the photographs were scandalizing Colombia by nightfall.

Years later, Judge Morales's family won a civil judgment against the Colombian government for the army's role in what came to be known as the La Rochela massacre. Her family received a damages payment equivalent to 1,000 grams of pure gold, as well as a lump sum representing her calculated future earnings until retirement. Baquero was eventually captured and sentenced to fifty-two years for his role in the La Rochela massacre. But the generals who sponsored and ordered the killings were never punished. In 1997, the newsweekly *Semana* interviewed Baquero and asked why he killed with such abandon. This was his answer: "When you have a godfather, in this case the army, you don't take into account the consequences. This is what happened to me. Because I had a godfather, I felt strong and we weren't afraid to do the filthy things that we did."

In the wake of the La Rochela massacre, President Virgilio Barco revoked the 1965 law (implemented after the attack on Marquetalia) that had legalized paramilitary groups. By then, though, the situation was well out of hand. In the same year, 1989, Escobar ordered the murder of Galán, the bombing of the DAS headquarters and the Avianca jet, and hundreds of other killings, often using operatives like Baquero and the killer boy La Quica to carry them out. The security forces made token efforts to dismantle MAS, but it was never more than public relations, to calm fears until the La Rochela massacre, like all of the others, faded in the public's mind.

That year, no one felt safe, even in the safest-seeming places. On March 3, 1989, for example, a gunman opened fire on José Antequera, a Patriotic Union leader, as he stood at the check-in counter in Bogotá's heavily guarded airport. Next to him was a rising political star, Ernesto Samper, who had stopped to chat. The gunman shot thirty-three bullets from a mini-Ingram submachine gun at Antequera, killing him. Five passed through Antequera and hit Samper, who survived. During his campaign for the presidency in 1994 (he won), Samper often let people unfamiliar with the incident conclude that he and not Antequera had been the target. At the time, politicians thought that an attack by traffickers burnished their reputations. In this instance, though, Samper had been caught in the cross fire. Antequera died face up on the slick airport floor. He was the 721st Patriotic Union member to be murdered since 1985.

Barco's decree did little to decrease MAS in size or modify its relationship to the Colombian army. MAS would move into an area, and behind it, like a hot wind, would fly helicopters and rocket-equipped fighter jets, the jangle of soldiers, leaflets promising massacres, *más de lo mismo*—more of the same. Of course, by then, the FARC would have melted away. All that would be left were the homes and cattle, the schools and barns, the soccer fields, the churches and bars, the beds and playpens and rocking chairs of the people who had the terrible misfortune, the life's burden, of living there.

ooooo

MY FIRST ENCOUNTER WITH MAS TOOK PLACE IN 1993, FOUR YEARS after it had officially been declared illegal. I was in La Uribe, the town

where, on December 9, 1990, the government had launched yet another full-scale assault on Marín's forces. At the time, the FARC's General Secretariat had been at Casa Verde (Green House), a camp near
La Uribe. The attack marked the surprising bitter end of Betancur's
six-year cease-fire. On that same day, millions of Colombians voted in
a special election for members of a Constitutional Assembly, which
would redraft the constitution as part of an effort to curb political violence. For some, the events were complementary; the country defended itself from extremists even as it perfected its democracy. Yet
many others saw it as the perfection of a mistake. In twenty-six years,
the military appeared not only to have learned nothing about the
FARC but also to have actually forgotten some of the useful things it
used to know. FARC spokesperson Raúl Reyes later claimed that during the attack on Casa Verde, they lost only thirteen fighters. None of
the members of the FARC's General Secretariat, its leadership, were
captured. The army had been bested at Marquetalia; it was bested at
Casa Verde. Marín emerged revitalized and with even less willingness
to negotiate in the future.

I was investigating reports that the army's Mobile Brigade 1 had
committed abuses during and after the attack and that MAS worked in
coordination with its men. The attack itself had been massive and, according to the FARC, unexpected. FARC spokesperson Raúl Reyes
later accused the government of taking advantage of the recent death
of Jacobo Arenas and the fall of the Berlin Wall to finish Marín off. For
Marín, it was just another in a long list of betrayals by the Liberal
Party.

In contrast to its attack on Marquetalia, the Colombian military
wasted no time on "civic actions" at Casa Verde. When I spoke to
them, local farmers could still recount the attack to me hour by hour,
as helicopters and small jets rocketed homes and trails. The soldiers
who came next captured fleeing residents and tortured them for information about the guerrillas' whereabouts. Behind them came MAS.
Once the battle ended, the Mobile Brigade took La Uribe as a temporary headquarters. Positioned in a cleft on the Eastern Cordillera, La
Uribe has 2,000 people, most from families that farm the surrounding
slopes. Like the FARC fighters who had preceded them, the soldiers
kept local business booming. La Uribe was dominated by bars, broth-

els, pool halls, and places to play *mini-tejo,* a horseshoe-like game that involves hurling compressed gunpowder at a wax backstop. Explosions as clear as rifle shots announce good scores. It is very Colombian.

Over the months preceding my arrival, the FARC had gradually returned to the heights, known as the Sumapaz. Its rugged valleys and the rivers that vein it hold transit routes that link southern Colombia, where guerrillas collect *coca* money and keep troop reserves, to central Colombia, where they can swoop down on towns, mount lighting roadblocks to seize travelers for ransom, and ambush the army as it lumbers up and down the roads. With support from cattle ranchers, local business, and the army, MAS had managed to occupy the towns that lay like beads between La Uribe, Villavicencio, and Bogotá. Yet combat was virtually unknown. Instead, armed men would kill people at roadblocks or drag them out of their homes to be shot. The residents of La Uribe were not in a unique situation; increasingly, Colombians in rural areas were finding themselves in the same predicament, with the FARC on one side, the army on the other and the paramilitaries with them, fighting for control by eliminating the civilians suspected of helping the enemy. At the time, the paramilitaries near La Uribe had adopted the rather cinematic name "Serpiente Negra" (Black Snake). On the streets of La Uribe, their war names were whispered like curses: Suckling Pig, Mosquito, Karate Man, Devil's Eyebrows, Grape Face.

They were MAS, or at least in the MAS model, transplanted to the *llanos* and run by the country's leading emerald broker, Víctor Carranza. He was the one Josué's group collected information on and the man, I feared, who would one day order Josué killed. Carranza was a squat, caterpillar-browed peasant whose only passion, other than emeralds and amassing wealth, was classical music. He was capable of a violence that rivaled that of Pablo Escobar. A former Carranza hit man who called himself "Travolta," after the movie star, once told government investigators that his duties included the murder of "anyone who was a guerrilla, kidnapper, mugger, thief, rustler, [or] member of the Patriotic Union." Sometimes, murders got ugly. At one farm, the target refused to come out of his house. "We lit the house on fire with our machine guns, and ten minutes later he and his mother turned themselves over; we took the individual two to three miles from the house [where the boss] gave the order that we waste him, and Crazy Joe [another killer] did it." Travolta later led investigators to a Carranza ranch called "La 60," where they unearthed a grave containing over fifty bodies. According to police, Carranza also kept cocaine labs on his ranches. One lab, Matacocos, was estimated to produce eight tons of pure cocaine a month.

Using Colombia's semantic custom, Carranza was a *"narcoesmeraldero,"* or a "narco-rancher." But these were not words used by either the Colombians or the Americans, who once sponsored an emerald trade fair where Carranza was an honored guest.

The residents of La Uribe were trapped. Yet they attempted to carve some semblance of normal life from the midst of constant tension, the "apparent calm" that defines permanent disaster in Colombia. Local shopkeepers sold to the FARC. They sold to soldiers. The prostitutes did not inquire about a client's political beliefs before quoting a price. If asked to place a phone call, the telephone operators did it. Some may have welcomed the soldiers. Others may have believed that the government would never pay attention to them unless the FARC backed demands with guns. But what they thought was irrelevant. The war was on them, among them, and the only escape lay along the long road out of town.

And that road was a problem. Patriotic Union candidates had been elected to La Uribe's town council but could no longer do official business in faraway Villavicencio. They couldn't perform their duties even ten minutes outside town. On the road, paramilitaries had permanent roadblocks and would stop vehicles to search for people whose names appeared on their lists. The council members suspected that the army had supplied the lists, but their protests only convinced the soldiers that they were doing the FARC's bidding, smearing the army with what soldiers said were false human rights claims.

The town council had invited me to visit, on one condition. They asked me not to identify myself as a human rights worker or even tell the army that I was traveling. My safety was not the issue. Theirs was. If they were seen talking to the representative of an international human rights group, they feared it would make the situation for them worse, not better. If necessary, I should think up another way to identify myself that had nothing to do with human rights.

I didn't like the idea of lying about who I was. It played into the very accusations that the army constantly made about human rights work and what our goals were. Still dominated by officers schooled in General Camacho's views, the army accused all human rights groups of being guerrillas or—when they made the effort to be polite—useful idiots, manipulated by Communists to further their campaign for world domination. The remains of the Berlin Wall, broken into pieces, had already been sold off as tourist mementos; but in the minds of most soldiers, it still loomed with menace. The town council members insisted. It would be best, they said, if I explained that I was there to visit a newly opened church. Perhaps I could describe myself as a Nordic nun? At the time, there were nuns living in La Uribe, although Josué could not remember which Scandinavian country they were actually from.

As the *campero* that served as public transportation climbed toward La Uribe, I worried about this request. Colombia is full of conspiracies and fake stories and outright lies. This is part of the linguistic gamesmanship, a kind of mental Hangman, that is constant. Fill in the blanks of the conspiracy, think of the most outrageous link or plot. If a right-winger like Álvaro Gómez, Laureano's son, is killed (as he was in 1995), the most likely suspect is not the FARC but his own extremist friends, who bet that his murder will be attributed to the guerrillas and will convince the government to forget about peace. It works the other way, too. Some particularly brutal massacres, with bodies dismembered and heads on pikes, were not the work of paramilitaries, some told me, but had been committed by the FARC, attempting to bump up outrage at paramilitaries at critical moments in its military campaign.

My intention in promoting human rights had not been to contribute to the tangle. I wondered how nuns looked in Colombia. The only ones I knew well were Sister Teresa, who had taken me to see Albeiro in Medellín, and Sister Nohemy, who worked with Josué. She wore a habit and crossed herself at every spot in the road were there had been a fatal accident, a shooting, or one of the frequent avalanches that bury traffic in mud and boulders. On one trip with Sister Nohemy, I had to avoid looking at her, since it seemed that every curve or bump marked the site of a disaster.

"Poor little ones!" Sister Nohemy would murmur. The souls of the dead wandered on the frigid heights looking for the path to the warmth of the valleys below, she told me. People left abalone shells at the roadside shrines to attract and bind them to the location of their deaths and keep them from haunting. On the climb to La Uribe, I wondered if I should start crossing myself. Was it left to right or right to left? I feared being caught like the American spy who failed to cut meat with the correct hand in wartime Europe. The question became moot when the driver's velocity, paired with the rough road, forced me to hang onto the metal rods bolted into the roof, to keep from crushing other passengers.

La Uribe was a place of scorching days and cool nights. The fields around it were a patchwork of chocolate, corn, papaya, and beans. Colombians from neighboring villages had hiked to town that morning to talk to me. I spent the day slipping in and out of houses and sheds in a most un-nunlike manner. The story that made the deepest impression on me related to an incident that had just taken place. Eusebio Ayure was a local farmer who had been in his fields when the army approached his house, where his wife and five daughters were working. The soldiers fired on his home, believing that guerrillas were inside. His eleven-year-old, Martha Cecilia, died instantly. A five-year-old was wounded. The army flew Martha Cecilia's body and the survivors to an army base without notifying Ayure, who was in his fields. This is how I wrote down his story in my notes:

> I asked [the army colonel] to deliver to me the daughters who had not been wounded in this episode. For six days, he tricked me by saying he would bring them until finally he insulted me and never brought them. . . . I hired an attorney and filed a claim. My wife was in the hospital for four and a half months. She left it handicapped [lost a hand]. My daughter is now handicapped [damaged leg]. I had to go up to my farm and work because the army finished off my entire crop. The house was destroyed. They killed my cattle. And to top it off, my dead daughter's body is disappeared, they never gave it back. . . . This is the greatest pain a parent can have . . . what pains me the most is that my daughter's body has not appeared.

By nightfall, I was exhausted. My hosts had arranged for me to stay with a resident who rented out beds to the infrequent travelers who stayed the night. I had a narrow cot in a windowless room. There was a water pump in the patio with a metal washbasin beneath it. It was a long and restless night, punctuated by *mini-tejo* explosions. Finally, a hard rain drowned them out with its battering on the tin roof.

A commotion woke me. During the night, several stores and the home where I slept had been painted with a huge red cross followed by a huge red question mark. In Colombian, it signaled who would be the next to die. Two members of the town council—the same people who had invited me—had received written death threats under their doors. The only people out at night were MAS and Mobile Brigade soldiers. My hosts made no distinction between them.

After breakfast, I visited the municipal official—the *personero*—whose duty it was to receive reports of abuses and report them to the authorities. These jobs are often filled by young people just out of law school. More experienced lawyers avoid them. Guerrillas kill the officials who report on their activities. So do paramilitaries and soldiers. These officials are also murdered when they report on local corruption or common crime. Only after the first threats would it suddenly dawn on the eager new lawyers why their more experienced colleagues had not competed for the position.

The La Uribe *personero* wanted to talk but didn't want me lingering in his office. He was terrified. As he opened his file cabinets to take out reports of killings, beatings, and disappearances, he kept a hand pressed to the metal, to muffle the sound. He had left the office dark, to hide my presence. That meant I had to peer at each document using only the sunlight that sifted through the dusty Venetian blinds. "It is difficult, almost impossible to do my job in a war zone," he said. "First, I must defend myself. The soldiers call me a guerrilla, a Communist, to my face. To me, it is clear that the armed forces are allowed a special kind of conduct. Instead of protecting the civilian population, the Mobile Brigade attacks it. Then, anyone who flees is called a guerrilla supporter."

There was no copy machine within fifty miles. I scribbled in the dark, trying not to write over what I had already written. There were names, villages I had never heard of before and that perhaps no longer existed.

The combat around Casa Verde had forced hundreds to flee, and many families had not yet and perhaps never would return. The man's voice trembled while his words emerged with the rush of confessed secrets. His reports to Bogotá had accomplished nothing. He corrected himself. They had only made him extremely unpopular with the army. The Mobile Brigade commander let it be known that he was displeased.

The man's head hung in the gloom. Even if a soldier seized my notes, I doubted he could have read them. Perhaps I could say that they were in Norse?

As I stepped out the door, the *personero* remained in the shadows. This was a man who would not live long, I was sure (several months later, I saw his name in the summary of murder cases prepared every three months by the human rights data bank). With that thought, I turned a corner. The Mobile Brigade commander stood ten feet away, apparently waiting for me. He looked like a caricature of a Latin American thug. His arms were folded over a burly chest. Under a billed cap, his aviator shades mirrored my surprised face looking back. His mouth opened. He looked surprised, too. I looked nothing like a Nordic nun.

I was spared by a miracle. Maybe one of Sister Nohemy's lost souls took pity on me. At that instant, a man stepped out of the bush a hundred feet down the road. Around him were children, jumping and laughing. The man carried something heavy in his arms. A slender peasant, the man strained under the weight. The children made such a racket that the Mobile Brigade commander turned. The peasant's shirt and pants were splattered with blood. The thing in his arms was tawny and long, and I suddenly realized that it was a mountain lion. Its eyes were white as eggs. Its mouth was frozen in a surprised roar. The man had skinned it, and from the neck dangled blood vessels and red strips of flesh.

The Mobile Brigade commander was transfixed. I slipped behind the building and headed to the *camperos* that would take me back down the mountain. Later, I learned that the commander had turned back ready to question me, only to find me gone, a soul that had found its path back down to the valley.

ooooo

THE M-19 CLOSED ITS PERFECT CIRCLE WITH ESCOBAR IN ITS OWN unorthodox way. On November 6, 1985, even as President Betancur tried to negotiate with the FARC, guerrillas seized Bogotá's Palace of Justice, where several justices were meeting to discuss the proposed extradition agreement with the United States. The M-19 claimed that it intended to hold a public hearing on President Betancur's failure to secure peace, which guerrillas charged was deliberate. The M-19 had seen its own efforts to negotiate with the government, separate from the FARC, fail. But some in Colombia dismiss the M-19's explanation and argue that the Palace of Justice seizure was not political at all, but rather payback to Pablo Escobar. He wanted Colombia's chief justice killed and the papers that constituted the criminal case against traffickers burned, to block extradition.

It was the beginning of the end of President Betancur's effort to negotiate an end to Colombia's conflict. By then, several M-19 leaders were dead or missing (Bateman himself vanished on a flight to Panama in 1983). The FARC seemed as surprised by the attack as everyone else. When President Betancur heard the news, he refused to negotiate and or even accept the anguished telephone calls of the chief justice, a hostage in his ruined office. The telephone was passed to the country's police chief, who himself received orders directly from army generals. Even as Colombia's radio news programs broadcast live the chief justice's pleas, the army arrived to encircle and blast its way past the building's bunkerlike walls. Tank rounds opened a path to the first floor and helicopters dropped troops on the roof. In twenty-six hours, the security forces retook the building.

Thirty-three guerrillas died along with eleven members of the security forces and eleven justices, including the chief justice. The government recorded forty-three other civilians killed, among them secretaries and janitors. However, the numbers of the dead, as is normal in Colombia, shift depending on who is telling the story. The government made only a token effort to identify all of the ninety-six bodies recovered from the building's ruins. The ones no one claimed were buried in a mass grave in Bogotá's South Cemetery, along with the bodies of dozens of Colombians killed in a 1985 mud slide in the town of Armero. Still more people were reported disappeared by the army after the Palace of Justice was retaken, among them cafeteria workers the army accused of helping the guerrilla operation.

Many things were done and undone in the fires that consumed the marble palace. The M-19 never recovered. In 1989, the M-19 negotiated its surrender. It is now a political party enmeshed in the same deals and scandals as the Liberals and Conservatives (though its aging members still trade on their fame as guerrilla commanders). The sword of Simón Bolívar that they had stolen to announce themselves in 1974, pledging to fight against exploiters of the people, was a loose end. In the 1980s, M-19 leader Iván Marino Ospina had given it to Escobar for safekeeping. Escobar had hung it like a trophy in one of his houses. After Ospina was killed, Escobar stashed it in a secret cache. When the M-19 prepared to sign its pact with the government, he returned it to them so that they could deliver it to the government in front of dozens of television cameras. At the time, few knew where and by whom the sword had been kept.

The sword's return was not the only deal the M-19 guerrillas struck before turning in their weapons. The government, after all, could not guarantee their lives once they became a political party. The M-19 feared the fate of the Patriotic Union. Within ten years of its first election, the Patriotic Union had virtually ceased to exist. In 1994, Josué and the few who remained filed a case before the Interamerican Commission on Human Rights, claiming that over 1,300 members had been murdered and dozens more had been forcibly disappeared. It amounted, the petitioners argued, to political genocide, the systematic elimination of a group based upon political party affiliation.

So, before turning in their weapons, the M-19 commanders sat down with MAS. The meeting took place in an elegant Bogotá restaurant. What better place for a "delighted chat" among enemies? The M-19 would disarm, that was clear. Henceforth, the M-19 would be a political party. Several of the leaders took part in the 1991 assembly to draft a new constitution and later went on to win seats in the Colombian Congress. At the dining table, the guerrillas offered MAS a deal. They would support a ban on the extradition of traffickers and an amnesty for paramilitaries and their army patrons. In exchange, they wanted a guarantee that the army and the paramilitaries would not hunt them down. At least, the M-19 wanted a warning first, before anyone was executed. The paramilitaries would give them one chance to get the person out of the country. Over drinks, the deal was struck.

Years later, I saw that deal honored. A Colombian prosecutor I knew had uncovered evidence linking the paramilitaries to a massacre in a northern state. Originally, he had not even been assigned to the investigation. But because he happened to be nearby when the killings took place–and no others wanted to go investigate–he took the case.

His investigation was supposed to be secret. But everyone knew who he was because he had shown up in person to sign the orders to collect the bodies. My friend had a common name, the equivalent of John Smith. Under his direction, the case advanced swiftly until the day I saw him in his office. The massacre file sat like a skyscraper on his desk. Prosecutors had few computers at the time, so each massacre, killing, or disappearance generated hundreds of sheets of testimonies, registries, certificates, autopsies, summaries, and the paperwork necessary to send one sheet of paper from office to office. The prosecutor had just signed the arrest warrants for the men he believed had carried out the massacre–local ranchers who had property near the site. Army commanders were also implicated and several were named in the case.

That morning, after the prosecutor had sent the paperwork for processing, he had received a phone call. It was from a friend, a human rights worker. The friend's voice, he told me, was trembling.

"It's my name," he said to me. He smoked, drawing the gray air deep into his lungs. "It's such a common name. The paramilitaries saw my name on the arrest order I turned in this morning. They confused me with someone who had once belonged to the M-19. So they thought they were bound by the agreement. They issued the warning. They called a friend of a friend of a friend. Finally, the warning got to me. My friend read to me the number on the license plate of my car, its make and color, the address of my house. They wanted to show me that they were serious. They've been following me for a while, it seems. I never noticed a thing. Of course, everything was correct. They know everything."

The prosecutor packed up his things. He left Colombia that night. There was no other option. In an instant, he had become a human target draped in clothes, a death foretold. Pacts between murderers are among the most reliable in Colombia. And of course, there was the phone call from a dear friend. Torturers know that the quickest confessions come not when the body of the captive is touched, but at the moment when the captive sees the torturer's hand reach for a spouse or child or parent. How creative, in this way, to force the friend to promise death, to cloak it as an offer of life! Colombia is, in its way, a great laboratory of human feeling, pushed to the limit of what is bestial, monstrous, unthinkable. But delivered with unmistakable élan. It is a beautiful car with a body in the trunk. It is incongruous, hideous, but has style to burn.

CHAPTER SIX

THE DEVIL'S TABLE

COLOMBIA'S NORTHERN PLAINS ARE CATTLE COUNTRY. CEBÚ AND THE Brahman-Angus hybrid called Brangus stand knee-deep in grass. The only shade comes from the widely separated bonga trees, as graceful as candelabra. The Sinú River occasionally wanders out of its bed and converts the pastures into a glistening marsh. When I visited in 1996, just such a flood had occurred. The Toyota Land Cruiser I was in functioned less like a car than the boat its name evokes, carrying us through the river itself as well as through places where weeks of water had made mud holes deep enough to grab the vehicle up to its headlights.

The sky was more populated than the ground. Herons, kites, and hawks whirled above us. I saw an egret resting on the hump of a steer, surveying us.

I may have heard the driver's name, but I tried not to. He was tall and burly, with a black mustache. That morning, he had appeared in the narco-hotel lobby as arranged. The previous evening, my colleague, Jennifer, and I had swum alone in the pool. We took a sauna and drank our Club Colombia beer in the silence of a building that would have been vacant but for the attentive staff.

Over the driver's shoulder was folded a *ruana*. As he drove, he manipulated two handheld radios. At the same time, the Land Cruiser radio softly played *vallenatos*, a type of Colombian folk music. The handhelds made sporadic buzzes that connected us, I supposed, to the place where Carlos Castaño, Colombia's paramilitary leader, was waiting for us. In the region, his forces were called the Head Splitters, the

Mochacabezas. Six times during the three-hour trip, the driver pressed buttons on the handhelds to signal our progress. There were no gas stations, billboards, or food stands. There didn't appear to be anyone in the occasional houses, either, or even in the single village that we passed through. I'm tempted to say that the feeling I had–a marriage of quiet and menace, the odd absence of people along the roads while I sat in close proximity to a man I neither knew the name of nor could trust if he told me, the spotless gray velour covering on the seats of the Land Cruiser, and the driver's buzzing radio–is a Colombian kind of feeling, when everyday scenes or familiar items of comfort or utility are set against a shocking potential for violence. At least I've felt it nowhere else.

I thought about the amulet Josué had recommended and that I had never acquired. Perhaps it wouldn't be such a bad idea. Certainly, Josué could tell me where to get one. We only spoke that one time about charms, but it was the kind of thing Josué always seemed to know a lot about. The next time we met, I promised myself, the amulet would be first on my list of questions.

ooooo

Castaño didn't call his men the Head Splitters. The official name was the Córdoba and Urabá Peasant Self-Defense Group (Autodefensas Campesinas de Córdoba y Urabá, or ACCU). Córdoba is the northern state where the Castaño family has ranches and other properties. Urabá is the region–including the Caribbean portions of the departments of Chocó, Antioquia, and Córdoba–that hugs the Gulf of Urabá, the poke into the eye of South America that seems to extend Panama's reach. Urabá is steamy and covered by banana trees. It was thinly populated until La Violencia pushed in thousands of refugees. In 1959, United Fruit set up a processing plant there, taking advantage of its proximity to the United States to ship bananas north. The work was exhausting, filthy, and poorly paid. But in a country struggling economically, it was something.

To arrange the meeting with Castaño, I had flown into Apartadó, the unofficial capital of the region, a sprawling, ugly town that serves the thousands of banana workers who care for the racemes destined to be split into bunches for the breakfast tables of the United States and Europe. The commuter plane descended and I saw what appeared to be dozens of bodies draped in white hanging beneath the broad banana fronds. As we touched down, I saw that these were the maturing fruits protected in cloth. The workers are predominately Afro-Colombian and have a singsong accent typical of the Caribbean coast. At night, they drink and dance and fight in Apartadó's discos, burning years in a matter of steaming hours. *Mapalé* is a distinctive beat melded from Guinea and Colombia's coast, and it seemed to pulse even in the relative peace of a Sunday morning.

Apart from the International Committee of the Red Cross (ICRC), the only other non-Colombians to request a meeting with Castaño had been a European group that was attempting to get him to stop attacking civilians. Their representative had worked in Colombia for almost a decade and had witnessed MAS's end, at least the end of the version set up by Captain Echandía. The La Rochela massacre as well as infighting and troubles with the traffickers had left most of the original leaders dead or in jail. After the government outlawed paramilitaries, groups calling themselves MAS or the Masetos continued to kill. Yet MAS had no center any more, no grand plan for beating guerrillas.

Until Castaño, that is. A European aid worker–"Celine," who continues to work in Colombia and asked me to use a pseudonym–said that he was something new, even though he had been part of MAS. As a youth, Castaño had volunteered as a guide for one of the army battalions that worked most closely with paramilitaries. He and his elder brother, Fidel, later set up their own version of MAS in the state of Córdoba, financed with contributions from cattle ranchers and business. To buy weapons and pay salaries, they also used the fortune Fidel had earned in cocaine. Fidel had discovered cocaine in the early days of the trade. But unlike the conflictive Escobar, Fidel had cashed out early. Fidel's achievement was visible as the Land Cruiser advanced, the seemingly limitless horizons of Castaño pasture as flat as Texas prairie.

What was new about Carlos—at least, for the residents of northern Colombia—was his willingness to use terror to fight guerrillas. MAS, of course, had killed with abandon. The massacre of Judge Morales and her team was a message to anyone who dared question what the group considered its right to eliminate perceived enemies. But with MAS, things rarely went further than a bullet in the head and the utilitarian slit in the belly, to ensure that the body sinks in water. Not so with the Head Splitters. They mutilated bodies with chain saws. They chained people to burning vehicles. They decapitated and rolled heads like soccer balls. They killed dozens at a time, including women and children. They buried people alive or hung them on meat hooks, carving them. They threw their dozens of victims like damp and flyblown trash to the side of the road. Rarely were their victims uniformed guerrillas. At the time, I was not aware of a single battle between Castaño and the FARC. Instead, Castaño's victims were civilians accused of supporting the guerrillas by supplying them with food, medical supplies, and transportation.

The Germans have a word for what Castaño did–*Schrecklichkeit*, meaning frightfulness. It was applied in their invasion of Belgium and France, to circumvent the civilian resistance that did not threaten but could delay troops. German soldiers burned homes, shot whole families, and pillaged and raped. It was not homicidal mania, but deliberate, part of the plan. The press called Castaño a butcher, bloody, remorseless, barbaric, cruel, demented, crazed, horrific. His face was a mystery to most, though as we drove, the image in my mind was a banal and obvious one, Marlon Brando playing the mad Colonel Kurtz in *Apocalypse Now*. I had heard that one of Castaño's favorite books was Joseph Conrad's *Heart of Darkness*. I was surprised he read at all, though it seemed, in the odd way that Colombia has of making seemingly normal things menacing, to be one of the scariest things about him.

What few appeared willing to say out loud what that Castaño's methods were working. For the first time since 1964, the FARC was in retreat, at least the units that Marín had deployed in Urabá. Even MAS, at its strongest, had never managed to completely dislodge the FARC from the Magdalena Valley. Castaño's success was especially important given Urabá's strategic value. The Gulf of Urabá and the 150-mile stretch of Caribbean coast that flanked it to the northeast were critical to the FARC's ability to tax cocaine shipments headed north and collect weapons and other war materiel headed south. Without Urabá, guerrillas were forced to acquire weapons in other ways (among them, the riskier air-dropping of gun crates, a technique that would later lead to the downfall of Peruvian intelligence chief Vladimiro Montesinos, who once sold the FARC 10,000 AK-47 assault rifles).

There was another thing about Castaño that people marveled at: He wanted to convert the Head Splitters into a political force. He was more, he claimed, than a warlord. He headed a political movement that represented Colombians sick of the guerrillas and their abuses— the *"gente de bien,"* the people like us. The ACCU had a plan not only to eliminate guerrillas but also to invest in Colombia, to bring back prosperity. In its day, MAS had launched a political party and used civic actions to broaden its appeal beyond killings. But the traffickers had poisoned the efforts and the political movement had failed. Castaño was more adept. At his camps, he regularly met with politicians, although the topics usually centered on their efforts to save the lives of constituents or villages on Castaño's lists of suspected subversives. But he could be reasoned with, people said to me. At least, you could make the effort. Castaño was known to begin each morning with a quick surf on the Internet. He would call Colombian journalists to praise or complain about stories. Some of his closest advisers regularly traveled between Colombia and the United States and with him would read the tea leaves of U.S. policy. He appealed to Colombia's middle class, beset by violence and kidnapping, fed up with the government's inability to keep them safe.

Like MAS, Castaño worked closely with the army. Sometimes, the Head Splitters and soldiers patrolled together. At roadblocks, they addressed each other as cousins. On patrols, soldiers would threaten villagers by saying that the Head Splitters followed in their wake and would massacre them if the villagers continued to support the guerrillas. These were not casual threats; Castaño's men followed close behind, chain saws at the ready. When Castaño planned an operation—in other words, when he sent his men into a farm or village to kill the civilians there, people he claimed were guerrillas in disguise—he let the army know, so that any soldiers who happened by the area would not make the mistake of intervening. They never did.

For me, what was most intriguing about him was personal: He had agreed to meet me. To my knowledge, no *pájaro* or MAS member had ever met with a foreign human rights monitor. Certainly Escobar hadn't, though a family lawyer had once argued to me over the telephone that the Americans' refusal to issue his family American visas amounted to a human rights violation (I disagreed and the man never called again). Castaño's willingness to talk was a sign. Perhaps he recognized that the Head Splitters were being measured against a standard that existed beyond Colombia's borders. If so, then I was ready to travel. I thought a meeting would demonstrate that his actions had consequences that crossed borders. Jennifer and I were portents. Our *mona* faces—the word Colombians use for "fair-skinned"—and tortured Spanish were the physical proof that a human rights movement could reach into the jungle where he had his fortress and address him directly.

That year, 1996, the human rights movement had won some small but promising victories. The case that would lead to Chilean general Augusto Pinochet's arrest was just beginning. Arkan, the Serb paramilitary, had been forced to disband the "Tigers." Already, I was lobbying the U.S. Congress to link human rights to proposals of military aid for Colombia, a tool to pressure Colombia's generals to break their ties to Castaño and pursue him in the field. Contact with the United States, I believed, was the only way to prevent Colombia's military from returning to its open alliance with paramilitaries.

Of course, there were big problems with my rosy scenario. Somalia and Rwanda were cautionary tales of grisly international inaction. Dutch soldiers had fled the U.N. safe area at Srebrenica just a year earlier, allowing Bosnian Serbs to slaughter Muslim refugees in the largest single massacre in Europe since the Holocaust. Human rights alone still did not move policy. But I was hopeful that there was real change afoot.

It was a long ride. Idly, I imagined making these forces visible, lightning brought down through my fingertips. I had put a fresh stack of business cards in my pocket the night before as I laid out clothes in preparation for a dawn departure. Familiar and symbolic of an ordered life, they disturbed me as I touched them. I imagined them scattered and crumpled in the marsh. Before requesting the meeting with Castaño, I had met Céline in a Bogotá hotel. I asked her if I would survive it. In a cloud of cigarette smoke, Celine encouraged me to go. Her conversation with Castaño, she reported, had been tense but productive. Just as the army did, Castaño accused human rights groups of working for the guerrillas. "All international human rights groups are shit and only accuse government security forces, while never denouncing the criminals from the other side who force us to act, and so on. What saved us was the public reading, translating in Spanish on the spot, of our last statement on Colombia where we denounced guerrilla violations," Celine said. She cut her hand through the air like a hatchet. "Pffff!"

Change in Colombia, I was convinced, could only occur as a result of personal encounters. It was one of the things I had learned from Josué. In another time, Pedro Marín had paused from violence to ask why. Couldn't the same be possible with Castaño?

Yet I had only read about Marín's transformation. This was altogether different. My feet shuffled in the foot well of the Land Cruiser. Had anyone been transported while crouching there? I also had this thought: I am silly and small. It was too late to turn back. Was it?

∽∞∾

THE CASTAÑOS ARE FROM AMALFI, A COFFEE-GROWING TOWN IN Antioquia similar to both Génova, home to Pedro Marín, and Pensilvania, home to Josué Giraldo. The Castaños owned a dairy and a house in town. Fidel was the eldest of twelve. One of the few photographs of him shows a square-jawed, moody face with large, dark eyes. While still a boy, Fidel left home. He made his way to Guyana's diamond mines and reputedly spent time in Brazil and Venezuela. When he returned to Amalfi, he had money. He bought a bar and half of his father's ranch. Soon, the neighbors whispered about his armed bodyguards and seemingly limitless cash. Although the family doesn't talk much about it, Fidel Castaño was a cocaine trafficker. He was also a thief, and he robbed anything with a ready market. As Carlos later said, Fidel was a family man, "but he lacked certain scruples."

Pablo Escobar was among his associates. For a time, Víctor Carranza worked with him, though Fidel concentrated on stealing the emeralds that brokers carried, not mining them like Carranza. There were rumors that Fidel had killed one of his girlfriends in a jealous rage. Occasionally, people in Amalfi would see Fidel jogging while followed by bodyguards in *camperos*. Fidel's dreams were much less grandiose than Escobar's. Cocaine was a means to pleasure: his ranches, a Medellín mansion, and enough money to dabble in modern art and purebred cattle. He frequently traveled to Paris and New York, and while out of Colombia preferred Ermenegildo Zegna suits and fine wines. In Colombia, though, he was a traditionalist. He barred television and air-conditioning from his ranches. The Ecuadoran painter Oswaldo Guayasamín painted a portrait of Fidel that captured his melancholy.

Fatefully, Fidel persuaded his father, Jesús, to sell the Amalfi property and move to the hot side of the slope that ends on the banks of the Magdalena River. The new ranch was called El Hundidor. There, Jesús Castaño lived by himself. He would go into town only occasionally, to buy supplies and do business. But everything changed in 1980. That year, the FARC abducted the elder Castaño. Likely, it was Fidel's fortune they were after. Earlier, the M-19 had grabbed Carlos Lehder, demonstrating that both guerrilla groups were eager to dip into what they imagined would be a bottomless pool of cocaine cash.

At first, the kidnapping seemed routine. Several of the Castaños had been sympathetic to the guerrillas' talk of social justice and an end to the corruption that permeated Colombian political life. Carlos admitted later that he had once toyed with the idea of joining the FARC. Relations between the family and guerrillas had been cordial. Carlos even knew "Boris," the *comandante* who ordered the kidnapping. Boris had been a childhood friend of several of the older Castaño children. Carlos described it as "a friendly kidnapping, really." At the time, Carlos was fourteen.

Fidel mortgaged his father's property. He arranged personal loans from friends. At least, that is the family's official story. By then, Fidel must have been a millionaire several times over. No one buys Italian suits with sacks of corn. In any case, the family paid. The FARC demanded more. The kidnapping stopped being friendly. Like so many other Colombian families, the Castaños felt powerless. The authorities were unable or unwilling to rescue Jesús.

A friend who once interviewed Fidel told me that he believed that this eldest son refused to pay from his cocaine fortune for a simple reason: He hated his father. Jesús Castaño was a taciturn and distant patriarch whose role in the lives of his children was to make them work and to beat them in preparation for life's inevitable sorrows. There were also rumors of rages and bisexuality, though it is only clear that Jesús drank a lot, typical in Colombia's backlands, where *aguardiente* flows as freely as coffee. Alcohol can harden the heart of a man against his children. As the eldest, Fidel may have absorbed most of his father's rage.

At least, this was my friend's idea, formed as he watched Fidel rock in his rocking chair. Fidel was surrounded by bodyguards who kept their guns off safety, ready to spray the shadows that surrounded his ranch. Later, my friend opined that the family had packed him off to a mental asylum, though that seems unlikely. The kind of rage that motivates a man like Fidel is too normal a part of Colombian life to be classified as illness.

Like the M-19, the FARC miscalculated the reaction of their prey. Perhaps Fidel thought that his family was better off without the old man. Perhaps he let those years of resentment creep into his decision. Perhaps his rage was simply infinite. Carlos later said that Fidel rejected the guerrilla demand for more money and sent them a final message: "I have never had that kind of money and if I do some day, I will use it to fight you."

In one of his first public interviews, Carlos told part of this story to Germán Castro Caycedo, a Colombian writer. Eventually, Carlos said, the family suspected that the guerrillas were delaying a release because Jesús was dead. They believe that the FARC shot Jesús in late 1980. The FARC counters by contending that Jesús Castaño, chained to a tree, bashed his head against its trunk out of fury when he learned that Fidel would not part with his cocaine fortune. Jesús Castaño's body has never been reported found.

Much later, the FARC delivered a kind of apology. Guerrillas told the Castaños that Boris had not been authorized to ask for so much money. But it was too late.

Carlos left school. He had dreamed of being a teacher, but he never returned to class. "My life divided into two parts, before and after the kidnapping of my dad. Now, it had a single purpose: to find the old man's kidnappers among the guerrillas."

Carlos, Fidel, and two brothers went to the Colombian army base in Segovia, the town nearest El Hundidor. There, they volunteered as guides. They offered to take soldiers to where the guerrillas camped and collected their supplies, to their favorite crossings and places where they could count on receiving medical treatment, a meal, a delivery of cash or weapons. The army caught the man who had seized Jesús Castaño, but a judge later released him for lack of evidence. The judge, Carlos later claimed, was really a guerrilla. So were the town's leaders. So were the members of the Liberal and Conservative parties in Segovia. The day that the alleged kidnapper was released, Fidel and Carlos followed him, then shot and killed him. One of Fidel's employees later told the journalist Alma Guillermoprieto that after Fidel located the place where his father had been chained and supposedly died, he and his men killed every man, woman, and child living along the river nearby.

These were the rules that Fidel had learned alongside Pablo Escobar: Kill or be killed. Strike first. Strike at the heart: the family, the home, the friends, the neighbors. Strike hard. Strike until the Borises of Colombia surrender out of sheer grief and despair. "Believe me that I understood that this was just," Carlos has said. "We had no idea what the word *self-defense* meant. We simply said—and I have to tell the truth—that we did it for vengeance."

In Colombia, stories of family tragedies and the vengeance they spawn have a name: *"culebras"* (snakes). The Colombian novelist Fernando Vallejo once wrote that *culebras* are "outstanding debts. As you will understand, in the absence of the law that is always being rewritten, Colombia is a snake house. Here, people drag behind them feuds sealed generations ago: passed from fathers to sons, from sons to grandsons: and the brothers fall and fall."

Culebras can poison an entire generation, even though some siblings or cousins may have nothing to do with the original grievance. *Culebras* know no political boundaries. Along with the Castaños and Maríns, Álvaro Fayad, an M-19 commander, saw his father executed by Conservatives. So did the ELN's Fabio Vásquez. Although Colombia's new president, Álvaro Uribe, did not see his father killed, he was told over the telephone that the FARC had invaded Guacharacas, an Uribe ranch, and shot Alberto Uribe. Sometimes it seems as if every alliance or every feud in Colombia begins with the killing or kidnapping of a family member.

I would occasionally meet families cored like apples by *culebras*. Sometimes, the aggressors seem to take pleasure in leaving some family members alive. It's like a savings account, something left in reserve for an emergency shooting. Once, I drove for several hours to meet a young man named Daniel, one of the few surviving males in his family. Over the previous decade, his mother, grandfather, sister, uncles, and cousin had been arrested and accused by the army and paramilitaries of supporting guerrillas. After a bar brawl, two uncles were killed. A brother and a brother-in-law were "disappeared." A nephew was shot in a market. Men hired by the family to work their farm had been murdered, tortured, raped, mutilated, and decapitated. Once, paramilitaries grabbed his sister, beat her, and threatened to cut off her head if she didn't tell them where her father and husband were. In all, seventeen family members had been murdered.

Daniel told me this in a matter-of-fact way, like the plot of a movie. I took down details with a sense of disbelief. He and his sisters were caring for over a dozen children left orphaned by the family's losses. I couldn't swear that none of them had joined the guerrillas. The area where they lived was firmly under guerrilla control, and it is common for young Colombians to imagine that guerrillas promise a life of adventure and romance. Or the guerrillas are seen as the only alternative to a life of crushing work and poverty. Yet as I counted up the family's losses, it seemed to me that the attacks against them went well beyond what one might expect if some of the children had joined the guerrillas. The *culebra* would not stop until the family had ceased to exist, like an infection cured only by excision to the bone.

Fidel Castaño was frustrated with what he saw as army delays and bureaucracy. In 1983, the family sent Carlos to Israel to take a yearlong course on anti-terror techniques offered by a private company operating near Tel Aviv. Meanwhile, Fidel hired about a hundred men. To the locals, they became known as the *tangüeros*, after Las Tangas, a Castaño ranch. A *tanga* is a tanager, common on the northern plains. It is an odd and somehow terrifying name for a death squad, taking the loveliness of a bird and harnessing it in the minds of people to horror. But it is not new; during La Violencia, *pájaros*, birds, were the worst killers. With the *tangüeros*, Fidel set out to drain the guerrilla sea in relentless, bloody gulps.

The press began calling Fidel "Rambo"(*First Blood,* the first Rambo movie, was released in 1982). The name didn't mean that Colombians considered Fidel's cause just. It meant that they recognized that Fidel (who, like Pedro Marín, never liked his nickname and preferred "Jaime," his nom de guerre) was capable of cinematic acts of violence. For Carlos, his brother's embrace of *Schrecklichkeit* was like a beacon of light in the darkness. "Since we could not combat [the guerrillas] where they were, we chose to neutralize the people who brought to their camps food, medicine, messages, liquor, prostitutes, and these types of things. And we realized that we could isolate them and that this strategy would give us very good results. Incredible."

Fidel spared no expense. He pitched in with Escobar and Rodríguez to pay the foreign mercenaries brought to train promising fighters like Alonso de Jesús Baquero and sent Carlos to study with them. Even as MAS expanded in the Middle Magdalena Valley, Castaño's *tangüeros* pushed south from the Córdoba plains. A young aid worker in Montería once ticked off for me the massacres they committed as if they had been particularly noteworthy soccer games. "There were at least sixteen in two years, all at night, all carried out by men wearing civilian clothes and hooded. The men have lists but they end up killing whomever they can get their hands on. There was Volador, Mejor Esquina, El Tomate, Toronto, Callemar, Puya, La Rincón de las Viejas, San Rafaelito, and Saisa-Palmira. Sometimes they force people out of the houses first and shoot them. Other times, they just lock them in and burn the house down with the people inside."

Later, I visited refugees from El Tomate, resettled in the misery belt that surrounds the city of Montería. Improbably, their slum is called Canta Claro (Bright Singing). The sun was down. A breeze blew in a hint of rain. In the distance, I saw flashes of lightning. People sat in wooden chairs outside their homes to escape the heat. From mud nearby, frogs croaked. A woman, Iris, said that the Maoist guerrillas called the Popular Liberation Army (Ejército Popularde Liberación, or EPL) had used El Tomate as a base of operations. People could not prevent it. Doing so would have marked them as pro-paramilitary. The guerrilla commander, known as "Marcos Jara," even paid the villagers to construct a building for them there. Then a clash between the *tangüeros* and the EPL near El Tomate left one of Fidel's men dead.

From the right, Sister Nohemy Palencia, Josué Giraldo, Gonzalo Zárate Triana, and a secretary with the Meta Civic Committee for Human Rights. After Zárate's murder in 2001, the committee disbanded. (© 1993 Robin Kirk for Human Rights Watch)

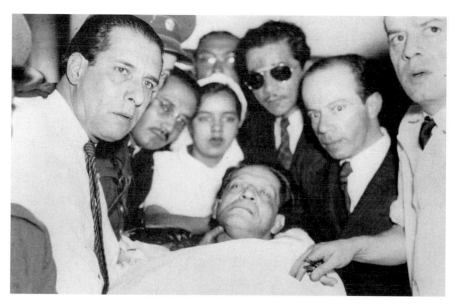

Jorge Eliécer Gaitán lies dying after being shot on April 9, 1948. (AP/Wide World Photos)

This family escaped paramilitary attacks and fled to
Villavicencio in 1993. They were among those helped
by Josué Giraldo and Sister Nohemy (center) of the
Meta Civic Committee for Human Rights. (© 1993
Robin Kirk for Human Rights Watch)

This Colombian family represents three
generations displaced by political
violence, the eldest in the 1950s.
(© 1993 Robin Kirk for Human Rights
Watch)

The M-19 seized the Palace of Justice in
1985. (© SIPA-Press)

FARC commander-in-chief Pedro Antonio Marín (left), known as "Sureshot," listens to the instructions of FARC southern block commander Jorge Briceño, known as "Mono Jojoy," minutes before starting a parade. (Photo by José Miguel Gómez REUTERS © Reuters NewMedia Inc./CORBIS)

Pablo Escobar holds his Colombian passport during a 1982 interview. (El Tiempo Archive)

After combat, Colombia's military often displays casualties, like these suspected UC-ELN members killed near Barrancabermeja, to the press. (Teun Voeten/Panos Pictures)

A cross followed by a question mark in La Uribe, meaning who would be the next to die. (© 1993 Robin Kirk for Human Rights Watch)

Albeiro and Sister Teresa with Albeiro's girlfriend in a Medellín comuna. (© 1995 Robin Kirk for Human Rights Watch)

An eclectic mix of VIPs watching an army parade and demonstration in support of the armed forces. Claudia Veláquez Angel, Miss Colombia 1996, gets more autograph requests than most. She is seated next to the army's supreme commander, General Manuel José Bonnet. (Teun Voeten/Panos Pictures)

Carlos Castaño, leader of the paramilitary group United Self-Defense Forces of Colombia (AUC), inspects his troops in a mountain hideout in northern Colombia. (REUTERS/Eliana Aponte/File photo, © Reuters NewMedia Inc./CORBIS)

Elsa Alvarado, Mario Calderón, and their son, Iván. (© CINEP)

Father Fabio with Jennifer in the Tierralta parish garden. (© 1996 Robin Kirk for Human Rights Watch)

A Colombian family lost six of its members to a culebra, the Colombian term for a feud carried out for political reasons. They rest together in this graveyard. (© 1993 Robin Kirk for Human Rights Watch)

In 1998, UC-ELN guerrillas caused the incineration of the village of Machuca. (© Jesús Abad, 1998)

A Colombian officer demonstrating new human
rights materials at Urabá's 17th Brigade. (© 1996
Robin Kirk for Human Rights Watch)

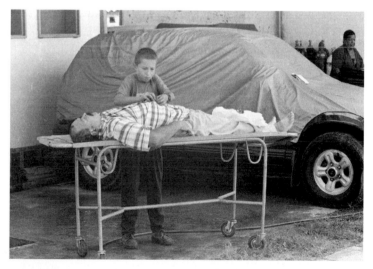

A child prepares the body of his father killed by the AUC.
(© Jesús Abad)

Opposite: General Rito Alejo del Río with the author
while he commanded the 17th Brigade. (© 1996
Jennifer Bailey for Human Rights Watch)

President Andres Pastrana (left) and the leader of the leftist FARC guerrillas, Pedro Antonio Marín, sign a joint statement in February 2001, to revive the peace process and resume talks. (AFP PHOTO/Luis Acosta © AFP/CORBIS)

President George Bush meets with Colombian President Álvaro Uribe in the Oval Office in September 2002. (AP Photo/Doug Mills)

Several days later, Iris said, the *tangüeros* arrived on the local bus. "They had already killed the five passengers and made the driver into their hostage. They went from house to house. People knew that they couldn't escape, so they waited to be killed. There were other men around the town, waiting to kill us as we fled. When they were finished, they tied the bus driver to the wheel and set the bus on fire. They killed fifteen people and burned twenty-two houses, one with a pregnant woman inside. They said that they would come back in a couple of days and kill anyone who didn't leave. So we left."

Fidel's relationship with local army commanders was excellent. After the massacres of seventeen workers on the Honduras and La Negra banana plantations in 1988, government investigators discovered that the gunmen who had executed them with shots to the head had first made a stop in Medellín to finalize plans. There, they had been hosted by the Colombian army intelligence officer who prepared the list of individuals to be killed. The officer paid their Intercontinental Hotel bill with his Diner's Club credit card. Subsequently, the judge investigating the case ordered the army officer's arrest along with Fidel Castaño and MAS leaders in Puerto Boyacá. MAS retaliated by ordering the judge's murder. She fled Colombia. But Castaño and MAS were persistent. A year later, gunmen killed her father in Bogotá. Then they killed the judge who replaced her, that judge's two bodyguards, and several witnesses. Terrified villagers abandoned their farms by the thousands. By 1990, guerrillas realized that they had a choice: death at the hands of the *tangüeros* or surrender. In 1991, the EPL signed a government amnesty and turned in its weapons.

Fidel Castaño was generous in victory. In response, he handed in 350 of his own guns and 2,400 acres of Córdoba ranch land, to be parceled out to amnestied guerrillas. The Castaños also set up the Foundation for Peace in Córdoba to dole out small loans. The director—a Castaño sister-in-law—told me that 897 families had been given land and hundreds of students had enrolled in Castaño-funded schools. Although they held title to the land, one condition of purchase was that former guerrillas agree to never sell or mortgage it. Among the villages the Castaños rebuilt was El Tomate. However, its former residents were never invited back. Instead, former guerrillas and their families received the newly built homes.

After the surrender, the EPL commander—whose real name is Rafael Kergelen—did well for himself. Along with other EPL leaders, he became part of a new political party, Esperanza, Paz y Libertad (Hope, Peace and Freedom). Esperanza, for short. He got a seat on the Montería town council, a gun, a sports utility vehicle, an apartment, and enough money to pay a dozen of his former fighters to be his bodyguards. These are *"reinsertados"* (literally, "reinserted ones"), guerrillas who accept an amnesty and return to civilian life. Predictably, the FARC despised them and what they derided as the government's buyout, *plata y puesto,* money and a seat in government. People like Kergelen and Antonio Navarro Wolf, a former M-19 commander who later was elected to the Colombian Senate, are, in the FARC's words, "traitors to armed revolution."

When I met Kergelen in 1992, a potbelly had erupted at the former guerrilla's waist. His complexion was pallid from too much rum and too many cigarettes. He had a pompous, too loud voice, which projected out his apartment window and into the street, where his bodyguards lounged in the building's shade. Before our meeting, I had been in Canta Claro with the refugees who had lost their homes twice: once to Fidel Castaño's *tangüeros* and a second time to the *reinsertados,* who seemed deaf to the irony of taking the land they had caused these families from El Tomate to lose. I was in no mood to hear his marvelous ideas about social justice. Kergelen had used, then abandoned them. It wasn't anybody's idea of a revolutionary fairy tale.

When I asked about the El Tomate refugees, Kergelen shrugged. He whisked his hand at the cigarette ash he had dropped on his new pants. Life was tough.

I couldn't rage against his lofty principles. He had none. "I am a Marxist capitalist," he said, grinning.

In quick order, he acknowledged that his men had made deals with drug traffickers, had used peace negotiations as a way to rest troops and prolong the war, had killed hostages through poor care or miserable conditions, and had cut a deal with the Castaños for cash. Kergelen told me how he had opened a channel of communication to Fidel Castaño by kidnapping his younger sister. When the EPL returned her without demanding a ransom, Fidel recognized the gesture as friendly.

Commander Marcos Jara was ready to get out of the region's persistent rain and sleep in a dry bed.

"On the whole, I would say that the results are positive, so far," he said.

As it turned out, Kergelen's respite was brief. He tried to use his cozy relationship with Castaño to eliminate his political rivals. He told Castaño that three local teachers had set a bomb in 1996 in front of the Castaño family foundation and the local ranchers' association, killing four and wounding thirty-five. Castaño ordered the teachers seized, then claimed to have tape-recorded their confessions. The *New York Times* later reported that a Castaño representative had played the tape for them, proof, Castaño claimed, of the men's guilt. Government investigators later told me that there was serious doubt about the teachers' involvement in the bombing. It was more likely, they said, that the teachers were Kergelen's political rivals. Kergelen was later arrested and charged as an accomplice in their murders.

When I left Kergelen's apartment, all this was in the future. Kergelen offered me a cigarette, a drink, a dance that night, and a ride to my next appointment or, in fact, anywhere I might like to go with the *comandante*, to see the sights of Montería. The twenty-something former guerrillas who were his bodyguards waited, like fruit flies on an old mango. All in all, I said, I preferred to walk.

ooooo

THE EPL'S SURRENDER LEFT THE REGION IN "APPARENT" PEACE. Colombians, I had learned, love the word "apparent"–*aparente*. "Apparent" has a complicated meaning: the situation seems all right but is actually impossibly tangled and you cannot get to the end of any story since the passions and the rancor from years past never entirely disappear but also never reappear in completely predictable ways. Since nothing terrible has happened for the past twelve hours (maybe less), or at least nothing has been officially reported, at any moment (maybe in less than an hour) bad things probably will occur not far from where you are standing or sipping your beer, but there is no telling and so, while you can, enjoy.

With the EPL's surrender in 1991, the Castaños believed that they had won. They had eliminated a guerrilla group and gained new recruits who didn't need to be trained to shoot a gun. The Esperanzados who got Castaño land became a kind of private security force, a buffer against attacks by the FARC. The farms were converted into listening posts, their children into watchers. The Colombian army was particularly pleased and declared Urabá "pacified." As the Toyota Land Cruiser I traveled in approached Carlos Castaño's location, those children were posted at each of the numerous gates we had to pass through, opening them as we approached and closing them after we passed.

The EPL's surrender was fortuitous for the Castaños. Their attention was elsewhere at the time. Fidel had remained loyal to Pablo Escobar until he learned that Escobar had delivered a huge cache of weapons to the ELN, part of his plan to promote chaos and force the government to block extradition. Fidel's anti-Communist core was offended. He confronted Escobar and later described their exchange as "heated. I never spoke to him again."

Carlos had already broken the tie. He was disgusted with Escobar and the problems he caused for MAS. Carlos said he began to deliver information to the authorities about where Escobar was hiding more dynamite and how he planned to kill a presidential candidate. The police found the dynamite and reinforced the candidate's security. Eventually, Castaño recruited other MAS colleagues to betray El Patrón. It was the beginning of what some called the "devil's table," a triangle that joined paramilitaries, the security forces, and traffickers tired of Escobar and his high-profile attacks. What Escobar had brought them, Castaño believed, was too much trouble. It was in everyone's interest to bring him down and return the business to reasonable men. When Escobar killed Kiko Moncada and Fernando Galeano in 1992, friends of the Castaño brothers, it was the last straw. A month after Escobar left the Cathedral, the Castaños convoked the meeting that would lead to the creation of the PEPES–People Persecuted by Pablo Escobar. MAS had been the fruit of an emergency meeting that included the army, local businesspeople, and traffickers; the PEPES drew from the same "devil's table." The Cali Cartel gave the PEPES an estimated $50 million, to pay informants, buy weapons, pay killers, and engage in ac-

tion where needed to hunt Escobar down. Known as careful businessmen, the cartel's leaders, Miguel and Gilberto Rodríguez, could defend
the PEPES as a wise investment. It eliminated not only a man who
had already tried to kill them, but a rival for the lucrative cocaine
routes north.

The PEPES were implacable. They killed Escobar's lawyers, his
couriers, and the people who shielded him from the law by signing his
legal documents. Fidel Castaño told the people too terrified to defy Escobar that they had a choice: Face Escobar's wrath or the wrath of the
Castaños, who would hunt down and kill every family member of the
person who gave Escobar any help. People chose to betray Escobar.
The PEPES showed Escobar that they knew where his family lived,
where they shopped, where his children went to school. In one four-
month period in 1993, the PEPES murdered five of Escobar's lawyers
and a lawyer's teenage son. One victim reputedly died of a heart attack
before the assassin's bullet finished him off. The PEPES also knew
where Escobar kept the things dearest to his heart, like the automobiles he had stored at a Medellín garage. The Pontiac that Escobar
claimed had belonged to Al Capone was a fake. But the charred and
twisted junk left behind when the PEPES bombed it was authentically
terrifying. The PEPES even kidnapped Terremoto de Manizales,
Roberto Escobar's Paso Fino stallion, and killed his groom. The
PEPES castrated the horse and left him tied to a post in a Medellín
traffic circle. Perhaps the PEPES were making an allusion to the famous scene in *The Godfather*, where Don Corleone orders his men to
place the head of the stallion Khartoum in his owner's bed. I suspect
that Fidel, who prized fine animals, could not bring himself to order
the stallion's execution. It was something he did not hesitate to do if
the target was human.

On December 2, 1993, the telephone betrayed Escobar. The PEPES
had demonstrated to him that his survival depended on a return to the
Cathedral. Escobar called his teenage son to arrange a magazine interview that he hoped would smooth a surrender. But Escobar talked for
too long, longer than the three minutes he knew the Americans
needed to fix his location. When he saw the police approaching, Escobar tried to flee but was cut down on the building's red tile roof. Journalists later described him as a fat man with a Hitler-style mustache,

unaware that the men who killed him clipped the mustache tips as souvenirs. One Medellín resident later wrote, "That day, a telephonic heart attack and a sudden downpour left a huge part of the city mute. These were the signals that showed that the battle between 2,000 men and the world's most wanted drug trafficker was over."

American technology found Escobar that day. Yet he would never have been vulnerable were it not for the PEPES. Castaño claims that the PEPES even bought houses for the police to install the American equipment used to capture Escobar's cell phone conversations. Diego Fernando Murillo, known as "Don Berna" and one of Castaño's main allies, frequently visited the headquarters occupied by DEA and CIA teams. The "devil's table," it appeared, had plenty of room for the American officials so determined to catch Escobar that they were willing to look the other way when the traffickers made themselves useful allies.

ooooo

FOR THE CASTAÑOS, ESCOBAR'S DEATH WAS WELL TIMED. IT AL-lowed them to return their attention to Córdoba, where the "apparent" peace that followed the EPL surrender was at an end. Infuriated by what they saw as the EPL's betrayal, the FARC began to hunt Esper-anzados, a macabre mirror of the extermination of the Patriotic Union. At the same time, the FARC moved into areas formerly held by the EPL and began kidnapping, collecting "war taxes," and taking their share of the robust traffic in illegal drugs and weapons. The Esperanza-dos responded by killing people they believed helped the FARC, among them members of the Patriotic Union and the Colombian Communist Party. The FARC didn't help matters by telling Colom-bians they stopped at roadblocks or grabbed on their farms to vote for the Patriotic Union or risk death. Peace pacts between the groups were negotiated and signed, but they lasted only as long as it took the ink to dry. In the heat of the banana groves, that is equivalent to the wink of an eye.

Carlos revived the *tangüeros*. But he had bigger plans for them. This time, he chose a proper name for them, the ACCU. He had helped his brother defeat the EPL. But Carlos knew that he had a far more formidable enemy in Pedro Marín. There was another factor that Carlos kept a secret for several years: Fidel was dead. According to what Carlos later claimed, Fidel was not in a Portuguese mental hospital (as the friend who had interviewed Fidel surmised) but had been killed in a skirmish with EPL holdouts on January 6, 1994. Fidel took a bullet to the heart. Carlos kept it secret to rob the guerrillas of a victory they were not even aware of. Fidel was the seventh of twelve Castaño siblings to die. These tangled wars—between the Castaños and the FARC, between Esperanza and the Patriotic Union, between the army and guerrillas, by the guerrillas and Castaño against the people who lived there—caused the homicide rate in Urabá to skyrocket in 1994, to 245 per 100,000 inhabitants that year. Even the most violent cities in the United States never top 50 per 100,000.

The same month that Fidel died, residents of an Apartadó neighborhood organized a chicken barbecue and dance to raise funds for a local widow and her ten children. After buying the chicken, the community, called La Chinita, had rented the loudest sound system in the region, packed in a pickup truck, and guaranteed to fill the hot night with cumbia, merengue, *mapalé*, salsa, and whatever else the DJ decided to spin. The speakers likely favored the guerrillas, who crept up in the midnight shadows of the banana grove that bordered the houses. Only feet from where 500 people danced, they opened fire. Thirty-four people died, including the DJ. Later, it was revealed that this was a FARC attack on suspected Esperanza supporters. But only one of the dead actually belonged to Esperanza. The rest were just poor people. The prosecutor who investigated the massacre later told me that the thirty-fifth victim had been one of the guerrillas, apparently executed when he refused to shoot.

Elected officials found themselves governing in a war zone without battle lines. The war intruded everywhere, even within city hall. The Apartadó mayor, Patriotic Union member Diana Estela Córdoba, was murdered. She had replaced a mayor who fled Colombia because of death threats, then returned and was killed. An ex-mayor was convicted of helping the guerrillas carry out the La Chinita massacre. Unable to fill the post, a coalition of twelve Liberals, Conservatives, and Communists chose a candidate that no one knew much about, so no one opposed: Gloria Cuartas, a social worker. A short, energetic woman, she had previously worked in the region on development projects. There was no other candidate. On election day, 80 percent of the eligible voters stayed away from the polls, leaving Cuartas with a margin of 7,120 votes to zero.

It was a candidacy, Cuartas later admitted to me, of lost causes and *culebras* impossible to untangle. When I interviewed her in the mayor's office, her determination to best the daunting odds fit her like a tight suit. Her round face was topped by a pageboy, the haircut of a woman with no time for or interest in fashion. She paced as she spoke, a torrent of words as thick as the rivers that vein the Urabá plain. In her speeches, she promised economic renewal and a voice for communities in municipal affairs. But plans were overtaken by bodies. "There is a lot of talk," she said, "but no one does anything to stop the violence."

For her, no ideology was at stake. She believed the fighting was essentially over money—money from the bananas, money from smuggling, money from drugs. "Of course, there are different political groups vying for power. If it weren't for the armed groups, I think we could reach a consensus on what the region needs to progress. But all the armed groups want is to control the economic question, and all are willing to massacre or murder or force people from their homes to win."

The week I spoke to her, the city had been overwhelmed by hundreds of refugees forced out of their homes by the FARC, in a maneuver meant to delay Castaño's advance. They were packed into a dust-floored arena that was filled with piles of clothes and blankets and children and the greasy smoke of cooking fires. I asked Mayor Cuartas if she had received threats. She waved her hand in the air as if to brush away gnats. "Of course! There are plenty of rumors. I don't know where they are coming from. Some are just for me, others are for the entire city council. Of course there is panic. Supposedly, there will soon be many massacres. What I want is to get the armed groups out of the neighborhoods and stop making civilians targets in this war."

But the civilians were the point of the combat, literally. Everyone was aiming at them. There was something—a relation, a job, a route used to go to work—that linked everyone to some supposed offense and could therefore be used to convert them into a target. The FARC and Castaño used bodies to speak—bone and flesh messages. When Mayor Cuartas took office, massacres had become an Urabá dialect. Paramilitaries killed eighteen customers in a bar frequented by Patriotic Union members. The FARC responded with a weekend's worth of murders in the towns of Apartadó and Carepa. The paramilitaries continued the conversation by killing in Turbo. The FARC answered by dragging twenty-six banana workers from a bus, binding their hands, and shooting them one by one. "The 'self-defense' groups took advantage of the conflict and selectively murdered individuals who helped the FARC and the EPL," Castaño later wrote in his memoirs of that period. He called the massacres *"carambolas,"* ripe fruits falling from a tree. "Every weekend, the armed groups spoke to each other with massive executions of collaborators or sympathizers. . . . I confess that I was not able to watch the nightly news and I believe that as many innocent as guilty people perished."

ooooo

THE TOYOTA LAND CRUISER LEFT THE PLAIN FOR SOME IMPROBABLE-looking hills—caricatures of hills, really, like the bumps drawn by my daughter under a smiling circle sun. We crested one bump, where there sat a house with a red-tiled roof. The driver got out and was replaced by two men carrying Uzi submachine guns. I did not ask *their* names, either. They were the first men we saw wearing uniforms—blue shirts and pants with ACCU baseball caps and armbands.

The new driver took a slippery track that cut sharply downhill. A forest thickened in the narrow canyon. The Land Cruiser fishtailed as if intending to slither all the way to the creek that marked the canyon floor. A horseman appeared. In front of us was a concrete pad with a roof of palm leaves enclosing a small kitchen. I felt immense solitude. I was cut off not only from the world I normally inhabit but especially and more precisely from any sense of physical limits. The trip had crossed and far outdistanced any limit I had previously set for myself in Colombia. I felt as if I could have exploded or flown. I could have curled up like a sow bug and rolled among the wet leaves.

A woman emerged from a kitchen. She had a cup of sweet coffee in a flowered demitasse with a chip at the lip. She had clearly been ad-

vised in advance of our arrival. The meaty steam of breakfast puffed
from a door as I got out of the car.

To my surprise, the shelter had a small lavatory. Jennifer vanished
into it. I sipped the coffee. There was a rustle. The plants themselves
seemed to grow hands and legs and heads sheened with sweat. There
were men in the bush or the bush was men. Which one was Castaño?
I had only seen an old photograph of Fidel published in *Semana*
magazine.

"Jennifer," I said. The men were young, slender. Seeing them elsewhere, I would have assumed that they were guerrillas. A man stepped
forward. I heard Jennifer behind me, a sharp intake of breath as she
saw them.

"Carlos Castaño," the man said. He held out a hand.

Castaño was shorter than me, fairer than the photograph of his
brother. He had a crewcut and ears that flared from his head. At the
time, he was thirty. He was no Kurtz; he was Captain Willard as
played by Martin Sheen. Castaño pulled a pistol from the small of his
back and placed it on a chair. I don't think the gun was meant to
threaten. It was the gesture of a man used to guns. I imagined that his
gun could be as annoying as a tie on a muggy day.

The woman who had given me coffee brought plates of pork and
boiled yucca. We ate in silence. Then Castaño began to talk. Dialogue
did not come naturally to him, particularly with such strange creatures
as American women. He was perfectly respectful during our four-hour
stay, never flirtatious or dismissive. Yet he spoke as if we were dim and
not particularly lovely children. He had no illusions, I imagine, of who
or what we thought he was. Yet he had difficulty, I saw, gauging us.

He began where most Colombians begin when telling their story to
outsiders: La Violencia. The FARC, he said, had begun as a self-
defense group. To fight it, the government had set up its own civilian
units. He skipped the turmoil of the 1970s and began the story of his
father's kidnapping and death. His telling made the decision to form
the ACCU seem inevitable and of a piece with the current of Colombian history. "It is impossible to defeat the guerrillas in Colombia just
using the same weapons and tactics as the army," he said. "It is an
unequal war, because guerrillas can always go outside the law. We un-

derstand this attitude. We chose to separate ourselves from the Colombian army, so that we could become a kind of guerrilla force and fight them using the same kinds of combat."

He acknowledged his time in MAS without naming the group. It had "lost its honor," he said, by getting mixed up with drug traffickers and foreign mercenaries. But the government, in his view, went too far in the other direction when it pursued MAS, in getting rid of the good as well as the bad. Listening to him, it all made a kind of organic sense. Fight fire with fire, use the enemies' tactics against them, hit them at their most vulnerable, along with the men and women who fed and clothed and cured them. But what of the massacres? The Head Splitters?

Castaño's voice got louder. He had a gruff, staccato way of speaking, appropriate for command but out of place in the quiet glade. *"¡Por dios!"* he said, the first sign of irritation. "My God! We don't kill the innocent. It's easy to blame us for any bad thing that happens." He claimed the press and the guerrillas hidden within human rights groups "satanized" him. "Look, guerrillas hide themselves within the civilian population, they manipulate the population."

To illustrate his point, Castaño told me the story of the meat butchers. "The guerrillas rustle cattle, they rustle maybe a hundred head, from the plains. They take the cattle to the poor farmers and they say, 'Look, we'll trade you five steers for your one steer.' So the farmer gets more cattle and the guerrillas are able to launder the stolen herd. Then everybody goes to the butchers, who dress the meat. Now the butchers know the brands of the stolen steers, they know that the cattle were stolen. So we send a message through the butchers. Don't be complicit."

Over the previous months, there had been dozens of reports of butchers killed, their bodies eviscerated, burned with acid, dismembered, beheaded, castrated, and dumped at the roadside. Not only butchers had been murdered; local authorities had lists containing the names of the truck drivers who transported the cattle and the shop owners who sold the meat.

"Do the butchers have a choice?" I asked. Castaño's "message" was apparently a bullet to the head. It didn't allow for much of a reply.

"¡Por dios!" Castaño said, even more irritated. "They know what they are doing. Now, they know it will no longer be tolerated. It is a problem that has been solved."

Fidel, he acknowledged, killed too generously. But he, Carlos, was different, he claimed. He started with 600 guns and as many machetes—curved knives long as an arm used to cut brush or crops. At first, his men sinned by what Castaño described as a "poor use" of their weapons. To cut human limbs? I did not speak, but the words tumbled in my head like dice. Castaño denied that his men used machetes or chain saws on the innocent. Only once had one of his men decapitated a victim, Castaño said. This fighter was a former EPL guerrilla whose sister had been raped by a guerrilla comrade. When the paramilitary realized that some guerrillas he had captured had fought under the rapist, his anger overcame him. He lopped off a captive's head with a swing of his machete. Castaño confessed that he personally regretted killing one person, a crippled boy. As he told the story, the boy had passed information to the guerrillas about the ACCU's location. "My blood boiled," he said. "Though I am the commander, I need someone to control me."

Castaño wanted us to see the ACCU as a work in progress. These mistakes were in the past. Now, he was "professionalizing" his force. He had divided them into a local force, which stayed in place to defend against guerrilla attack, and what he called his "Shock Force," specially trained men able to move where they were needed. He also had urban commandos in the cities, among them Medellín.

There were ten commanders on what he called his general staff. At the time, he claimed over 2,000 trained and uniformed troops, close to an entire army brigade. For Castaño, however, the key to victory was not troops but intelligence: knowing where guerrillas received support, who advised them. In his telling, guerrillas were ubiquitous, with spies and fighters out of uniform everywhere, in the offices of mayors, in hospitals, in schools, even the Presidential Palace. The ACCU had a system, he claimed, to evaluate intelligence and confirm it. The information came from many sources, including the army.

From his olive-green backpack, Castaño drew a stack of papers. These, he said, were intelligence reports that identified guerrilla supporters. I remarked on their professional appearance. The text had been

assembled on computers and printed on ACCU letterhead. The letterhead itself was oddly pastoral for such a relatively monied war. It featured a male farmer spreading seed from a mesh bag, superimposed on
an outline of Colombia. I didn't add that the Colombian ranchers and
traffickers who supported the ACCU didn't seed from mesh bags, but
inspected their properties and the work of the hired help from Toyota
Land Cruisers, accompanied by heavily armed bodyguards, a cell
phone and beeper at the ready in belt clips. The laborers they inspected
were the ones typically killed by the ACCU as suspected guerrillas.

Castaño was flattered. He volunteered that he had sociologists, historians, and anthropologists working for him. It was true. One of them,
Isabel Bolaños, had even done work for a well-known human rights
group before becoming a close Castaño adviser (and was later arrested
and convicted of aggravated homicide and forming paramilitary
groups). Castaño had never finished high school, so the fact that intellectuals had pledged his cause was a source of pride. He patted the
stack. He had positioned it on the battered canvas of his backpack, too
precious, it seemed, to expose to the splintered plank of the table. I
asked if I could have them.

"No."

"May I look at them?"

After a pause, he handed them to me.

The first report dealt with the plight of the elderly in Córdoba. Another examined social welfare policies enacted by the central government to assist poor and abandoned children. The language was taken
straight from the lexicon of a hundred left-leaning think tanks. I sup-
pressed a smile. It was a victory of sorts, albeit semantic. A private
army built by traffickers to defend their brand of savage capitalism had
morphed into the war weapon of the "oligarchy" of the FARC's petri-
fied vision. Yet somewhere along the line, Castaño had soaked in a social conscience. Was this more evidence of his peculiar genius?

In the reports, the ACCU was positioned as a group that was political, not military. It represented an identifiable constituency, the middle
and upper classes. Just as the FARC did, the ACCU described Colombia's institutions as unjust and oppressive. The reports advocated reform and greater equity. The conclusions stopped short of advocating
the government's overthrow; but there was nothing in them that my

most left-leaning Colombian friends would object to. It was all, in theory, what the Colombians currently killing each other were fighting
for. This was the kind of plan that the FARC claimed it wanted, so
long as it did not arrive on letterhead featuring a bowed peasant toiling
on someone else's farm.

So why did Colombians fight? It was a question that I posed to myself often. No differences in race, ethnicity, religion, or language separate Colombians. I could see that in the men who made up Castaño's
personal guard and lounged nearby. To my eye, they were drawn from
the same pool as the men guarding Rafael Kergelen: white, black, mestizo, some with the scraggly beards and the broad, flat cheekbones of
Colombia's indigenous communities. "Strange country," wrote one
Colombian violentologist in an essay about the roots of Colombian violence, "where all of the parties to the conflict claim they fight for the
same reason." Castaño himself once admitted it, in an interview with
the Spanish newspaper *El País:* "Why do we kill each other when
what we are searching for appears so similar?"

I flipped through the last report as Jennifer and Castaño talked. Jennifer had a technique that helped smooth difficult interviews. She
smoked. When Castaño offered a cigarette, she accepted, leaning close
to light it on his match. I would have liked to have taken a picture
there: an attractive blonde with her eyes narrowed against the smoke
and Castaño, grizzled, dirty, but newly curious as he examined this
marvel, an American human rights worker, at his table. Jennifer had
smoked with the ELN. She had smoked with the army and police. She
smoked with other human rights workers and government ministers
and mayors. If I ever write a textbook for human-rights school, I will
dedicate a chapter to smoking as a critical investigatory tool. Non-
smokers like me are like skiers afraid of heights; we lack that subter-
ranean mastery of the game.

The last report in the stack was a history of the Jesuits in Colombia.
The document began with St. Ignatius of Loyola's decision to found
the Company of Jesus and summarized the order's history in modern-
day Argentina and Paraguay, where it had once run extensive missions
among the Guaraní people. The conclusion stopped me and I no
longer heard even Castaño's loud voice. The document claimed that
there was evidence that the Jesuits were part of an international Com-

munist conspiracy. In itself, it is a familiar charge, one that has been leveled against the Jesuits for several centuries, as persistent as the blood libel against Jews. But the document was specific. It identified Jesuits at a nearby parish, in the town of Tierralta, as guerrillas. The report followed with their names.

My thoughts narrowed like one of those science films that begin with a frame of the blue globe of Earth, then narrow to a continent, a country, a state, a city, a park, a person, her skin and hair, in my case, prickling uncomfortably. The letterhead, the Courier typeface, and the study, I realized, were elements in a death list. It was peculiarly Colombian, sophistication and modernity around a rotted core. I recognized the names. The previous day, Jennifer and I had lunched at the parish house with one of the people on the list, Father Fabio. He ran the local chapter of the Colombian Red Cross. Father Fabio had been the one to alert me to the murders of the butchers, truck drivers, and store owners who had been the object of Castaño's "lesson" about working with guerrillas. Father Fabio told me that these same people were threatened by the FARC, which would kill the butchers who refused to slaughter the meat, the drivers who refused to transport it, and the store owners who refused to sell it.

The parish had a quiet inner garden with a gazebo sheltering a table and chairs. There, Father Fabio laid out maps that showed where the guerrillas were using refugees to push back the army and the ACCU and reopen supply lines. More than 3,000 people from thirty-six different villages had packed up their few belongings and converged on Tierralta that week. Those who refused had been executed. That day, the families were camped on the town's outskirts, flooded like the rest of the Upper Sinú plain. As the Red Cross representative, Father Fabio had to cope with the misery that the FARC's maneuver had provoked. He later drove us through the settlements, a repeat of my tour through the refugee shacks with Josué years earlier. "In the hills, there are tiny fiefs, like small dictatorships, where people are at the mercy of this or that commander, from either of the armed groups," Father Fabio told us. "We've tried to form health brigades or cooperatives or local committees to at least address the most basic problems. But every time that we try, we are accused of helping one or the other side."

At first, the Tierralta mayor wanted to block the families' exodus.

He could not pay for shelter or food. After Father Fabio spoke with him, he relented and sent the town's trucks and even road-grading equipment to pick them up. Still, there was only food enough for a week's worth of lunch. "There is a generalized panic," Father Fabio said, "one rumor will start and then it is like a snowball that grows huge in people's minds. Last year, it was the paramilitaries who forced this movement, because they wanted to empty out the land as a way of cleansing it of people they thought supported the guerrillas. Now it is the guerrillas. It is part of a dialogue, with words of human bodies and flight."

As his fingers traced strategy on the maps, they trembled. In 1989, Fidel Castaño had ordered the Jesuit who ran the same parish, Sergio Restrepo, killed. The FARC also killed priests whom they accused of betrayal. If any of the refugees complained to the guerrillas that they were being poorly treated, the blame would fall squarely on Father Fabio. Each day he lived was the gift of the FARC commanders or Castaño, not God, it seemed.

According to the document I held in my hand, Castaño was preparing to withdraw his gift. In it, Father Fabio was accused of supplying guerrillas with tents, food, and medicine. Indeed, we had spent much of the previous day viewing those same supplies. There were so few of them that Father Fabio worried that an epidemic of dengue or cholera would break out and wipe out families who were already sick and malnourished. What the report identified as support for the guerrillas was actually humanitarian assistance.

I packaged my alarm as a question to Castaño. Was he aware that this priest represented the Red Cross? That he couldn't possibly know or be required to know who among the needy were guerrillas? That the priest's job was to help people in need? That many of the refugees were children who couldn't possibly have a political affiliation?

"Perhaps," Castaño allowed. "My intelligence sources may be incomplete." However, he added, there was no room for doubt about one thing. The parish was a nest of guerrillas.

I put the document on the table. How many names had I missed? The director of a senior center, the truant officer, the day care teacher? It was too late to grab the documents again and scan them for names. Castaño, annoyed, began putting them in his backpack. Although in the morning newspaper, reports of massacres and murders seem senseless, without logic, in fact each has its reason. Sometimes the reason is flawed or casual. But it is a reason. Of the bodies found in Colombia, 90 percent show signs of torture, meaning that the victim had time to explain, to correct, to plead. It rarely matters. As another priest once remarked to me, "No one dies without a reason in Colombia. It doesn't mean the reason is right."

A tapping on the rush roof signaled rain. I wanted to stay, but we risked being marooned in the vast marsh that would soon rise to isolate the house. Our good-byes were rushed. Since we had brought our bags with us, the driver took us directly to the Montería airport. Once in Bogotá, Jennifer and I went to the Jesuits' office and spoke with Father Fabio's colleagues. The next day, Father Fabio was reassigned to Bogotá, effective immediately.

I thought I had solved at least that one problem. There were other names from Castaño's report that we shared, though no one else appeared to be in imminent danger.

The price, of course, was that as of that day, there was no longer a Red Cross representative in Tierralta. Therefore, there were no more tents, food, or medicine. There was no one there to record the refugees' deaths, marked only by freshly turned ground in the cemetery. Over the next weeks, people returned to their villages. They had less than they had taken away with them and there were fewer of them. But that, too, seemed part of someone's grand plan.

ooooo

ALMOST A YEAR TO THE DAY AFTER I MET WITH CASTAÑO AND SAW Father Fabio's name in the report, armed men entered the Bogotá apartment building where Mario Calderón lived. He was one of the people whose names I culled from Castaño's report. For several years, Calderón had worked in Tierralta as a priest. Later, he left the Jesuit order. He married Elsa Alvarado, and they had a son. For a time, he worked for a Jesuit-run human rights group. Then he gave advice to communities in the Sumapaz region interested in ecologically sound enterprises. Despite its proximity to Bogotá, the Sumapaz had been a FARC stronghold for decades. Nevertheless, Calderón believed that working on behalf of the greater good while keeping the authorities informed of his work would avoid any misunderstandings about the nature of his endeavors.

It was a new path, different from what he had done and who he had been in Tierralta. But Colombians often say that stories never truly end in their country. Calderón was in a *culebra*, though perhaps he didn't know it. Near midnight, armed men forced their way into the lobby of Calderón's apartment building. They took the elevator to the seventh floor and blasted into his apartment. Witnesses later said that they heard no voices or screams, only the thunder of automatic weapons fire. Below, a police car passed on its normal patrol but noticed nothing unusual.

Elsa's parents happened to be visiting. Elsa's mother managed to shut her eighteen-month-old grandson into a closet before being wounded. She survived, but Mario, Elsa, and her father, Carlos, perished. Both Fidel and Carlos Castaño were charged with ordering the killing, though by that time, Fidel was three years dead according to family reckoning. Government investigators later used the panicked telephone call made by a lookout in the lobby when the police car passed to identify the gunmen. They belonged to La Terraza, a band of criminals Castaño used to murder in the cities, where his armed and uniformed Shock Force could not go. Named after the Medellín ice cream parlor where they met, members of La Terraza had previously worked for Escobar, then for "Don Berna" during the PEPES campaign.

Calderón's colleagues believe that Castaño and the army had decided that it was time to send a message to human rights defenders that all of their chat about rights and the law was just a guerrilla facade. It was a message that Castaño had not given to me, perhaps because of his restraint in dealing with foreigners. It was not a restraint he felt regarding his fellow Colombians. Apparently, Castaño and the army colonel in charge of intelligence looked for a person that they all could agree was a guerrilla using human rights as a trick. Castaño remembered Calderón from Tierralta. The army had recently stopped him at a roadblock in the Sumapaz. It was not hard, it seemed, for them to agree on a name.

Afterward, the government offered human rights groups what it described as "protective measures" to foil similar attacks. Some accepted. Even they realized, though, that such things only delay the inevitable. "You can install as many panes of bulletproof glass and video surveillance equipment in these offices as you can and wear bulletproof vests and walk about in a swarm of bodyguards and you would still be in danger," one colleague said to me. No real effort was made to arrest Castaño for the murders. Many Colombians simply accepted that Castaño had found a link between Calderón and the guerrillas, just as many believed that the execution of the teacher who had been delivered to Castaño by former EPL commander Rafael Kergelen was justified by what had to be convincing information. *"Por algo será,"* people say: It must be for something.

A year after the Calderón attack, Castaño struck at human rights defenders again, ordering the kidnapping of two men and two women who worked in Medellín. Again, it was La Terraza that grabbed them, stole their money, jewelry, and belts, then delivered them to Castano. I had worked closely with these people and knew them to be dedicated human rights activists, not guerrillas. But in statements to the press, Castaño called them "parasubversives" who would be tried and executed, like the Córdoba teachers whose bodies were never found.

An international outcry may have helped save their lives. Within ten days, Castaño released the two women. The men were released a month later. One of them told me that Castaño had talked with them for hours and not always about the war or their supposed guilt. Perhaps he was intrigued by the fact that one was a historian and the other a philosopher. He had an ignorant man's respect for education and must have valued their advice on what new books he should add to his already large library. Castaño wanted to know how it felt to ride Medellín's new metro, which he had only seen from afar. He said that when the war was over, he wanted to finish high school and study sociology. He also wept. He wanted to let them know that he was a man of thought, not a monster.

Castaño has this vulnerable side, that part of him that sees what he has become and is aghast. Again and again, he publicly recognizes his guilt or what he calls the "stupidities" that stain his cause. In the same breath, he defends them as regrettable, but necessary. Of course, this is rude and familiar, the way any killer can writhe out of accountability. Yet it remains unusual in Colombia, where so few of the violent men who drive the war ever reflect, at least in public, on the nature of the actions they take. Sometimes, Castaño reveals hard truths, among them why he decided to murder Carlos Pizarro, the M-19's presidential candidate. In the memoirs he published in 2001, called *My Confession,* Castaño recounted how he personally trained the boy who shot Pizarro while the candidate traveled on a commercial airliner in 1990. The boy carried out his task, then was killed by Pizarro's bodyguards.

Castaño accused Pizarro of being the "useful idiot" who would help Pablo Escobar achieve his dream of total control of Colombia. Castaño claimed to have witnessed a 1985 meeting between Escobar and Pizarro at Nápoles. There, Castaño said, the traffickers paid the M-19 $2 million to kill Colombia's chief justice and destroy the criminal case against the mafia during the taking of the Palace of Justice. People who have studied what happened in the palace doubt the story. But what appears beyond dispute is that the traffickers, among them Carlos and Fidel Castaño, agreed to supply the M-19 with some of the weapons used by guerrillas in the assault.

Certainly, the "stupidities" that Castaño reveals are selective, careful. In them, like weeds in the cracks of a sidewalk, are the lies and evasions that lurk at the heart of his brand of atrocity. He lies about his ties to the army. He lies about his links to drug trafficking. His relationship to drugs is, as he will freely admit, a weakness. Repeatedly, he has offered (through the press and never in person) to surrender to U.S. authorities for trial on trafficking charges. His only condition, he claims, is this: "If the United States government guarantees that I won't be prosecuted for my political crimes stemming from the counterinsurgency campaign, I am willing to turn myself in to the appropriate American authorities to defend myself against this slander." In 2002, the U.S. Department of Justice formally requested his extradition to stand trial in the United States for trafficking.

I find Castaño's truths more disturbing than his evasions. His life is a testament to gray, to the power of *culebras* to twist and poison lives. Yet his ideas are as stark as the bars of a cell. Either with him or against him. Either right or wrong. Perhaps in some cases, Castaño was right;

his target was a guerrilla in disguise. But Colombia had taught me that these cases are incidental, almost flukes. In most of the killings, Castaño had been starkly, tragically, and demonstrably wrong. Occasionally, he will admit it. But by then, it is usually too late. There was Father Fabio, who escaped. There was Mayor Cuartas, who also managed to finish out her term. Then there was Jesús Valle, a human rights lawyer like Josué. In 1998, Valle presented to the courts and the media evidence showing how Castaño's forces had coordinated with the army to carry out a massacre in his hometown. Like Josué, Valle had been raised a Conservative, though he never left the party. When I sat with him one December in his Medellín home, his sister Nelly served tea and cookies. Built like a truck driver, Jesús held the cup by a slender handle, masked completely by his thick fingers. He had been offered asylum in Europe, since the threats on his life had multiplied alarmingly. I told him I could get him a ticket out that afternoon. He finished his tea. His place was in Colombia, he told me. He would have nothing to do with bodyguards or guns or bulletproof vests or surveillance cameras.

Before Castaño, he was unarmed. He had only words and his outrage. To get rid of Jesús, Castaño chose La Terraza. On February 28, 1998—my son's birthday—two men and a woman talked their way past Nelly, who worked as Jesús's secretary. Perhaps his name had also been in the documents Castaño showed me. Was I too stunned or slow to see it? In Valle's office, they pulled out their guns. He asked them not to kill Nelly or the clients who were unaware in the waiting room, but he did not plead for himself. The killers complied. They bound Valle and shot him dead.

ooooo

IN 1997, CASTAÑO ANNOUNCED THAT HE WAS FORMING AN ALLIANCE of paramilitary groups under the name United Self-Defense Force of Colombia (Autodefensas Unidas de Colombia, or AUC). Over the next three years, he went on a media blitz, agreeing to dozens of interviews with the national and international press and even appearing on television for the first time, in a carefully orchestrated interview with one of Colombia's leading television newsmen. The AUC posted its own web site, featuring Castaño's political commentary as well as the media articles he liked and even a game that allows web surfers to shoot guerrillas in a fictional village called "Aguas Blancas." In Colombia's war, few of the people who die actually wear a uniform. But in the game, the targets are conveniently marked. As far as I can tell, the paramilitary shooter always wins.

My Confession caused a public sensation, particularly the revelations about his role in Pizarro's murder and the tale of his brother's death. The book begins with Carlos's exhumation of Fidel's secret grave at Las Tangas, threatened by the flooding of the Sinú. At Las Tangas, Fidel lay not far from some of the people he had trucked to Las Tangas and executed. To anyone with a memory, the AUC roster was depressingly familiar: former MAS leaders, well-known traffickers, former military officers cashiered or convicted of coordinating massacres with Castaño's men. Castaño's power over them was tenuous. Like Pashtun warlords for whom the world ends at a riverbank or mountain range, they take convincing.

Once, Castaño was forced to mediate a dispute between Ramón Isaza, who is a MAS veteran and head of a branch of the Middle Magdalena paramilitaries, and the multinational Coca-Cola. Without warning or explanation, in 1998, Isaza's men banned Coca-Cola products and blocked trucks from delivery routes. Executives with the Colombian bottler Panamco, which had the Coca-Cola contract, were stunned. They were used to harassment from guerrillas, who had kidnapped drivers and burned trucks to force the company to pay a "war tax." But threats from the paramilitaries were unheard of. To the contrary, Colombian labor unions have accused other bottlers of colluding with paramilitaries to break strikes and kill bottling union leaders.

Panamco arranged an emergency meeting with Castaño and Isaza. As a peace offering, their representatives brought cases of Coke. Isaza claimed that Coca-Cola's former bottler had failed to pay its debt to a friend. Since Panamco had the new contract, Isaza said that they should pay it. Like Castaño, Isaza had lost several family members to violence: one son and several nephews killed on Pablo Escobar's orders and another son ambushed and shot by the FARC. He was not the sort to take orders from a kid like Castaño. So Castaño had to reason with him. To a journalist from the magazine *Cambio*, Castaño explained: "It was made clear to Ramón Isaza that, no matter which soda he preferred, his problem was the war on guerrillas, not the war between the sodas."

Other allies were not so malleable. In order to achieve his dream of becoming the "armed wing of the middle class," Castaño realized that he had to reduce "stupidities." He ordered "Cabezón," responsible for the Pueblo Bello massacre in 1988, executed. After "Camilo Morantes" dragged over twenty people out of the city of Barrancabermeja, shot them, and burned their bodies in a heap in 1998 (this is according to "Camilo Morantes" himself, since the remains have never been found), Castaño ordered him killed. La Terraza also felt his wrath. After La Terraza began robbing cars and killing on its own, Medellín families complained to Castaño. Castaño lured the gang's leaders to a meeting, then ordered them executed.

By 2002, Castaño claimed almost as many fighters as the FARC, at least 15,000 men and women. Paramilitaries matched the FARC's battle savvy, in part by luring away guerrilla commanders who had already proved themselves on the field. It was a macabre brand of free agency. In his memoirs, Castaño estimated that he had 600 former guerrillas and 300 former military and police officers under his command. "This war is overflowing with men and even women who want to grab a gun," he told the journalist who wrote up *My Confession*. "I've found that I have to turn down requests to join [the AUC]."

The presence of former guerrillas made massacres particularly deadly. Men and women who had once threatened civilians into helping them now fingered their former victims. Then, they had them shot. In the village of Chengue on January 17, 2001, for example, the paramilitary commander was a former guerrilla who called herself "Beatriz." Trained as a nurse, Beatriz had left the FARC over a dispute about her handling of the unit's money. The people of Chengue knew they were in danger. The village was among thousands of similar ones *"macartizado,"* as one official said to me, by paramilitaries. They accused residents of being pro-guerrilla. I puzzled over the word until I realized that it was taken from English: McCarthy-ized, referring to Wisconsin Senator Joe McCarthy and his witch-hunt of Communists in the 1950s. During the months before the massacre, Chengue's elected leaders had pleaded with the police and military to increase patrols in order to avert a tragedy.

Yet when the paramilitaries finally moved, a young police lieutenant was the only one who raised an alarm. Head of a local base, he received reports from patrol officers who saw two trucks pass carrying heavily armed paramilitary fighters wearing the AUC armband. When the paramilitaries saw the police, they swerved to try to run them over, calling the officers sons of bitches and snitches. In contrast to the military, the police had refused to help Castaño's forces. The lieutenant filed a detailed report. But none of the navy units sent to protect Chengue from attack responded until late the next morning, when bitter smoke hung over what had once been the village.

In all, paramilitaries killed twenty-six. Or forty-six, according to the later confession of one of the men who helped Beatriz that night. Bodies slip in and out of view, appear and then vanish like sets of keys. While the men did the killing with stones, she lit the houses on fire. Beatriz ordered the bodies piled in front of Chengue's health clinic. Later, Castaño seemed to regret her macabre sense of humor. He was convinced of the guilt of the dead; yet he also realized that displays of savagery hampered his bid to win public support and avoid international outcries.

Human rights defenders generally shunned the bulletproof vests that the government's interior ministry had begun to hand out. When I walked with Régulo Madero, a human rights leader from Barrancabermeja, the same month that the Chengue massacre took place, he was armed only with his cell phone, which trilled like a pesky bird every few minutes. Castaño's men were reported to the north, to the south, within blocks. Madero took it all in with practiced calm. The only way to keep the fear at bay, he told me, was to fight the uncertainty, not knowing where the threat came from and who it sought. "Information is one defense," he said. How thin, though, it seemed to me as we walked a deserted Sunday street, Madero oblivious to the stream of *parrilleros*–at that hour, men with their girlfriends or with small children between their knees as they went to Mass–that passed us.

In 2002, Castaño's commanders signed a pledge to avoid what they called "unnecessary killings." Yet overall, more Colombians than ever die. Instead of heaping them in piles, paramilitaries disperse bodies along roads or disappear them altogether, in rivers or the holes in the ground that glow like ovens on the scopes of ground-penetrating radar. Dispersion keeps the news crews away, since few reporters are willing to make the slog just to record the death of a teacher or a clerk. Briefly, Castaño announced that he had disbanded the AUC. Several subordinates had refused to dissociate themselves from direct involvement in drug trafficking. Although he did not elaborate, one of those commanders was another elder brother, José Vicente. The *culebra* that has coiled its way into the family continues. Weeks later, the AUC was reunited, its web site featuring two Colombian "martyrs": Jesús Castaño and Fidel, his son.

Escobar erased limits on violence. Castaño made violence ordinary, what Colombians now accept as part of the day. It's like the weather. Will it be cloudy today or clear? Will there be a massacre or just bodies along a road? Mostly, it is something most Colombians barely notice, except on days when it interferes with some personal task. Like when you prepare a picnic and it rains, or when you wear clothes too heavy for a warm day. It is like when drizzle grips the Upper Sinú for days on end. It's a drag, but inevitable. What can you do? Just wait until the sun returns. It makes the rain into a memory and a memory into something that you forget, since it is just part of the rush of days that are the blood and breath of our lives.

CHAPTER SEVEN

PATAQUIVA'S LAMENT

I FIRST MET CAPTAIN GERMÁN PATAQUIVA IN COLOMBIA'S DEFENSE
Ministry, a 1960s-style building midway between Bogotá's city center
and the airport. The commanders of Colombia's armed forces and its
civilian defense minister have their offices there, encased in glass and
with a bristle of antennae and satellite dishes and snipers on the roof. I
needed the army's permission to interview brigade and battalion commanders about the rules governing modern warfare and how those
rules shaped operations in the field. Pataquiva was to be my guide and
help arrange meetings with army commanders. My plan was to look at
Colombia as a war, not just a political conflict. The distinction was
meaningful. It gave me the legal foundation I needed to investigate
crimes committed by guerrillas as well as by Castaño when he acted
independently of the army.

Strictly speaking, human rights can only be violated by states, since
only states are parties to the treaties, conventions, and other legal
instruments that define them. In contrast, the laws of war apply to in-
surgents as well as governments. Once an insurgent group can be said
to meet certain criteria—among them, that it operates under a central
command and controls territory—it is subject to the rules governing
conduct: the Geneva Conventions and Protocol II (added in 1977 to
address internal strife or rebellions like the one taking place in
Colombia).

Colombians can be pedantic when it comes to legal questions. I
can't count the number of times I have been trapped in lectures on appropriate jurisdiction and points of procedure and statutory limita-

tions until I was ready to jump out any available window. But on this question, even noted legal scholars would get narrow-eyed and blustery, with my precise language. "Do only guerrillas have human rights?" one had once said to me. He handed me a photograph of a soldier captured while off-duty by guerrillas, then dismembered and stacked like chopped wood. It was not a question with an answer, but an accusation.

So I stopped mentioning these technicalities in Colombia. Instead, I used the phrase "human rights" more broadly, to mean abuses by all sides.

Since General Camacho's day, Colombia's military has made a sport of bashing human rights groups for their alleged bias in favor of guerrillas. The generals who worked in the Defense Ministry were convinced that human rights groups ignored—or worse, justified—guerrilla atrocities. Their suspicions fed on this narrow use of the phrase "human rights" and the fact that some groups only publicized allegations against the security forces and paramilitaries while remaining mute on guerrilla crimes. The press contributed to the military's paranoia by mining our reports only for the most scandalous material, usually linked to official misdeeds, while ignoring the equally painstaking accounting of guerrilla atrocities.

To counter what they claimed was bias, the generals began publishing full-color reports on guerrilla abuses. I had to reserve a high shelf in my office for them, after my five-year-old daughter pulled out a report to read. I found her cross-legged on the floor, parsing the geometry of the human genius for destruction in a photograph of a body blown to bits by a gas cylinder bomb. Ironically, my decision to use the laws of war as a frame for an investigation prompted criticism not from my usual adversaries, the generals, but from some of my human rights colleagues. They opposed describing Castaño as in any way separate from the Colombian military. While I agreed that Castaño's forces coordinated closely with the military, as they had at Chengue, it was also true that Castaño could move independently. In *My Confession*, Castaño complained that his forces had become "the sweetheart, the mistress that you have hidden and only visit when you need to."

I once described this dispute over the essential nature of Castaño's ties to the military to a Colombian army colonel I often talked to. The colonel had served with the United Nations in El Salvador and knew in detail how its army had set up death squads and murdered suspected subversives who were nothing more than government critics. In Colombia, he said, the relationship between the military and paramilitaries was both independent and dependent, close and fraught with mistrust, like most any relationship in Colombia. He mulled over his answer. "It's like the affair between a married man and his mistress," he finally concluded, echoing Castaño. "One has one, but doesn't bring her home to meet your family."

Using the laws of war did not mean that state forces were any less responsible when they helped Castaño commit abuses (just as a mistress may have other men, as the colonel helpfully elaborated). Yet like the generals, Castaño had perceived in the laws of war a useful tool to make his case internationally. His forces, he argued when Jennifer and I spoke with him, were not "Head Splitters," but a pro-government guerrilla force, dedicated to restoring democracy. He invited the ICRC to instruct his fighters on proper humanitarian behavior and issued regulations. It wasn't faked. With me, he had been able to discuss the intricacies of how these laws are applied in the field. We talked at length about such issues as how to distinguish between a military target and a protected civilian structure. Of course, the distance between his words and the actions of his men remained vast. When pressed—for instance, with the examples of the butchers he had ordered killed—Castaño's discourse crumbled. To me, he advocated a "creole" version of the laws of war, which allowed him to declare certain people or places "military targets" at will.

The guerrillas used the same arguments and even the same phrases, among them "military target." The use of the phrase would increase dramatically when the two groups were fighting for control of a region, as they sought to justify the murders of civilians who they claimed had helped their enemies. Its official sound gave a new twist to business-as-usual atrocities, but I also saw in it that familiar Colombian genius for language. Fighters invested a book-bound phrase loved by lawyers with powerful new meaning. Often, Colombians active in politics would announce to me that they had been declared "military targets," proof of their importance even as the phrase placed a virtual toe tag on their feet.

Some of my colleagues worried that holding guerrillas accountable for violations would doom peace talks and be used to justify direct U.S. intervention. Guerrillas themselves rejected the idea that they could be held accountable to any law that they had never agreed to. To them, it felt like an imposition from humorless Switzerland (though they also accepted training from ICRC workers, who made the treks to their camps like missionaries bent on saving a pagan, vicious tribe). The FARC dismissed prohibitions on kidnapping or gas cylinder attacks as simply "another instrument of war waged through propaganda, manipulation and political cynicism."

Once, I had asked ELN leader Felipe Torres if the guerrillas would prohibit the execution of captured paramilitaries, as the laws of war demanded. At the time, Torres was in a comfortable prison outside Medellín. In his suite—several light and airy cells connected by halls carved through the cell walls—he had a substantial library, a television, and a VCR. Fellow prisoners worked as servants. His video collection included mostly Disney movies dubbed into Spanish, for when children visited. Torres has a weather-beaten face and the thinning, long hair of an aging hippie. "Nonnegotiable," he replied, with a slash of his arm across the air between us.

What about civilians—in other words, not combatants or spies—who might provide the authorities with information that led to the arrest of guerrilla leaders? Torres himself had been captured after a tipster alerted the police and collected a reward.

Torres drew his hand across his throat.

Some days, it seemed to me that Colombia was living a familiar science-fiction narrative, the one about the alien capable of inhabiting human bodies and mimicking voices and habits. All of Colombia's armies seemed to assume, barring clear proof to the contrary, that everyone in their path was suspect, a potential "military target." Contact was contamination and contamination was death. Had a store owner bought from or sold to a guerrilla? Death. Had a telephone exchange operator placed a call for a paramilitary? Death. Had a teenage girl danced with a teenage boy who happened to be an army recruit? Death. Once, paramilitaries had executed several boys who wore sneakers like the ones guerrillas had stolen days earlier from a truck. The FARC had shot an elderly couple, hands clasped, then burned them beneath a statue of the Virgin Mary because they lived on a street where the paramilitaries has set up an office.

In the tiny town of Guintar, Antioquia, fear was like the perfume of the blooming trees that shaded its lovely, deserted central square. Several months before my visit in 1997, paramilitaries had taken Guintar and accused its residents of supporting guerrillas. The fighters forced everyone from their homes, then chose one local man and cut off his nose. One of the paramilitaries told the store owners that if they opened for business, he would return, cut them open alive, and string their entrails from the manicured bushes. The reason? Paramilitaries knew that store owners sold food and medicine to the FARC, which had operated in the region for decades.

Weeks later, the FARC came to Guintar. To underscore their resolve to remain in control, they killed the mayor, a town councilman, and a resident they accused of supporting paramilitaries. That night, no one turned on any of the electric lights, since to do so would have risked renewed attack by appearing to do business. The local priest was the only one to challenge the darkness. It was December. He hung a single strand of Christmas lights over the church door. Then someone hung lights above a nearby door and window. To welcome me, one store owner opened his coffee shop for the first time in four months to brew a cup of coffee. To do it, he risked his life. "I have eleven people in my family, so how are we supposed to live?" he said, not expecting an answer.

Several of his neighbors had moved to Medellín, the nearest large city. A mixture of fury, fear, and humiliation twisted the store owner's boyish features. "The minute we see them coming again, we are going to run for our lives."

"Them" was any of them, all of them. It was as all-encompassing as the war itself.

I could follow the massacre stories and execution stories and "military target" stories like steps on a path. All were brutally logical. Yet once outside Colombia's extraplanetary atmosphere, I would read my notes with a sick horror. It was all crazy. I developed a mnemonic trick to tell atrocities apart, since they ran together so quickly, like frames in a movie. "Bajo el Oso" was where the FARC had laid out its victims like beads on a chain beside the festive bus called a *chiva*. So it was the *chiva* massacre. There was also the "basketball court" massacre and the "teen hikers" massacre and the "soccer ball" massacre, when witnesses had accused paramilitaries of beheading an elderly resident, then kicking his head between them like a soccer ball. Sometimes, all of the arguing and rationalizations and manipulations made me want to pack my files and send them to whatever archive would be willing to store them until someone with a better idea came along. I lacked the Swiss patience for endless discussion followed by the same old crimes. I enticed myself by calling each trip to Colombia my last. This would be the last time I would take notes on obscenities. This would be the last time I would force myself to nod and not scream. This would be the last time I would press a witness to repeat a story that had left her with "view paralysis."

At least, these were some of the thoughts that motivated me to make the appointment at the Defense Ministry and get myself through the first checkpoint. But they weren't enough to get me up the broad stairs that led to the offices of the military's commander in chief. Around me, men in full battle gear clanked and squeaked and rubbed. A *gringa* was in the house. Eyes flicked to my Washington suit and pumps, which dug raw trenches into my heels.

I imagined another incentive, something Josué had sent me earlier in the week via a friend: a bottle of rum. "Rum, rum, rum," I thought, waiting for me in my narco-hotel. On those imaginary fumes, I made my way up the hall to where Pataquiva waited.

ooooo

OF THE FOUR ARMED FORCES—THE COLOMBIAN ARMY, NAVY, AIR Force, and National Police—Colombia's army is the largest and most influential politically. Until 1990, its status was reflected in the choice made for defense minister, always an army general. President César Gaviria, elected that year, was the first to break with tradition and appoint a civilian, a sign that he intended profound change. It made a difference but did not extend as deeply or broadly as he must have wanted. *Doctores* loyal to the president and palatable to the generals would take up temporary residence in the minister's office, a gaggle of other civilians brought in as speechwriters and policy wonks. Reliably, they were kept away from most decisions of substance.

One retired general and former defense minister once fussed that civilians were not the "natural" leaders of the armed forces, suggesting, I imagined, a ritual of selection where men stripped to the skin do battle with their fists and teeth. So the generals handled it by putting the civilians in charge of administrative matters (ensuring that everyone got paid and that there was coffee available in the kitchens). Meanwhile, the generals took care of "public order." The pact agreed to forty years earlier to end La Violencia held.

I could see its effect in the waiting room of the defense minister, a civilian. It was dark and stuffy, furnished with black Naugahyde couches that seemed to have been dragged from a bankrupt disco. In contrast, the room adjoining the offices of the chairman of the Joint Chiefs of Staff, where Pataquiva stood, was bright with sunlight. Well-tended plants cheered the room and its milk-chocolate-colored leather chairs looked newly stuffed. This division of labor had its flaws. For instance, it left the military staff with the difficult task of winning without being able to spend what they thought they needed to get the job done, since the budget was controlled by the civilians. The generals had 120,000 troops, less than the per capita equivalent in any other Latin democracy facing an insurgency. Worse, Colombia had faced a dozen, the FARC being only the largest and most experienced. Defense spending was similarly low. The situation appeared even more dire when the generals counted just combat-ready troops. Subtracting administrative staff, underage recruits, maintenance workers, and troops assigned to guarding oil installations, bases, bridges, buildings, and dams, the generals had no more than 40,000 men available, barely more than the number of all of the guerrillas and paramilitaries combined.

Many families of means bought their sons out of military duty, obligatory for high school dropouts but only requested of all others. Every time the army tried to increase the defense budget or recruit more young men, the editorial pages of the nation's newspapers screamed. Wealthy Colombians offered to write the checks as long as someone else fought. "There is no sense of sacrifice," one American diplomat who had served in Colombia once said to me. "Colombians don't feel they should have to bite the bullet and rescue the country."

The contrast with Castaño's army was stark. Castaño had given the AUC a sense of mystique and purpose that eluded the generals. It also eluded the FARC, which by the end of the 1990s was relying increasingly on desperation, not inspiration, to draw in new fighters. Many among them were children. One aid worker told me that you could tell by the guerrilla casualties lined up by the army after every fight. The boots and hands that peeked out from beneath bloodied plastic sheeting were those of adolescents. In areas the AUC controlled, Castaño ordered billboards to be erected with advertisements for the paramilitaries: *"La mística del combate integral"*–the mystique of total combat. Former guerrillas switched sides. People who had lost family members to guerrilla violence volunteered. In his frequent interviews, Castaño described himself as a patriot and drew deliberate parallels between his cause and the American Revolution, as well as the campaign waged by Simón Bolívar to liberate the Americas from Spain.

It was beneath a huge oil portrait of Simón Bolívar that Captain Pataquiva stood. He had a slender build and a fresh, boyish face that made him look barely old enough to have graduated from the War College. He introduced himself as part of the army's newly created human rights office.

He ordered coffee, the first step of almost any meeting in Colombia. *Servicial*, I thought to myself. It was a new word I had learned. To my English ear, it sounded negative, like "ingratiating," someone who groveled, a hanger-on. In Colombian Spanish, however, *servicial* is a compliment. It means obliging or solicitous. Pataquiva was being *servicial*, gracious.

That had not been my typical reception at the ministry. *Berraco* was what the generals usually were, another word I had picked up. *Berraco* means tough or difficult, complicated, ruthless. Colombia was *berraco*. Pablo Escobar was very *berraco*. Carlos Castaño was the most *berraco* of all.

Once, a general I had not previously met told me that he had seen me before. He said I was in Villavicencio, where he had recently commanded the army's Seventh Brigade. I had been walking with a man, he said. He described the man in detail. "Interesting," he mused. I realized he meant Josué. The eyes I had thought I felt in Villavicencio were real.

This general's office was tastefully decorated. Photographs of his family crowded the shelf behind him. Sunlight bounced gold and silver beams from the medals on his chest. I fought a temptation to run. Of course, panic was what the general wanted. With casual malice, he was letting me know that my movements had been watched and recorded, then distributed among the right people.

When I met Pataquiva for the first time, the human rights committee that Josué had helped start was preparing to close its doors. Letters and fliers and invitations to their own funerals arrived in the mail or were slipped under the office door or faxed from unknown locations. Around Villavicencio's shaded square circulated SUVs and *camperos* driven by hard-eyed men and identified by license plates from Middle Magdalena towns. At night, the men would park their cars and have a coffee in the open-air cafeterias. They cleaned their guns in the blue glow of the fluorescent lights. The only thing the government offered by way of security was what is called "hard" protection: a bulletproof vest, a bodyguard or two, bulletproof glass and metal detectors for offices. The really important people got a bulletproof car, a lumbering behemoth that felt (the times I had ridden in one) like a moving casket.

Protective measures were something. Or they were nothing at all, since assassins routinely found their way through such defenses by killing people on their way to work or walking with their mothers on Sunday or at their homes, like Mario Calderón. In 1996, paramilitaries had launched a rocket at the bulletproof car of Aida Abella, the Patriotic Union president, as it idled at a Bogotá intersection. She survived, but only because their aim was poor. She left Colombia soon afterward. Exile was the closest thing to a guarantee.

Another general had directly accused me of writing lies in my reports for Human Rights Watch. This was part of a guerrilla campaign, General Manuel Bonett had said, to smear the Colombian army with "false reports" and hobble it in its battle with what he called "narcoguerrillas." The word slipped off his tongue like an oiled fish. It was supposed to be a category-killer and end debate. It was 1997 and the U.S. Congress was beginning to debate new military aid for his troops.

Suddenly, the word "narco-guerrilla" was everywhere, the magic spell that would ease millions out of the American treasury.

Bonett had a rubbery, elongated face, with crooked teeth that jutted over his lower lip. One U.S. embassy official had dubbed General Bonett and his advisers the "Apple Dumpling Gang," referring to the Disney movie featuring actor Don Knotts, whom Bonett closely resembled. The moniker conveyed the Americans' low opinion of the Colombian military's fighting skill, which the official had described to me as "pathetic." In U.S. government reports and the congressional testimony of administration officials, Colombia's military was described as little changed from the disorganized and largely passive force that General Yarborough had assessed in 1962. The Colombians had not changed; but Washington had, now convinced that the only way to wage war on drug trafficking was by increasing the firepower available to Colombia's soldiers. Strengthening the army was necessary, American drug warriors argued, because the FARC units that controlled the *coca* fields were themselves heavily armed.

Until that time, Colombia's military brass had resisted the conflation of the drug war and counterinsurgency. They wanted no part of chasing down traffickers or busting labs, a dirty job better suited to the police. In 1992, the Colombian military had flatly rejected a U.S. offer of $2.8 million to set up army counterdrug units. Of course, anyone who followed Colombia also knew that the traffickers themselves had been important army allies through MAS and Castaño's Head Splitters. The generals also wanted nothing to do with human rights talk, which inevitably accompanied American dollars.

But by the mid-1990s, things had changed. Even with Castaño's help, the generals continued to lose the war. Regularly, Marín's forces outmatched soldiers. In 1996, at Las Delicias, Putumayo, the FARC seized a heavily guarded military base, killing (guerrillas claimed) twenty-seven soldiers, wounding thirty, and capturing sixty. Meanwhile, millions in U.S. aid—money, equipment, helicopters, and training—was bolstering the army's bitterest rivals, the Colombian police. When I sat in the Defense Ministry, workers were busily recasting Colombia's forty-year-old war into a drug-war mold. Grudgingly, they also had to neutralize the arguments of human rights monitors like me, who continued to write about abuses and their links to Castaño.

The military added human rights training to officer courses. Generals learned to use human rights terms in speeches and public statements. Yet the reality on the ground remained unchanged. It could not be swatted away with rhetoric. Human rights leaders continued to appear in military intelligence reports as "facades" for the guerrillas, on no more evidence than their occupation. Occasionally, the majors, sergeants, and privates tasked with delivering the weapons to paramilitaries or coordinating via radio or protecting Castaño's men as they murdered were later caught or confessed, implicating their commanders. But colonels and generals were rarely prosecuted. The few who were charged saw their cases closed or settled with only minor sanctions by military tribunals.

I pointed this out to General Bonett. I also reminded him that the U.S. Congress was likely to put human rights conditions on military aid, something that had helped convince his predecessors to turn down previous offers. The general's eyes sparkled. Over the previous weeks, he had met with dozens of political and peace delegations from the United States and Europe. It was part of the military's campaign to convince the world that it took human rights seriously. At these meetings, I had seen General Bonett squirm as if his underwear were laced with itching powder. Unlike many of these groups, I did not advocate a ban on military aid, since I believed this would only convince the army to embrace Castaño openly. I wanted aid with strings attached, so that U.S. officials would be the ones pressuring the generals to change. My goal, in other words, was to put human rights words into the mouths of the American military officers who often preceded me into these meetings or followed me after I had been escorted out. Military aid was a hunk of meat to a starving tiger. If you want the Black Hawks, my message was, you need to eliminate the Head Splitters.

My colleagues and critics warned me that the tiger might simply swipe the meat and eat me. Of course, they were right.

General Bonett was a devout Catholic. A huge Bible lay open and lit by a special light on a lectern. He wagged a bony finger at me. Did I know that lies about these spurious links to paramilitaries were sins that would land me in Hell? With a well-manicured finger, he stabbed toward my face. "In Hell!"

I scrambled for what I remembered of the faith practiced by my

Turkish friends. In my religion, I replied, there was nothing like the Christian Hell. The general blinked. It was a tremendous lie, a hurl at his sanctimony. I had heard that General Bonett had a sense of humor. Would it emerge even in a meeting with a human rights *gringa*? Heaven was spectacular, I continued. In Heaven, there was food and drink and perpetual spring. Medellín without the killer boys and the slums and the vile blood sausage that is considered a *paisa* delicacy. In Heaven, I added, there was sex with seventy of the handsomest men imaginable. Except, I added (thinking of the female virgins promised to suicide bombers), I hoped that they were very experienced.

General Bonett's mouth opened wide enough for a hard-boiled egg. It was like hearing that Pedro Marín was moving to South Beach to do aromatherapy with his "life partner." Or Carlos Castaño was giving it all up to spend more time with his children. The meeting sputtered to an end.

Later, though, I suspected that not everything had been lost on General Bonett. He fancied himself an expert in classic Greek literature (and after retiring, was appointed to Colombia's embassy to Greece). While still military chief, he proposed, only slightly tongue-in-cheek, that guerrilla women take a lesson from Lysistrata, Aristophanes' fictional heroine. In the play, she leads a conjugal strike of young wives meant to force their husbands to end the war between Athens and Sparta. Within weeks, General Bonett promised in a radio interview, "they'll be tamed and they'll propose peace out of desperation."

ooooo

Captain Pataquiva wasted no time in making his pitch. The army, he said, may have made some mistakes with human rights groups in the past. Unfortunate! His eyes were damp and eager. Things were different. Things had changed. Now, he promised, he was prepared to offer transparency.

"Transparency" was another one of those words that meant something slightly different in English. Pataquiva intended it as a synonym for above board, open to scrutiny. The army was transparent, meaning ready to make its behavior and methods and doctrine available for examination. In English, though, it was an adjective that could be coupled to nouns like "manipulation" and "spin." Was transparency on a list of words that some Beltway lobbyist had drilled into Pataquiva's head? After "narco-guerrilla," but before "war on drugs." Or was the word "transparency" the fin in the water that marked the first fruits of U.S. pressure on human rights?

I imagined long coaching sessions led by buff *gringos* with Kosovo medals on their chests. We were in a new age of military thinking on human rights. Inevitably, the hope for change in Colombia lay with officers like Pataquiva, capable of transforming the way the military thought and moved and acted. If this thirty-something officer was beyond change, so was Colombia, at least in my lifetime.

There was something special that Pataquiva wanted to tell me, he said. He had a personal story to discuss. Would there be time during my visit?

Before he could elaborate, the door to the office of the chairman of Colombia's Joint Chiefs of Staff opened. The chairman himself was not available, Pataquiva said hurriedly. The only navy officer ever to hold the post, the admiral had replaced an army general hastily retired after accusations of drug corruption. But the admiral was traveling. Instead, I would be received by the army commander.

The news both pleased and disturbed me. General Harold Bedoya Pizarro was the real power within the military. As he rose to shake my hand, I noted that he already seemed at ease with the admiral's furnishings (not long afterward, he moved the admiral into retirement and claimed the post and office as his own). I had not met him before. But I had no trouble recognizing his profile and iron-gray hair. He was what I have heard called a fine-looking man. To me, though, his uniform seemed to enclose a controlled fury. General Bedoya appeared often on the nightly news and in the newspapers, the epitome of the kind of military man Colombians adored, feared, and hated in equal measure. He was tough but smart, capable of great violence but free of formal legal charges, able to charm and intimidate in the same conversation. I was surprised only by his eyes. They were chips of sky-blue porcelain in his face.

Unlike General Bonett, Bedoya didn't entertain me with bluster and religious invective. I felt like a mouse being considered by a very calm snake. There was nothing *servicial* or transparent about him. Known as a *tropero,* a soldier's soldier, Bedoya inspired fierce loyalty among some subordinates, including Pataquiva. The reaction among human rights groups was the reverse: revulsion. In the 1970s, then Lieutenant Colonel Bedoya, a protégé of General Camacho, had been linked to the Triple A, the death squad accused of "disappearing" activists and planting bombs in public places in order to cast suspicions on the left. The allegations were never properly investigated. As a rising army star, Bedoya had been repeatedly linked to MAS, but again with no formal charges ever filed.

His disdain for human rights groups was notorious. Once, he came to the United States bearing a document that he claimed proved that Human Rights Watch was in the direct pay of the FARC. A friendly journalist passed me a copy. It was a photocopy of a check stub that registered expenses reimbursed under the category of "recruitment." For Bedoya, "recruitment" meant fighters for the FARC.

The stub was real. It had accompanied a reimbursement check sent to a former Colombian government official who had flown to the United States to interview for a job with Human Rights Watch. In 1995, this official had forced the retirement of one of Bedoya's colleagues, General Álvaro Velandia Hurtado, for his role in the arrest and murder in detention of an M-19 guerrilla. Velandia was the first Colombian military officer of this rank discharged for a human rights violation (he had also been named by the government as a MAS supporter in 1983). A noted legal scholar, the government official was later forced to leave Colombia because of threats on his life.

The journalist was perplexed when I explained the story. Was General Bedoya naive enough to mistake a public job search for guerrilla skulduggery? Or did he knowingly attempt to deceive? Either way, rather than raise questions about human rights groups, General Bedoya revived fears about the extremism in the army first nurtured by General Camacho.

Yet Bedoya also reflected a generation newly influenced by the ideas of General Ruiz, the architect of Plan Lazo. Like General Ruiz, General Bedoya believed that civilian support was the critical factor in a winning strategy against guerrillas. Where he differed from Ruiz was in how to get it. Civilian support was not something he believed the army had to build through good works. In his view, civilians owed the state support. Those who refused it or even hesitated were no better, in his view, than the guerrillas themselves. In fact, they were guerrillas, since their passivity was what would allow a guerrilla victory. "Concerning the delinquents, no one can be neutral," he once said in an interview with the daily *El Tiempo*. "The civilian population should be the ally of the authorities because it is the guerrillas' most frequent victim. What would have happened if the civilian population, during the War of Independence, had declared itself neutral? Bolívar would have lost the war. No, neutrality is not possible. You are with the terrorists or you are against them."

I never heard him point to MAS as a model for a successful campaign. But the Middle Magdalena was the region General Bedoya constantly held up as an example of ideal cooperation between the military and civilians. In our meeting, he urged me to go there to see what cooperation could achieve. As we spoke, I realized both of us were feinting with words whose meanings were different. General Bedoya answered my questions about Castaño by rejecting the word "paramilitaries"; he claimed they did not exist. He parried with the "delinquents" or "terrorists" who disturbed "public order." The *"gente de bien,"* good people, were the ones who helped the army. To me, this phrase was the verbal rock that covered the military-paramilitary alliance. In the field, soldiers allowed the "good people" through roadblocks or lifted roadblocks when they knew they planned to pass. Paramilitaries advised them of their movements and plans in advance, often using information gathered by soldiers to make the lists of people they planned to kill. Once they had finished an "operation"–like a massacre in a village–the military allowed them to vanish, arriving only later to record the bodies and destruction left behind. This strategy allowed the army to get out of the dirty war by subcontracting it to Castaño.

After General Bedoya took command of the army, human rights groups like my own noted a drop in the number of allegations that implicated soldiers directly in abuses. The drop was more than offset by the rise in the number of abuses perpetrated by paramilitaries, usually in heavily militarized areas.

A few army officers spoke out against this strategy. Colonel Carlos Velásquez won fame in the early 1990s for helping bring down the Cali Cartel. In equal measure, he earned ridicule after falling into a trap set

by the cartel, which hired a prostitute to pose as an informant, then se-
duce the colonel in a love hotel wired for video and sound. The tape of
the married colonel cavorting prompted the army to reassign him to
Urabá, a punishment. He became chief of staff of the Seventeenth
Brigade in 1995, just when Castaño was driving south through the banana fields.

An urbane, soft-spoken man, Velásquez told me his story in the
restaurant of an upscale Bogotá hotel. He reminded me of photographs of my grandfather as a young man, with a narrow face, clipped
mustache, and tender, sad eyes. Ideologically, he was firmly in the "sociological" camp descended from General Ruiz. After his first weeks,
he concluded that the best way to fight both Castaño and the FARC
was by making common cause with local leaders, among them
Apartadó mayor Gloria Cuartas. With the support of the general in
command of the brigade at the time, he began deploying troops to defend the population, particularly the banana workers who were targeted by all sides. Colonel Velásquez measured success by an overall
drop in the killings and massacres of civilians, not the body counts
used by most other brigades. "The challenge became how to defend
the civilian population from all attacks, not simply generate lists of
guerrillas killed in action," Colonel Velásquez told me. Too often, body
counts were inflated with civilians executed by roving patrols or "legalized" by paramilitaries, who killed civilians and delivered the bodies to
soldiers to be included in their tallies.

Velásquez's strategy ended with the arrival of a new commander,
General Rito Alejo Del Río, in 1996. A corpulent, whiskey-faced man
with close ties to Bedoya, Del Río had made a name for himself by
working with MAS in the 1980s. "The first thing he did was remove
troops from areas where they were protecting civilians from paramilitary attacks," Velásquez told me. Local officials were no longer invited
to meetings about area security. Del Río accused them of being FARC
supporters. "The army went back to chasing only the guerrillas, leaving the civilian population vulnerable to paramilitary attacks. That was
a terrible year for massacres."

When I met General Del Río in 1996, the effects of the army's strategy were diagrammed on the satellite-generated map that covered

part of his office wall. The map featured tiny flags marking army and FARC positions. The areas controlled by Castaño had no flags at all. I asked why.

"Obvious!" the general replied. "That area is completely under control."

The effect of Del Río's arrival was swift. While speaking to residents of an Apartadó neighborhood, Mayor Cuartas watched unbelieving as two young men grabbed a twelve-year-old. They may have known the boy or simply picked him out of the crowd. "They took off his head and they raised it and the terror that this provoked in me was so great, I mean so incredible, that all I remember are the wide-open eyes of the other children, my hand on my mouth, and a complete silence."

Mayor Cuartas believes that the men were paramilitaries and the boy's murder was meant to frighten her. She accused Del Río's troops of standing by while people were brutally killed. Del Río responded by accusing her of slander. Years later, several cases against Mayor Cuartas were closed for lack of evidence; in one, prosecutors discovered that General Del Río had paid witnesses to falsely accuse her and required him to pay a fine.

Velásquez was concerned enough to report to his superiors that Del Río did nothing against the paramilitaries. Velásquez also provided details about Del Río's meetings with a retired army major who worked with Castaño. The report made it to General Bedoya's desk. His reply was unequivocal. "He said I was being disloyal," Velásquez told me dryly.

Del Río countered by accusing Velásquez of meeting with known guerrilla sympathizers, meaning Mayor Cuartas and human rights groups. He claimed these meetings were proof that Colonel Velásquez was mentally unstable. An army investigation ordered by Del Río contended that Velásquez's behavior was "more than sufficient to [withdraw] confidence in an officer . . . who maintains a great friendship with people and institutions that have openly declared themselves enemies of the army."

General Bedoya cashiered Velásquez. For the record, his crime was insubordination and failure to promote *"compañerismo,"* esprit de corps, within the army.

For his part, General Del Río served an unprecedented two tours in Urabá, even as the air filled with the *carambolas* of massacres and revenge massacres and massacres to revenge the revenge massacres. Then the army promoted him and moved him to a plum post in Bogotá. There, he sent troops into the building belonging to a leading human rights group, to catch the supposed guerrillas within. Among those he found was Josué's friend Sister Nohemy, forced to kneel as soldiers chuckled about the ease of on-the-spot executions. Del Río's career ended in 1999, when President Pastrana dismissed him from service. That same year, the United States withdrew his visa, reportedly for his ties to paramilitaries. This last charge stemmed from shady deals that may have involved cocaine shipments off the north coast. The dismissal and visa withdrawal provoked howls from the military, whose leaders declared him one of their brightest officers.

In Washington, I would try to explain to the young aides responsible for developing policy what lay behind the Colombian military's Power Point reports, part of their campaign to win U.S. support. In them, Colombia's war of gristle and bone was a column on paper, with numbers neat as budget totals. Over coffee in the Rayburn Cafeteria, I spun stories of brave colonels like Velásquez and threatened mayors like Cuartas and the quiet of the banana farms as armed men crept close, confident that no matter what they did, they would never be made to pay. What was at stake was not percentages, but lives. On General Bedoya's graphs, there was no calculation for them.

General Bedoya was *berraco*. No prosecutor in the land would sign so much as a traffic ticket against him. It would be like shaking the very rocks beneath the Defense Ministry, ripping the cables from the telephones and the antennas from the radios on the roof. It would be ripping the supple leather from the seats and tossing coffee into the air, with the cups and saucers and tiny spoons and silver tray and cubes of white sugar. It would be suicide–in a word, unthinkable, as radical as refusing air.

At the time, it was the air that Colombia breathed. Only aliens like me, living on some kind of tanked fume, believed that it could ever, really, be any different.

ooooo

AFTER MEETING GENERAL BEDOYA, MY FIRST STOP WAS THE CITY OF
Barrancabermeja, on a bend in the Magdalena River. The river is the
color of wet cement. From its depths, fishermen dredge up a spotted
catfish they call *bagre*. At the port-side restaurants, it is served steamed
and unappetizingly whole on a mound of rice, a spined monster
dredged from a child's midnight closet. Just downriver from Escobar's
former ranch and the birthplace of MAS in Puerto Boyacá, Barranca
(as the locals call it) is painfully ugly, but prosperous. The country's
largest oil refinery dominates it like a huge Erector set. Its chimneys
are topped by a perpetual lick of orange flame from the gas produced
by the refining of crude. In the lowland heat, the refinery's twenty-
four-hour-a-day operation seems to boost by several degrees the heat
that already squeezes the city.

Many residents work in the refinery and nearby drilling sites or run
businesses that cater to oil workers. Barranca literally runs Colombia,
the gasoline it manufactures filling the tanks of the trucks, cars, trains,
and airplanes. Barranca also has a role in the drug trade. Thieves
siphon gasoline from the pipeline and sell their contraband to cocaine
laboratories, which use it to refine cocaine, avoiding controls on the
sale of so-called precursor chemicals.

The refinery contributes to the city's poverty and violence in an odd
but typically Colombian way. Many employees work as contractors,
well paid when times are good and broke when contracts go unre-
newed. For several decades, Colombia's oil industry ran on what was
known as the "twenty-eight" system. Workers were hired for twenty-
eight days at a time, exempting the companies from paying benefits or
guaranteeing a job. Often, contractors were told to never hire the same
person twice in a row, to prevent them from gaining any right to a permanent job. This also meant that three or four men—and the families
behind them—would compete for the same job, only pulling in a paycheck a couple of months out of the year.

In Colombia, wealth—or the fight over who gets it—spurs violence,
not poverty. This is one of the most striking things about the country.
Violence concentrates where there is money and industry. In contrast,
Colombia's neighbors—Peru, Ecuador, Venezuela, and Brazil—have the
more familiar problem of violence in the midst of poverty, with the
rich able to screen it from their enclaves.

Guerrillas took advantage of this dynamic in Barranca. While the FARC and MAS battled in the South, the *elenos* controlled the city and parts north, up the river's left bank as it cuts by the San Lucas Range. There was never much *coca* there, so the ELN demanded that the contractors working with multinational oil companies pay what it called "war taxes." Guerrillas punished refusals and late or short payments by laying an explosive charge under a piece of Colombia's 7,400 miles of pipeline—longer than from Miami to Seattle and back again—or shooting holes in it with their machine guns. The pipeline's metal skin is no stronger than paper against the dynamite guerrillas use to blow it up. Out of the gash spews crude that covers the ground and tributaries with an iridescent sheen. A single pipeline—the 485-mile-long link between the Caño Limón wells and the Caribbean port of Coveñas, co-owned by U.S. oil company Occidental Petroleum—was bombed more than 700 times between 1986, when it was opened, and the end of 2001. Over 2 million barrels of oil spilled, nine times the amount left in Alaska's Prince William Sound by the *Exxon Valdez*.

Occasionally, damage was apocalyptic. In 1998, guerrillas blew the Central Pipeline in a defile near the Pocuné River, which feeds the Magdalena. A clump of vaporized light crude slid down an incline and jumped the water, landing on the other side where the settlement called Machuca lay. It took six minutes to make the trip. The vapor arrived near midnight, when many residents were asleep. But someone had a flame burning. The gas ignited. In the flash produced by vapor meeting flame, seventy-three people were burned to cinders. Thirty-six were children. Later, I saw in the Colombian army report photographs of their bodies, like Pompeiian remains charred into fetal curls. The explosion sucked so much oxygen out of the river water that for days, fish washed up suffocated on the Pocuné's banks.

The ELN claimed the attacks were to protest the role multinationals played in extracting crude; yet they never shut down the industry entirely. It was too important a cash cow. Just as the FARC used cocaine taxes, the ELN used oil extortion to clothe and feed and arm its fighters. Driving in from Barranca's airport, Jennifer and I passed the shantytowns where most of the city's residents lived, misery in the midst of what should have been plenty. At a spot where pavement turned to dirt, the driver turned right. This was the ELN side of the city, less than a mile from Barranca's center and the refinery. On the rare occasions that police or soldiers carried out a sweep, they had to use armored vehicles. The ELN would ambush them with land mines or rocket-launched grenades (though usually destroying only market stalls and passers-by while leaving the armored vehicles unscathed).

Previously, Jennifer had contacted several Catholic priests who lived in a parish house at the heart of one slum. Father Abel, our host, had met us at the airport. As we drove, he explained that the guerrillas had sentries at virtually every corner. The sentry could be the boy fixing a bicycle or the woman chatting with friends. We were able to enter only because he and the taxi driver lived there. To me, this tight control was invisible. The houses and shops looked like any other slum in the hot lands, with shoppers and children and the inevitable scrub dogs nosing in the garbage. Father Abel–not his real name, for reasons that will become clear–had recently graduated from seminary. At the time, he and another priest were working with refugees forced to the city by the war, some by paramilitaries and others by guerrillas. Like Father Fabio, they worked against time and short resources to palliate the worst of the war's damage.

His reasons for offering to help us were straightforward. Father Abel was relatively new to Barranca and lacked important contacts with local officials. By helping us to set up appointments, he was able to meet people who would otherwise ignore the efforts of yet another priest to do good. Father Abel was particularly interested in meeting the commanders of the army and navy units in Barranca. Although people like Father Abel often knew much more about what was happening in places I visited and knew exactly what needed to be done to solve problems, they were often ignored by officials until some stranger, preferably an American, met with the authorities and delivered exactly the same message. Suddenly, food would arrive or detainees would be released or a swift raid would be launched against a paramilitary camp that had existed in that same spot for months.

Afterward, things could return to normal. But sometimes, these visits were like evolutionary leaps, saving months of waiting. Of course, they could also backfire. One humanitarian aid worker had once accused human rights groups of indirectly creating Carlos Castaño by pressuring the military on human rights, thus forcing it to subcontract

the dirty war. It had been easier, this person argued, to deal directly
with the military, since it was possible to discover which soldiers had
committed crimes and get the generals to put them on hard duty. Still
others accused me of only "fiddling" with what they believed was
General Bedoya's criminal arrangement, my efforts on behalf of human rights irrelevant in the midst of such atrocity.

These were not issues that Father Abel, Jennifer, and I discussed
when we drooped into the steamy parish sitting room. There was
sweet coffee ready and a barely perceptible breeze. What I asked yet
again was whether Father Abel realized that he and his colleagues
risked being perceived as too close to a controversial human rights
group. The relationship could leave them in more danger, not less,
once we had left. Father Abel was built like a wrestler. He had a cap of
curly brown hair and a habit of saying *"¡Miércoles!"* ("Wednesday!")
when he was surprised, dismayed, or amazed. It was the equivalent of
saying "darn" instead of "damn" (or *mierda,* shit).

Priests and nuns were among the few still considered neutral in
Colombia's war. When General Del Río had forced Sister Nohemy
and the other nuns to kneel as his soldiers searched the human rights
office, the news had provoked outrage among many Colombians who
otherwise would have accepted without comment his argument that
guerrillas were working within the building. Yet this protection was increasingly fragile. There had been a disturbing increase in the murders
of religious workers deemed too partisan or critical. Jesuits like Sergio
Restrepo and Mario Calderón had been murdered by the Castaños.
The FARC had executed several priests during or after mass, accused
of speaking too forcefully in favor of peace. With its history of recruiting priests—at the time, the priest Manuel Pérez was just beginning to
succumb to the hepatitis B that guerrillas claimed killed him in 1998—
the ELN created a particularly dangerous context for Father Abel. The
parish priest who had lived in that same house for the past decade as-
suaged the tension with liberal shots of Johnny Walker Red in his coffee. Father Abel had assumed that because he was simply trying to
help the refugees, he was immune from attack. For him, it was like
ministering to the sick or dying. Who could doubt his motives?

That was what many thought they were doing before they were attacked, I said. It depended on who the sick and dying were or where

they were or who the men with guns thought they were. It wasn't a question of doing the right thing.

"*¡Miércoles!*" Father Abel murmured.

Father Abel was still new enough to Barranca to be surprised by almost everything that happened. The poverty was unlike anything he had ever seen in his comfortable Bogotá home. So was the heat. So was the way people died, sometimes, he said, even before they were actually dead. "Just last week," Father Abel continued, "some children ran up to tell me that a certain neighbor had been killed. I thought I would go to the house where he lived to express my condolences. Just then, I heard a shot. It was at that moment that the man was killed. Somehow, the children knew it and already counted him as among the dead."

A dedicated reader, Father Abel said that the incident made him feel like he was living out a García Márquez story. Except it did not feel magical at all. As he spoke, his brown eyes blinked quickly as if still reacting to the report of a gun.

Father Abel decided to accompany us to the meeting Captain Pataquiva had set up at the local army base. I was to interview its commander, responsible for the 1,000 troops guarding the city. The army base is set on a promontory that reaches into Miramar Swamp, a lagoon off the Magdalena River that serves as a natural defense between the city of Barranca, the base, and the refinery beyond. The swamp is distinguished by an eighty-nine-foot-tall iron Christ with fingertips that can shoot out water. Called "Petroleum Christ," it was designed by a local priest and welded by oil workers. Not long after our visit, the guerrillas tried to rocket the army base from a sculpture park nearby. There, the oil workers has set up a menagerie of iron animals to frolic at Christ's feet. The guerrillas were careful to aim away from the Christ, lest they damage a popular icon. But their explosive missed the base and hit the houses that lay east of it, killing several residents.

As promised, Captain Pataquiva was waiting for us. A whisper of a breeze slid off the swamp. Pataquiva showed us what looked like a green room, part of the extensive garden that softened the familiar lines of a military installation. The plants seemed to absorb our polite conversation, creating a feeling of intimacy as Jennifer and I waited for the real interview to begin.

Pataquiva was anxious. There was something he wanted to say. Without preamble, he began his lament.

∞∞∞

"LAMENT" MAY SEEM OVERWROUGHT. IT IS A WORD WITH A LOT OF drama for one young captain. To test my choice, I later looked it up in a dictionary. "Lament: to mourn, to express sorrow for, to grieve and to wail aloud."

Pataquiva did not wail. If he had, a dozen soldiers would have rushed to his aid, convinced that the human rights activist they suspected of being a disguised guerrilla had finally revealed her true form, ripping off her human skin to show the fangs of the basilisco within. Yet there was grief in his voice, and sorrow. In an instant, those emotions seemed to fill his frame.

He had been wronged, Pataquiva said. He had suffered a cruel and unjust fate. If only he could explain how lies had ruined his good name! Perhaps those people did not even know that what they believed was based on lies, good people, *gente de bien,* Pataquiva said, who were duped.

I recognized the preamble. This was the military's case against human rights groups. We waged war through our reports. We were as dangerous—sometimes more so—than foot soldiers. For many within the Colombian military, human rights is simply a facade for international communism, a disguise in a century-old war. As one defender of the army once noted: "The best Colombian officers are not defeated militarily by the guerrillas. That job is accomplished by their political wing: the nongovernmental organizations that serve them and the prosecutors who share their phobias."

In other words, human rights groups singled out officers like Pataquiva—the best ones, considered the most effective against guerrillas—and tarred them unfairly as human rights abusers. The army had several names for it: the *guerra jurídica,* the legal war, "that each year leaves thousands of officers and soldiers literally out of combat," according to one general. Human rights groups were even said to cause a kind of sickness, called the "Procuraduría syndrome," after the office of the inspector general. The syndrome was caused by the fear of being

charged unjustly–*empapelado,* literally "papered over"–with accusations of human rights crimes. Officers thus targeted would experience
a weakness in action or strategy and panic provoked by lawyers. As a
result, they would ensconce themselves in their bases rather than combat the enemy.

As I listened, I had this curious sensation: I was hearing the groan of
change provoked by the newly vocal human rights movement, what I
had envisioned emerging as lightning from my fingertips on my way
to see Carlos Castaño. Here it was again, proof that something was
happening. Although it was phrased as a lament, it was audible and
real. Sometimes, all the reams of paper I generated from my computer
seemed to me to be as irrelevant as invitations to a party whose date
had passed. Yet they were not, at least to this young captain. I admit
that a kind of morbid joy filled me; the lament showed that my work
was not in vain.

In 1992, Pataquiva said, he had been arrested, handcuffed, and
charged with being an accessory in over 140 separate murder investigations. All of the alleged murders had taken place between 1987 and
1990 in or near the town of El Carmen de Chucurí, about four hours
by truck from where we sat. The town was in the foothills of what
Colombians call the Coward's Range. It was the birthplace of several
ELN leaders and was considered a guerrilla stronghold. The charges
dated from the time Pataquiva was assigned to the El Carmen army
base. When he first arrived, he said, residents refused even to say hello
to him. They were terrified that guerrillas would punish them for
speaking to an army officer. Guerrillas routinely executed teenage girls
who were seen dancing and drinking with soldiers. Even chatting with
an officer could raise suspicions that a local was passing intelligence to
the army.

Perhaps a few residents supported the ELN, Pataquiva allowed.
Certainly, guerrillas slipped into town to eat and drink and dance. In
his view, though, most residents were forced at gunpoint to construct
fortifications around guerrilla camps and plant defensive mines along
the mountain pathways. Again and again, farmers and their children
and animals were killed or maimed when they inadvertently tripped
what were called "foot-breaker" mines.

What Pataquiva was telling me was the sad story of hundreds of

Colombian towns. There was nowhere in the country, as far as I had been able to tell, where support for guerrillas ran deep or broad. Most Colombians collaborated through fear or because they despaired that anything could be different. Most people's concerns—jobs, education, health care, security—were not things that guerrillas talked about convincingly. By the time I sat with Pataquiva, Marín's methods—the targeting of civilians through killings, kidnapping, and extortion, the use of gas cylinder bombs, the recruitment of children—had deeply eroded his popularity.

Pataquiva described his effort to win people's trust house by house, family by family. The mayor of El Carmen was won over. Local farmers began to pass information and guide troops to the guerrillas' secret spots. Pataquiva sponsored public works, health clinics. Soon, the town was behind him, he claimed. The guerrillas were furious. Pataquiva told me this as if his "hearts-and-minds" campaign had all been his new and wonderful idea, something that he, a bright young man, had thought up on those dark nights as he sat on his cot, alert for any sound that would reveal a guerrilla attack on the town.

"What of MAS?" I asked.

No such thing! Here, Pataquiva cleaved to Bedoya's insistence on calling them only "good people." "We committed the sacrilege of dedicating ourselves to serving the civilian population," Pataquiva said, "helping them turn their backs on subversion."

The appointment with the base commander appeared delayed. We had been stuck in that green room for an hour. With a rush that sent a splash of color to my cheeks, I realized that this was deliberate. My joy became irritation. General Bedoya had meant for Pataquiva to make this appeal to me, the physical manifestation of the international human rights groups that were causing so much trouble for him. Pataquiva was not a liaison. He was a messenger.

"*¡Miércoles!*" Abel said.

I had seen the photographs of El Carmen taken while Pataquiva was there. The town's walls had been covered with MAS graffiti. "FARC-UP-ELN! GET OUT! MAS IS WAITING!" "GUERRILLA SUPPORTERS: ONE BY ONE THEY WILL FELL [sic] MAS." I imagined that some of it had appeared overnight, much as the question mark and cross had appeared during my stay in La Uribe.

Pataquiva's lament contradicted another compelling story I knew about El Carmen. I had heard it from a young tailor named Orlando who had been born and raised there. Orlando had lived a relatively peaceful life until the mid-1980s. There was growing conflict between the guerrillas, MAS, and the army. But what changed Orlando's world was spiritual. A Catholic, he was drawn to a new project begun by the local priest, Bernardo Marín (no relation to Pedro Marín), another El Carmen native. In seminary, Marín had learned about liberation theology and the work that was being done with lay people in "base communities," parishioners who studied the Bible with an emphasis on what theologians like Gustavo Gutiérrez were calling Christ's "preferential option" for the poor. The idea, as Orlando explained it to me, was to raise an awareness that the Bible could be read as a call to action against poverty and powerlessness, not as an admonishment to surrender to God's will.

Under Marín's guidance, Orlando began to lead Bible discussions. People seemed to like it, he told me. "They were used to having the priest visit them every six months or so, or once a year, very rarely. But now the people were beginning to take part more frequently. We led meetings about every eight days, I mean that we gave people material to read, biblical texts, reflections on the life experiences that these farmers had ... it was a new thing to meet without the parish priest present."

Without realizing it, Orlando was part of a movement then taking place across the Americas to press for social justice using the Bible as a foundation. Several of the meetings key to the development of liberation theology had taken place in Colombia. Yet it was a particularly hostile environment, given the conservatism of the Colombian Catholic Church and the history of La Violencia, waged in part as a defense of Catholicism against creeping communism. Marxist ideas informed liberation theology. The ELN—with its guerrilla priests, several of whom had followed a similar path before choosing to take up weapons—was to many the confirmation that these ideas could be deadly.

Father Marín was not a guerrilla. Most of the Catholics who embrace liberation theology abhor violence. But to others in El Carmen, simply thinking thoughts influenced by Marxism was proof positive of its poisonous reach. They saw the basilisco at work among these newly enthusiastic Catholics. For MAS, liberation theology was a guerrilla sneak attack, a chalice stolen from the altar. One of the most emotional charges MAS supporters leveled at Father Marín was that he refused to give local soldiers communion, something I could never confirm.

MAS organized from the Middle Magdalena Valley up into the mountains. Father Marín and Orlando went from the heights of El Carmen down toward the Magdalena River. Clashes were inevitable. When MAS guerrillas found evidence of a base community, they banned it. In turn, the base communities exhorted their members not to join MAS. In 1988, locals–among them representatives of base communities–organized a march to the state capital to protest the government's failure to invest in road repairs and other development. Although the march wasn't organized by Father Marín, the army and MAS saw it as evidence that the Communist ideas embedded in his sermons were bearing fruit.

Soldiers stopped the marchers at a place called Llana Caliente (Hot Flat). After a five-day impasse, shots were fired. The soldiers claimed guerrillas hidden among the marchers started it. Orlando told me a different story, with all of the classic Colombian elements of betrayal, heat, confusion, guns, rage and outrage, death, and lots and lots of alcohol.

What happened was that there was a guerrilla deserter there who was working for the army, he was the bodyguard for the colonel [commanding the troops]. That Sunday, the soldiers were celebrating the colonel's birthday and they had been drinking. So they went over to the marchers to rough them up. First it was just with words, insults, and the people got heated up, too, and responded in kind. In the middle of the drunkenness and the agitation, the colonel ordered the soldiers to fire on the marchers. The soldier, who was from the area, refused, so the colonel took out his pistol and shot the soldier dead. When he saw this, the guerrilla deserter took out his rifle and shot the colonel, a lieutenant, and some others. That was when the shooting really began against the people. Twelve of the marchers died. But there is a river that passes nearby, and there [they threw bodies], and there were many people disappeared, more than one hundred.

Death threats against Father Marín followed. He had to leave El Carmen. Orlando tried to keep the base communities going. But a local woman soon passed him a message. "She said, 'Look, they are going to kill you, they accuse you of giving information to [the authorities], for taking the place of Father Marín, they think you are sending him information. And this group, called the Masetos, they are going to kill you.'"

"One thing is crystal clear, you are either with them or you die or you leave," Orlando finished when he told me this story. "There are the three options. With them, leave, or die."

Orlando refused to surrender entirely. He began passing information to government investigators, who were already inundated with information about MAS killings. In 1992–the same year that Pataquiva was arrested and three years after the government had declared paramilitaries illegal–the government pulled together a team of prosecutors and police to arrest the El Carmen mayor and two dozen others and charge them with murders linked to MAS.

What happened next was more farce than the "legal war" that the army accused human rights groups of using to cripple them. The prosecutors knew that they had to arrive unannounced and swiftly, so they bypassed the army and arranged for police helicopters. The challenge of locating the more than two dozen civilian suspects remained. The prosecutors had written descriptions and photographs but wanted an eyewitness, someone who knew the town and would not make mistakes. They told Orlando that he would have to come along. Orlando described to me what happened next:

> They were going to disguise me with makeup, anything to make sure I was not recognized [by the residents of El Carmen]. On March 29, I went. There were about thirty-five police officers from an elite unit and five DAS [Administrative Security Department] agents and five judicial investigators, a judge and another judge, and a prosecutor, which is to say the highest levels of the government. Well, they failed me. What I mean is that they did not do what they had promised. [He had to apply his own makeup.] I was immediately recognized because I had lived my whole life there. When I was recognized, everyone knew that I had left and had given information [to the authorities]. Immediately, people be-

gan to say that there went a guerrilla. I had asked the [police] colonel to order some of his officers to apply makeup as well, since otherwise I would have been the only one with makeup on. Because if the people saw only one person with makeup, they could have killed me. So a captain, a lieutenant and five other officers had makeup. Eight total. It was camouflage makeup. I wore a police uniform and had my face painted and sunglasses on. But the people still recognized me. The army was supposed to provide security to the operation. But when the soldiers realized that it was to capture the paramilitaries, a captain stood next to where I was and said that these were whoring guerrillas, etc. They were the ones who began to heat up the atmosphere. And since it was a Sunday, there were a lot of people in from the villages, so the security perimeter that had been established fell apart. People began to flood the soccer field where our helicopters had landed. The police had grabbed six paramilitaries. Well, since the army was egging the people on, the people rushed us and took back five of the detainees. In the end, the police managed to arrest only one.

In the end, the prosecutors and Orlando were lucky to leave El Carmen alive.

The incident at El Carmen reached a national audience when an influential editorialist, Plinio Apuleyo Mendoza, adopted it as the model case for how guerrillas were, in his view, faking human rights claims to weaken the army. In his columns, Mendoza portrayed Pataquiva as the hero who bravely stood up to subversion only to be smeared by Communists disguised as priests, human rights workers, and government officials. Mendoza did not contend that liberation theology was the basilisco itself. Instead, it was part of a "brotherhood of ideas" tainted by the beast. Therefore, the crime is not to become a guerrilla; that is just one possible outcome. The real crime is to have an idea branched from a poisoned tree. Mendoza is no crank; he is a close friend to writer García Márquez and an author himself. In 2001, Mendoza's version took on new life when the *Wall Street Journal* reprinted his El Carmen argument just as Washington was debating a new tranche of military aid to the Colombian army.

My own work for Human Rights Watch had frequently been the object of Mendoza's fury. To him, Human Rights Watch was one of many "facades of the Communist party ... [causing] Tirofijo and Jojoy to rub their hands with contentment, very thankful for their allies in the legal war." In Colombia, Mendoza's columns can have devastating impact. The human rights group that documented the El Carmen case had to send its director, a Jesuit priest, out of Colombia for his safety after Mendoza repeatedly described him as a member of the ELN's general staff. Meanwhile, Pataquiva was acquitted by a military tribunal and promoted. Mendoza and the military are especially hard on government officials like the one who received the reimbursement for his interview trip to Human Rights Watch. Only rarely do these officials manage to actually put an officer in jail; however, Mendoza regularly prints their names in his columns and describes them as guerrilla members, a kind of "death threat" journalism. In that, he is a Colombian Robert Brasillach, the French collaborator who during World War II published in his newspaper the names and addresses of hidden Jews and resistance members. Mendoza has even accused the U.S. State Department and members of the U.S. Congress who express concern over human rights of belonging to a "fifth column" of Communist agitators.

A prosecutor and friend of mine awoke one morning to find that she was featured in a Mendoza column as a subversive "encysted" in the government. In his eyes, she had proven herself a guerrilla by filing charges against a navy officer and because of her last name, shared with a ranking member of the Patriotic Union party (not a relative and someone she had never met). Brave beyond description, my friend went to Mendoza's home and defended herself face-to-face in his comfortable study. Thus vanquished, Mendoza published his first–and I think only–retraction.

I saw that Pataquiva was close to tears. The case against him was the result of guerrillas "encysted" in the government, he claimed. The attorney general's office was filled with them. So was the office of the public advocate. So were all of the government offices and, what's more, so were human rights groups, even European groups, even American groups. The guerrillas even had, he said, people in the State Department, people in the American embassy (this in a whisper) who promoted the guerrillas' cause. And the United Nations? Without a doubt. The U.S. Congress? Pataquiva had reliable information on that. Would it surprise me to hear, he asked, that some human rights groups—of course not my own, he quickly said—were even in the pay of drug traffickers? That all of this campaign against the army was really an effort to ship more and more cocaine into the United States?

In his mind, the line linking communism to human rights was as crisp as the crease in his pants, which held despite the heat. Pataquiva lowered his eyes. For the first time, I noticed his thick black lashes. Father Abel—poor Father Abel, who had thought my presence would help his tiny assistance group get started—looked at me, aghast. What was I? Sometimes, Colombian *culebras* became so tangled and intricate that I wondered where they would end or even if an end was possible.

Finally, Jennifer and I were escorted to the meeting with the colonel. What else would Pataquiva say to the young priest? Before turning away, I glimpsed the two of them hunched together, brows almost touching. Their lips moved, in prayer or conversation, I couldn't tell.

ooooo

THE COLONEL WE MET WITH SUPPLIED AN IMMEDIATE CORRECTIVE. Clearly, he had failed to get word from General Bedoya to deny that MAS existed. A harness for weapons banded his chest like the rings on a whiskey barrel. He had bright red hair, close-cropped into curls. "There are commands where you are expected to work with the paramilitaries and commands where they are not as powerful. It's a fact of life," he said after the usual pleasantries.

I could have kissed him.

It was not often that I found officers who admitted what was plain to everyone, but I did have my private list, men I occasionally call or contact by e-mail as a way of testing my information or gauging the news. Perhaps one day, these officers will not be in the minority, trying, like this colonel was, to get his next assignment in a unit where working with the paramilitaries wasn't a prerequisite. He made no apologies. "What you do pains me, but it's necessary," the colonel said. "How else would we change?"

I asked about El Carmen. Was there still fighting over who was in control?

"Not at all," the colonel said. "The paramilitaries won."

The colonel offered Jennifer and me a ride to El Carmen. A helicopter sat like a battered mosquito in the parade ground outside his door. To go by land was tedious and presented the usual risks: roadblocks, common crime, who knew? He couldn't vouch for our safety at either the hands of the paramilitaries or the guerrillas. "They'll bring out the people who've had their legs or arms blown off by the guerrilla land mines, if that is what you want to see. They have a presentation."

The colonel felt compelled to warn that the helicopter was not his own. It belonged to the state oil company. Occasionally, bored guerrillas would shoot at it from the ground. The rounds usually fell back harmlessly, like a sudden shower of metal rain. He couldn't guarantee that a round or two would not penetrate the helicopter's unarmored skin. Besides, he confessed, it was leaking oil. "A lot of oil."

I watched the rotor turn in the soggy air, a fine black spray coating the inner blades. A trip could wait.

By the time we left the colonel's office, Pataquiva had vanished. Father Abel's brow was furrowed as we drove in silence back to the parish house. The old priest seemed to divine the mood. He poured everyone a finger of his precious Johnny Walker Red. "That man is very hurt," Father Abel said.

Over the next several days, we touched on the captain's lament several times. Pataquiva had tested Father Abel's perception of the war and the stories that it produced. For the first time, Father Abel perceived that these stories were not always clear, that people had radically different views of what was happening. Even if you saw and heard a story from someone you trusted absolutely, there could be doubt. Father Abel never directed his doubts in a direct question to me: Is what Pataquiva said true? Have you been unjust? Are your motives other than the ones you described to me? The question was written broad as the frown on his face.

Truthfully, I asked myself these questions all the time. Had I been fair? Did I know the whole story? What were the interests of the person talking to me? If Colombians could not even agree on why they fought, how could any of us trying to understand the conflict tell what was the real and absolute truth about any story? The lies were easy to detect. It was the selective truths, the overstatements, the shadings, that were hard at times to grasp. Sometimes, I would feel like a Ping-

Pong ball, batted between two opponents in a game. From one meeting to the next, the version I carried in my head of a single event would radically change or bust up into pieces.

The question meant more to me than getting something right or wrong in a report. If I did not know the truth or could not gauge people's motives, how could I craft the best way to defend human rights, to promote justice? My work is not just reporting on abuses but trying to create the right strategy to promote better protection. Having the wrong version of what happened meant I was likely to propose the wrong cure, not helping Colombians but adding to the confusion. Pataquiva was also proof that more was at stake than accuracy or analysis. If we were wrong–if we did promote false accusations–lives could be shattered. As my interview with Colonel Velásquez and the Barranca colonel showed, not all of Colombia's officers embraced General Bedoya's strategy. If the human rights movement was to have any success in Colombia, it meant being able to identify the officers willing to change and not tarring them with the same brush.

In my notebooks, I have written down dozens of the possible motives I have heard for Colombia's war, none completely convincing. One farmer once said to me that the war was rich people's way of grabbing poor people's land. For him, the terror waged by paramilitaries was an immense and nefarious real estate swindle, meant to force people from their farms, drive prices down, and grab land for agribusiness. He described guerrillas as his only hope, since with their weapons they could resist these efforts by threatening and killing land speculators (a view Marín promotes).

A police major in the Colombian Antinarcotics Police told me that the blame lay with drug traffickers. They wanted to control Colombia, to convert it into a narco-state tailored to their business needs. To him, there was no difference between the armed groups. The guerrillas and paramilitaries were all puppets manipulated by kingpins. Their master plan was to buy out Colombia's leaders with oceans of fresh cash (a view many Americans have come to embrace). Others ascribed the war to habit, custom, rivalry, politics, sex, power, status, need, greed, justice. I have heard it said that mass murder can have a pace all its own, that people grow used to it, are entertained by it, like sport.

A noted Colombian economist and politician, Miguel Antonio

Caro, once wrote that in reality, Colombia has no authentic political life, only "inherited hates," *odios heredados*. Castaño and the army blamed the guerrillas, terminally infected by the basilisco that would not allow them to rest until they had toppled democracy and installed a Marxist dictatorship. The only hope, then, was to fight them to the death. By decade's end, this view had gained considerable currency with many Colombians, who had witnessed how President Andrés Pastrana sacrificed his term to what became a chimera of peace with the FARC.

Negotiations had been the centerpiece of Pastrana's 1998 presidential campaign. A Conservative and son of a former president elected in what some suspected had been a rigged vote (the date of which, April 19, was later appropriated by the M-19 guerrillas), Pastrana was handsome in the airbrushed way of a television anchorman (which he had been before becoming mayor of Bogotá). Pastrana met with Marín at a secret camp before his inauguration to demonstrate his willingness to agree on the details that would allow the FARC to work out an end to the war.

The photograph of the two men together left Colombians thrilled and amazed. Marín seemed ready to end his feud, perhaps to find some farm to retire to where he could spin the tales of his exploits to journalists eager to write his life story. To satisfy a FARC demand, Pastrana agreed to cede Marín a Switzerland-sized swath of southern Colombia long under their de facto control. The police and military were withdrawn from five towns and the land that lay between them, land that joined La Uribe and the Ariari region to the jungles surrounding the town of San Vicente del Caguán. The town became the temporary "capital" of a region that became known as Farclandia.

There, on January 7, 1999, the government and guerrillas held a ceremony to officially open negotiations. For the celebration, a raised dais draped with Colombian flags had been erected. The agreement was to be sealed with a handshake and an exchange of speeches between President Pastrana and Marín, the money shot that had drawn dozens of news crews from as far away as Australia. Although reporters described it as a "demilitarized zone," there was nothing unmilitary about it that day or afterward. Heavily armed FARC guerrillas patrolled. At the time, the weapons seemed almost part of the decoration. Soda sell-

ers did brisk business. Salsa bands played. Some visitors took note of
the beauty and frank gazes of the guerrilla women, whose dress uniforms included a pouch for lipstick and mascara.

President Pastrana took his seat. The crowd searched for Marín. His
appearances are rare, and he almost never gives interviews to any but
the most fawning reporters. But Marín never showed. Later, a FARC
commander told journalists that they had uncovered evidence of plans
to assassinate Marín. It was an absurd claim, given that the FARC far
outnumbered the handful of policemen sent as Pastrana's escort. The
empty chair cast a pall over the proceedings that did not lift for the
next three years. Pastrana gamely continued with his prepared remarks, ad-libbing that Marín's absence "cannot be the reason to fail to
inaugurate the dialogue table." One guest later said, "Pastrana is like
the bride all dressed up and left at the altar."

Joaquín Gómez, commander of the FARC's Southern Block, eventually trudged up the dais steps to fill in for Marín. Like his commander,
Gómez was of peasant stock, and his brown, weathered face revealed
more about the guerrillas' intentions than any speech. He did not sit,
but read standing as he gripped pages in his hands. The statement began thirty years in the past. Gómez ticked off a long list of complaints
buried in garbled history. For instance, he identified 1964 as the year
President Kennedy "designed a counterinsurgency plan for Latin
America in order to suppress that growth of other revolutions," forget-
ting that Kennedy had been assassinated a year earlier. All of the people Gómez accused of betraying the FARC were long dead (among
them Laureano Gómez; his son, Álvaro; and General Rojas). Gómez
listed Marín's losses in the 1990 attack on Casa Verde as if reading a
complaint in small claims court—"300 mules, seventy riding horses,
1,500 cattle, forty pigs, 250 chickens, ducks and turkeys, fifty tons of
food," and the sacks that contained seeds for the next year's harvest.

After that day, the 130,000 residents of the region found themselves
in another country, without rights or guarantees beyond the whim of
the guerrilla commander in charge. Some told journalists that they
willingly sacrificed for peace. But if peace talks failed, they all knew
they would pay a steep price. For the paramilitaries, anyone who remained there was by definition a guerrilla. The guerrillas answered
with their own paranoia, targeting Colombians they accused of sup-

porting the paramilitaries, including members of a Gnostic Christian community who had been arranging to purchase land just outside Far-clandia. The FARC admitted killing three Gnostics, though the actual number may be as high as thirteen.

Pastrana understood that negotiation was the only way to end the protracted war. No matter how many troops or tanks or men he sent to the generals, they would never be able to completely eliminate the guerrillas, who had proved again and again their talent for survival. Yet the terms he laid down for them were fatally flawed. In return for granting them Farclandia, Pastrana got nothing but a commitment to talk. The inaugural ceremony had a circus-like atmosphere that per-sisted for the three years Farclandia lasted. Thousands trooped to San Vicente to get a glimpse of the FARC, among them personalities as di-verse as Jim Kimsey, the founder of America Online, and Queen Noor of Jordan. To the press, Kimsey explained the flight in his private plane in July 2001 as an effort to get the FARC's approval to bring in "Oper-ation Smile"–free reconstructive facial surgery for children born with deformities. But the visit had the unmistakable flavor of adventure tourism racheted to a new level, with Farclandia like a game park where the captains of the information age could observe virtually ex-tinct Marxist guerrillas in their natural setting.

The *guerrilleras* staffed a "hospitality house," where new arrivals would put in their requests for interviews with the elusive *comandantes:* Mono Jojoy with his Land Cruiser and bottle of rum, the more sedate Simón Trinidad, a former banker strapped with guns, or the ultimate prize, Marín himself, the alchemist attended by a young and doe-eyed *guerrillera.* One journalist who knew the commanders well described to me how he had visited the farms they had appropriated from Colombians who had fled the region. He described the commanders as content with their cattle, crops, and morning coffee. Some, like Mono Jojoy, seemed to thrive on media attention, posing for photog-raphers and flirting with the female journalists who took down their every word.

Outside Farclandia, guerrillas continued their increasingly brutal war. Two years after the inaugural ceremony, the FARC executed a Colombian congressman who was traveling to meet Marín and discuss peace. Guerrillas stopped Congressman Diego Turbay Cote, chair of the Peace Commission in Colombia's House of Representatives, and six others, forced them to lie face down on the road, then shot them in the head. Outside San Vicente, guerrillas set up weapons production facilities and allegedly brought in IRA explosives specialists to teach them how to aim their cylinder bombs better and plant more sophisticated remote-control bombs. Units slipped out to attack or ambush, then rushed back, protected from pursuit by the government's commitment to peace.

One Colombian friend described this to me as the FARC's "autism. They are demanding things that the government won't or can't do, yet making it politically impossible for the government to do what it can and says it wants to do."

President Pastrana readily acknowledged the negotiation was flawed, but he once told me that even an imperfect peace was acceptable. "If this doesn't work," he added, "we'll see each other again at the same table 10,000 deaths later."

In three years, the stop-and-start negotiations produced a prisoner exchange (guerrillas for captured police and soldiers) and a breathtaking increase in violence. To many, it was clear that within the FARC, there was no consensus about peace. In words oddly reminiscent of pro-gun propaganda in the United States, Mono Jojoy told journalists that the guerrillas would never agree to a cease-fire or to disarm. "Don't you see that the rifle guarantees any agreement? As long as the human being does not order it to fire, it does not fire. It depends on the person carrying it. If we had no guns, no one would respect us."

Some guerrilla negotiators may have had genuine hopes for an accord. But they were in the minority. The ones who carried the day treated Farclandia as a way to leverage a military advance, moving from a war of ambush to a war of positions. For all intents and purposes, Pastrana's negotiation sliced Colombia into three parts: the north for Castaño, the south for the FARC, and Bogotá for President Pastrana, who went from sleek to gray and careworn during his four-year term. On the radio, an announcer once joked that Pastrana was the most successful president in Colombian history. "He was given one country and he made it into three!"

The last straw came in early 2002, when the FARC hijacked a commercial airplane. Guerrillas forced the plane to land on a country road, then kidnapped a Colombian senator on board. At the time, a U.N. peace negotiator was located permanently in San Vicente, and the ambassadors of six European countries, along with Canada, Mexico, Cuba, and Venezuela, had been frequent visitors. The diplomats were aghast. Weeks earlier, the FARC had kidnapped three German aid workers and a former governor of the state of Meta, pulled from his seat in a U.N. vehicle.

Pastrana declared the experiment over. He lost his gamble and his legacy. The generals sent troops back, but they found little resistance. The beautiful *guerrilleras* faded into the jungle like shadows at sunset. The army chiefs blustered about how they would encircle and capture the FARC leadership and Marín himself, always said to be on the verge of capture. But even Mono Jojoy's substantial rum gut slipped through the generals' fingers.

Reading about it, I was reminded of what U.S. army colonel Harry G. Summers once said to a North Vietnamese counterpart after the war ended. "You never defeated us on the battlefield," Summers boasted.

"That may be so, but it is also irrelevant," the Vietnamese veteran replied.

ooooo

THE POINT OF COLOMBIA'S WAR ELUDES ME. I'M NOT ALONE. WRITER Antonio Caballero once wrote that despite a war that intensifies each year, nothing actually happens: *Nada de nada*. Because of that, things worsen day by day.

"The country aflame, rampant misery, the putrefaction of the political class, the disintegration of our institutions, the complete lack of security for our lives and possessions, flooding rivers, the proliferation of criminal mafias, the extinction of our wildlife, all are inevitable consequences of our stubborn conviction that here, nothing happens. The country comes apart in our fingers, over our heads, under our feet, because of us, precisely because we want nothing to happen, and when it happens, we deny it, saying, 'It's over, it's finished, *ya pasó*.'"

It might be more accurate to say that everything happens, yet nothing is done. Or what is done is washed away or made irrelevant by the flood of what happens. When peace talks ended, Colombia was stopped cold, a fly in the amber of violence with no visible way out. A study by the Interamerican Bank showed that Colombians were just as poor in 2000 as they had been in 1990. Meanwhile, the casualties caused by political violence had more than doubled.

Since 1984, ten illegal armed groups have demobilized, 7,000 people have "reinserted" into civilian life, and there have been a dozen peace negotiations. Yet in that same time period, many more Colombians joined illegal armed groups. In 2002, the authorities estimated that the FARC had 20,000 members, the AUC had 12,000 members (and was swiftly increasing), and the ELN had 5,000 members. Increasingly, the FARC and AUC faced each other on the battlefield, a new phenomenon.

To my mind, Marín seems to have accepted war as an end in itself. I can no longer perceive in him that figure of a provincial salesman who had once struggled to find some logic to La Violencia, a reason to fight beyond just more killing. Of course, the FARC continues to talk social justice, land reform, a fight against corruption. But its behavior in the field is like static that distorts the message, a sign that something very different is at stake. War keeps Marín's family and followers fed, clothed, and occupied. It got him his farm, at least for a time. Field commanders advance in salary and rank. They wield a power and status that few can aspire to as "*reinsertados*," amnestied guerrillas. What awaits Mono Jojoy if he surrenders, becomes a *reinsertado?* The *reinsertados* I knew were, like the M-19 and Esperanza, either part of the devil's table with Castaño or dead or afraid of being dead. Since 1994, when the Colombian government opened an office to assist *reinsertados*, over 700 of them had been murdered. Once they surrendered, what most likely awaited them was a bullet in the head.

The bargain was made real to me one afternoon as I sipped cappuccino in a Medellín restaurant with a *reinsertado* from the ELN. As a guerrilla, Fernando had been known as Commander Jacinto. He was trim and graying at the temples, more like a stockbroker than a jungle fighter. As I understood his story, Fernando had not meant to leave the ELN but had been secretly exploring with friends ideas for negotiating a peace deal. Discovered, he faced a choice: firing squad or surrender.

A woman I knew had arranged the meeting and watched us from a distance. Fernando had chosen the meeting site not for its elegance but

for the security guards that fancy restaurants in Colombia keep as part
of their permanent staff. Like Rafael Kergelen, he had his own bodyguards, too. They lounged at the entrance in too-big jackets and pants
that bulged at the waist. They could have been Kergelen's or Castaño's
men. For that matter, they could have been Father Abel, hardened by
war. The government had given Fernando a seat in Colombia's House
of Representatives, a vehicle, and a gun.

Fernando positioned himself with his back to the wall. As we talked,
his eyes followed an oval between my face and the entryway, where
well-dressed men and women came and went, oblivious to the fact
that they traversed a potential firing line. With my back to a potential
assassin, I estimated that I had, at most, two seconds to duck.

I was halfway through a too-sweet cappuccino when the assassin
appeared. Fernando leaped up. In a silver blur, he pulled out the most
enormous pistol I had ever seen in my life. I dedicated the next moment to cursing the woman who had arranged my meeting with him.
She had assured me that every consideration had been taken for his
safety and, I had assumed, mine.

It was not that she had lied. As I pushed myself on my belly to the
women's bathroom–thinking that the killer boys would not look there
if they meant to kill Fernando–I remembered that she had told me
that the city was experiencing "apparent" calm. It was that word
again–"apparent."

Fernando crouched behind a rubber plant. Had Commander Jacinto's instincts compelled him to the only shred of jungle in sight? The
enormous gun was aimed at the door. I realized that Fernando had
been holding it even as we chatted, his hand inserted in the briefcase
that, I remembered in retrospect, he had kept in his lap. The shooting
stopped as suddenly as it had begun. Fernando's bodyguards rushed a
wounded colleague to the hospital, leaving Fernando with me. Of
course, we also had the enormous gun and the woman who had set up
the meeting. She was *"paniqueada,"* panic-ified, a new word I later
scrawled into my notebook. We took a taxi to Fernando's office, hoping that the killer boys hadn't left a backup team to finish the job.

Thick rivulets of sweat ran down the taxi driver's face. He had been
quicker to notice Fernando's gun.

Marín had seen this happen with the Patriotic Union. He had seen it happen with other guerrilla groups (and had ordered his forces to kill some of them). It was unreasonable to expect him to tread the same treacherous path. By staying at war, the FARC avoided this fate. What they achieved was immediate and tangible: money, food, weapons, safety, cocaine (the means to more money), power. Of course, they lost something, too: their political vision. Their pronouncements and manifestos and calls to action had a tired, mechanical feel, as if generated by a piece of software made to mix Marxist words with the FARC's standing demands for land titles and investment in roads and schools. It was an excuse for war. For Marín, after so many years of fighting, fighting seemed enough.

Nothing happened. The Colombian government rebuilt Machuca, burned to a black crisp by the ELN. Everyone got new clothes and furniture and pots and pans, in the exact spot where a gas cloud could easily end lives again with a lick of flame. They were just as poor. Guerrillas and paramilitaries still came by to take their children and their food and threaten them if they dared help the enemy.

The refugees from El Salado—the "basketball court" massacre—also wanted their village back. That is, they wanted everything except for the village name. "It's that the name El Salado is like a sign of bad luck, and it makes us seem as if we are destined for bad things. That's why we are going to change the name, so now the village will be called Villa del Rosario," one resident said. "The new name is a symbol that, as of this moment, we are protected by the Virgin of the Rosary."

Most of Colombia's more than 2 million displaced people had nothing to go back to. Even the words to describe their tragedy were too dangerous to speak. "It's worse to report these things than remain silent," Pabla, a refugee, once told me. When she fled her home as paramilitaries approached, the only thing she had been able to grab was underwear. For weeks afterward, the only thing she could truly call her own was a fistful of faded panties.

ooooo

I TRIED TO ARRANGE ANOTHER MEETING WITH PATAQUIVA, WITH NO luck. I wanted to talk more about his story, to try to stitch together with words the two versions I had, like a sleeve on a shirt. Was there any point at which the patterns would meet? But he never called back. His lament in the garden became something ghostlike to me, a cipher for the things in Colombia that remain fraught and elusive.

For me, it wasn't, in the end, a question of the truth or the falsehoods in the captain's lament. I had no real doubt about the strength of Orlando's story. Yet I was struck by how little, in the end, the stories matched. Orlando and Pataquiva seemed to live on different planets, different galaxies. If we could not even agree on the basic facts of what happened—who were the *"gente de bien,"* in a way, and why they had died or killed others—then how could we ever agree on the far stickier questions of how to find justice, who to punish and when, and what the shape of a Colombian society without political violence would be? This is not a unique problem, but it bedevils almost any story in Colombia. What is your version of the story and why do you tell it? Who is behind you and what interests do you serve?

Father Abel ended up leaving Barranca, leaving the priesthood, then leaving Colombia entirely. A sensitive man, he was overwhelmed. We never spoke of the young captain again.

CHAPTER EIGHT

THE MAGIC KINGDOM

JESÚS, MY DRIVER, WAS BENT OVER THE STEERING WHEEL. I HAD FIN-
ished my interview and was walking toward the spot where he had
parked his Toyota. The afternoon sun hung just over the valley that
holds Bogotá. Its light was fading against the red brick houses that line
the street. As I approached, Jesús was motionless. As things had gotten
worse in Colombia, I had stopped using taxis. As a foreigner and
therefore a person of some means, I risked getting taken for a *paseo mil-
lionario*, a million-dollar ride. This happened when thieves stole a taxi,
picked up a promising-looking passenger, then took the passenger
hostage. The taxi would drive to the nearest cash machine, where
thieves would force their captive to withdraw money. Then they
would steal what the captive carried, including glasses. Passengers
were lucky to be left on some corner with the clothes on their backs.

There was also the possibility of being picked up by undercover police, soldiers, paramilitaries, or guerrillas. Once, I had managed to get
the same taxi driver three times in one day, about as likely as winning
the lottery. The driver kept his eyes on my face in his rearview mirror,
only occasionally glancing at the rush hour traffic.

Jesús worked with foreign reporters and knew all the secrets of getting through the city. Bogotá was built for the 1950s, without freeways,
interchanges, or broad arteries that could funnel workers from the
neighborhoods to downtown offices and back again. Every morning
and every afternoon, traffic snarled across the city. Motorcycles–the
assassins' vehicle of choice–would scream between stalled vehicles,
their drivers anonymous behind mirrored visors. One friend had tried

to convince me that it was possible to read Colombia's class struggle in the daily traffic jams. "These buses and the chaos of the transportation," she said, "it's all a way of saying I'm better than you, I'm just a little more important. You have the regular buses for the poor, then the slightly quicker and smaller *busetas* for a slightly higher fare. Then there are the 'executive' buses, then the buses with movies and a waitress. Some buses have plastic seats, some have cloth, some have leather. And you choose the bus that fits your status, pay your fare, and wham! You are stuck in the same traffic jam as everyone else. Too bad! Because no one is willing to give way, to cede their position, to give up a peso."

Like many professionals, Jesús had lost his real job. He took up driving to keep the family's small house in a northern slum. A slender, balding man, he looked like a university student, though he had a wife and teenage son. As we drove to my appointments, we would discuss the *X-Files* television program, his favorite. A delight in conspiracy theories is something Americans and Colombians share. Was Jesús asleep? The street was empty. I wasn't sure whether Jesús fully grasped that driving a human rights worker was more dangerous than driving a journalist. We had discussed my work and possible threats, but Jesús had dismissed my concerns about his safety. Indeed, he seemed to enjoy the extra thrill.

His granny glasses were pushed up to his forehead. Through the open window, I heard the sound of Spanish mangled by an American. It was the radio. Jesús was laughing so hard that tears glistened on his cheeks. He was listening to *La Luciérnaga* (The Lightning Bug), an afternoon radio show that spoofed the news. A host was doing a mock interview with the American ambassador, Curtis Kamman, who spoke Spanish with a heavy accent. Kamman looked like a Latin American's second-worst nightmare of an American (the first being the beefy, red-cheeked businessman): a drawn, gray-faced parson, as warm as the auditor who provokes George Bailey's epiphany in *It's a Wonderful Life*. It was 1997 and the United States was planning how to equip and train new battalions within the Colombian military to use in the "war on drugs." Colombians were buzzing about what some feared–and others hoped–would be the imminent arrival of U.S. troops to fight the FARC.

But *La Luciérnaga*'s hosts were having none of the serious debate that preoccupied the pundits. The false ambassador was crooning a love tune. Weren't Colombians in the mood for love? He wanted to sing about Caribbean breezes and hot salsa, not Black Hawks or night-vision scopes. He wanted a mail order bride, a juicy *negra* from the Chocó or perhaps a coffee princess from Caldas with lips as red as ripe beans.

"Señor Ambassador, Señor Ambassador!" the hosts insisted. "What about the guns you are sending to Colombia?"

"All I need is love!" Ambassador Kamman trilled.

Jesús accepted a tissue to wipe his eyes. Curtis Kamman was a *Luciérnaga* favorite.

American ambassadors have a special position in Colombia, as they do in most of the rest of the world, unlike any foreign ambassador in the United States. The American ambassador is usually the most powerful of the resident diplomats, able to move aid or apply sanctions that can save or cripple a nation. In Colombia, the ambassador's moods and foibles are immediately broadcast to the populace and are important elements in the daily drama of events that unfold in the news. Rarely, of course, is the person seen as only the mouthpiece of American foreign policy, a dutiful employee following orders from Washington. In Colombia, the policy and the person conflate in the public eye. The individual becomes the incarnation of intent, a personality that can be fickle or determined or angered and thus punish or reward an entire nation.

After my meeting with Ambassador Kamman, Jesús questioned me closely about his mood. Was he angry? Had the Colombians done something to set him off? I imagined that in Jesús's mind, the ambassador was like a potentate with an army poised on the border. If the meat served at dinner was too lean, would he order his forces to invade?

In these exchanges, I would try to explain to Jesús that the ambassador, as quirky as the person might be in private, was a bureaucrat following orders from afar. Certainly, personality plays a role in world affairs. It certainly served Colombia to get an intelligent person. Yet an ambassadorship was also a post into which different people were inserted depending on time and circumstance. Some things changed and some remained the same. Yet Colombians seemed to greet the arrival of each new American ambassador with a hope that finally, finally, the American would see the light and do something to help the country and not push it further into violence.

Usually, I managed to keep my cynicism from Jesús. My occasional displays risked throwing him into a funk for the rest of the day. Jesús worried most about his son, who had already had several scrapes with the gang in his neighborhood. What future awaited him if Colombia's war only intensified and even more businesses closed down or fled? Jesús's business would thrive, of course. It depended on foreigners coming to chart the country's demise. But Jesús was too responsible a man to take any pleasure in that.

Once, I described my own opinion to him. In fact, the American ambassador seemed to be the least-well-informed person in Colombia. I explained it this way. The European and Latin American and Canadian ambassadors gossiped constantly, sharing information and updating each other on the latest developments in the president's close circle or in the brigades that provoked the worst atrocities or in the inner circle of the FARC surrounding Marín. For them, the businesspeople with interests in Colombia were invaluable sources. These ambassadors traveled constantly and without the armature that by necessity moved with the American.

But they didn't necessarily share this information with their American colleague, for fear of Washington's quick temper at any perceived meddling in its backyard.

"But the CIA!" Jesús protested. His knowledge of the agency was based on the generalized perception in Colombia that anything bad that happened could be traced back to a CIA plot, including the fact that drug trafficking continued to be robust despite decades of eradication efforts, an indication of the CIA's vested interest in keeping the cocaine industry booming. The agency's alleged dabbling in the trade in the 1980s had forever colored it in the minds of Colombians. I imagined that he envisioned a CIA operative like a melding of Cigarette Man from the *X-Files* and MacGyver. Perhaps the paramilitaries were a secret force trained by Washington, Jesús said. Perhaps Washington itself promoted drugs, to pacify the unruly blacks, poison protest, defuse justice, engineer world domination, lull the people's will to freedom. Ignorance never drove an *X-Files* plot. All is known and planned down to the split second. The Americans had to know. That was irrefutable. So, he mused, what was the purpose? How then could the Americans simply shut their eyes or stop their ears to what any Colombian could easily point out? His wasn't an isolated view. And for all I knew, Castaño might be a wholly owned subsidiary. News of CIA ties to known traffickers and abusive military officers in places like Guatemala had been widely covered in Colombia. Castaño himself claimed to have negotiated the surrender of some traffickers to the Americans.

Perhaps, I allowed. I was sure, I said to Jesús, that the CIA knew a lot about Colombia that it had never and would never share.

The FARC certainly believed that Americans were up to permanent no good. Any American was suspect: bird-watchers, missionaries, scientists, activists. In 1999, guerrillas seized and executed three Americans who had come to Colombia to help an indigenous group, the U'wa, prevent oil drilling on land they claimed as their own. Likely, the rebels had known who the Americans were. At the time, the FARC wanted drilling to proceed, so it could "tax" the oil companies. Previously, FARC guerrillas had executed ELN guerrillas who backed the U'wa and their efforts to stop oil drilling. The activists' grisly death—bound and handcuffed, they were forced across the border between Colombia and Venezuela and made to kneel before they were shot—underscored how risky it was to be an American anywhere in Colombia that was not firmly in the category "tourist destination" (of which, it must be said, there are very few). At least the bodies of the activists had been found. Two American missionaries kidnapped by the FARC in 1993 remain missing, their families' last word of them a garbled transmission from a radio somewhere in the Darien Gap.

At the same time, it was my perception that there was a lot that most American ambassadors didn't want to know about Colombia. That is, too close a knowledge of Colombia itself could cripple an ambassador's ability to effectively promote U.S. policy. In that sense, too much knowledge was a bad thing. In 1972, Richard Nixon was the first president to use the phrase "war on drugs." A decade later, Ambassador Louis Tambs went a step further when he coined the word "narco-guerrilla" to refer to the FARC, since the group levied taxes on cocaine. There was both manipulation and truth to the description. When Tambs used it, the relationship between the FARC and drug trafficking existed, but it was no more pronounced than the FARC's relationship with any other business. He could have called them "cattle-guerrillas" or "oil-guerrillas." Guerrillas "taxed" *coca* and charged fees but did not themselves make or sell cocaine. Nevertheless, the choice of term served a political purpose. It worked as a hinge to connect what had been a war on communism to a new campaign, waged with the same tools and against similar targets.

But "narco-guerrilla" and "war on drugs" also deceived. Certainly, the "war on drugs" makes for excellent newspaper copy and rousing campaign speeches. Kingpins like Escobar and the Rodríguez brothers were killed or jailed and hundreds of others were swept into Colombian and American prisons on the strength of coordinated actions by both countries' police and military. Since 1995, when the United States began spraying *coca* bushes with herbicide, thousands of acres have been destroyed. Police and customs agents have seized millions of pounds of pure cocaine in ships, airplanes, submarines, and trucks. Every day, passengers enter the United States, their intestines holding condoms or balloons filled with cocaine; they either shit it out or die trying.

Yet in 2002, the CIA reported that there was more land planted in *coca* than ever before in Colombia's history. Despite all of those efforts, there is more *coca* now than ever before in world history. In fact, there is more than enough powder to cover all of the seizures and losses and still keep prices low and make a fabulous profit. Illegal drugs continue to cause immense damage in the United States–from lives and families lost, to the economic stagnation caused by moribund inner cities, to the rising social cost of more prisons and increased law enforcement. Colombia's drug entrepreneurs are so confident in their ability to produce that in the 1990s, they made an investment in opium poppy, a new twist on the South American repertoire. At the turn of the century, speculators transplanted South American rubber to Ceylon (now Sri Lanka) and Malaysia to spur a new boom. Decades later, Colombians imported Asian opium poppy plants to the rugged northern mountains, where they flourished. Once, smugglers even packed street-grade heroin into the nose cone of Colombia's presidential aircraft as it readied to take the country's president to address the United

Nations in New York in 1996. Clearly, traffickers understood the mantra of Wall Street: diversify, diversify, diversify.

The trade persists for a simple reason. As long as there is demand, there will be supply. It is a truth as immutable as addiction itself or the human thirst for pleasure and escape, impossible to fumigate from our beings. Politicians know this. They also know that at least for the foreseeable future, it is political suicide to admit this and propose policies that accept illegal drug use as inevitable.

In other words, it doesn't necessarily benefit the American ambassador in Colombia to make a close study of the country a priority. Certainly, an ambassador with a will can avoid the issue of Colombia altogether. Such an emissary can spend an entire tour without ever leaving the magic space that encloses an ambassador in its protective sheen, allowing easy movement from cocktail party to chamber of commerce speech to embassy and the occasional cultural function. The usual suspects fill the space at each venue and all visitors are carefully screened. In cables sent home and internal recommendations, Colombia itself becomes a kind of virtual version of reality, tailored to Washington and encouraging more of the same. Because, of course, the people to whom the ambassador ultimately answers do not live in Colombia, nor do they see the effect of U.S. policy there. Their concern is how it plays at home.

Some ambassadors stretch the boundaries that come with the office, too wise or unruly to submit entirely. Born and raised in Chile, Myles Frechette, who served from 1994 to 1997, was among that group. He spoke flawless Spanish. His quick wit and passionate opinions delighted many Colombians who may have disagreed with his statements but enjoyed the fireworks that he provoked. The press dubbed him "Proconsul," and he was usually good for a controversial quote or an off-the-record analysis that laid bare Washington's failings and Colombian chicanery. Famously, he once welcomed a Colombian defense minister to his office wearing a vampire cape and fangs, playing on press accusations that the Americans proposed sucking Colombia dry of natural resources. While Ambassador Frechette ran the embassy, the United States publicly accused Colombian President Ernesto Samper's presidential campaign of accepting contributions from the Cali Cartel. The accusation was based, among other things, on evidence that members of his staff had arranged for the payments, once delivered in a box wrapped in Christmas paper. The investigation became known as the "8,000 investigation," a media-friendly round number assigned by the attorney general.

Samper denied that he had known about the contributions. Eventually, he blamed his campaign finance chief and, later, defense minister (the same one that Frechette greeted in a cape and fangs). In an unprecedented rebuke, on July 11, 1996, the United States announced that it had canceled Samper's visa to the United States on the grounds that he had links to traffickers. For the Americans, this signaled the "political death" of the president. The cancellation was especially painful since Samper's wife, Jacquie Strauss, is the daughter of an American pilot killed over Cambodia during the Vietnam War. Samper responded by accusing Ambassador Frechette of treating all Colombians as "latent criminals" who needed to be taught a lesson between right and wrong. Invited to the general meeting of the United Nations in New York soon afterward, President Samper had to travel on a special U.N. document in order to legally enter the United States (and it was his plane packed with heroin). It is the same mechanism used by other heads of state barred from entry, among them Fidel Castro. Samper felt so persecuted that in his memoirs, he compared himself to the character portrayed by Italian actor and director Roberto Benigni in his film *Life Is Beautiful,* a poignant tale about one man's spiritual triumph over the Nazis. Samper saw himself as the irrepressible Italian hunted by jackbooted drug warriors. Samper called the visa cancellation a "despicable weapon."

In preparation for his stay in New York, Samper had a pharmacist friend prepare for him a cyanide capsule, to take in case the Americans placed him under arrest. He claims he kept it in the back pocket of his pants during the entire visit. Worse than being barred from the United States was being placed under arrest there. As the Medellín Cartel once wrote, "Better a tomb in Colombia than a cell in the United States."

Samper's interior minister and former campaign chief, Horacio Serpa, delighted the press when he publicly ruminated over the suggestion that the DEA was plotting to kill Samper's attorney and topple the president. "*Me suena, me suena,*" he said, "it sounds right." For months, the phrase was repeated to cover any and all outlandish theories about why Colombia was falling apart.

The issue of visas is perhaps among the most sensitive between Colombia and the United States. Although some Colombians denounce American imperialism and meddling in national politics and business dealings, there is an equal and growing hunger for American products, American food, American music and, most of all, America itself. Although many of the Colombians who visit go no further than Orlando, the promise of a visit is seen as a right, not a privilege, the reward for belonging to the First World. Samper himself recuperated in Florida after being shot in the attack that killed Patriotic Union leader José Antequera. Carlos Castaño claims to have brought his children to Disney World in 1994. Before he became the world's most wanted man, Pablo Escobar toured Tennessee and had a photograph taken of himself standing with his son in front of the White House. Until 1999, the reward for army officers who excelled was a week at Disney World with their families. That ended in 2000, after the army chief publicly excoriated the United States for its "offensive treatment" of officers applying for visas in preparation for trips to the Magic Kingdom. At the time, the consulate was required by law to ensure that visa holders were not being prosecuted for alleged human rights violations or support for paramilitary groups. This was part of a growing effort to link proposals for U.S. military aid to human rights. Several officers had received letters informing them that their visa requests had been turned down because of their links to acts of "international terrorism," the phrase used to describe human rights violations committed by paramilitaries with military support. Instead of the Magic Kingdom, the army began offering its officers outings to the Caribbean.

For Jesús, the promise of an eventual trip to the United States, perhaps a job there and a little house for his family, was a beautiful dream, as playful in its way as Benigni's fable of wartime Italy. Once, he paid a shyster lawyer to arrange fake visas, a relatively easy task. More difficult was confirming that they would actually work on a Miami customs agent and not convert Jesús into another deportation statistic. Like so many Colombians, he was torn between attachment to his home, a realization that things would get far worse before there would be any hope for improvement, and a powerful desire to make things better for his son, so that at least he wouldn't end up himself stuck behind the wheel of a cab, his only distraction the crooning of the fake ambassador on the radio.

ooooo

THERE IS NO BETTER PLACE TO SEE THE EFFECT OF THE UNITED STATES in Colombia—both from the purchase of drugs and the destruction of drug-producing crops—than the state of Putumayo, which forms part of Colombia's southern border with Ecuador. The state has a split personality. Its capital, Mocoa, sits atop a flank of the Andes and is surrounded by lush forest. The larger and more prosperous part of the state lies east, in the rolling jungle hills, with their plentiful water and steamy climate perfect for *coca* bushes. Unlike Peru, where *coca* is grown and used by a significant number of indigenous Peruvians, in Colombia only a small number of people continue to chew the leaf. The *coca* grown in the Putumayo is primarily for export. The people who grow it treat it as a cash crop, like Carolina tobacco. In the 1980s, when I lived in Peru, most *coca* was grown in that country's Upper Huallaga Valley, then flown as bricks of *base* into Colombia for final processing and packing. But several forces—among them, a fungus that ravaged the Peruvian bushes and the arrests of Cali Cartel leaders, who purchased most Peruvian *base*—led other traffickers to shift production into southern Colombia. In the end, the shift from Peru did not result in less *coca*, but much, much more, this time centered in Colombia (where the fungus is, as yet, unknown).

In Colombia, there was a second, more serious repercussion from the crop's shift north. *Coca* happens to flourish in the regions historically under the control of the FARC. Marín's ragged little band, his orphaned Marxists, were hand-delivered a fabulous, inexhaustible, and easy source of wealth. By the late 1990s, General Charles Wilhelm, then head of the U.S. army's Southern Command, estimated that the FARC made one-third of its annual income from the taxes and fees it levied on the cocaine industry.

I saw the boom first in 1992, when I traveled in the Putumayo. I was with a Colombian and an Ecuadoran colleague. We went from town to town in a mustard-yellow *campero* driven by Don Vitervo, a local, whose sound system was dedicated to Cuban *son* from the 1930s and 1940s. He had strung Christmas lights around the inside of the roof and they twinkled to the intoxicating beat of Guillermo Portabales and Celina and Reutilio. The smell of smoke from forest burned to clear land for *coca* bushes hung in the air as a permanent haze. Everywhere I saw signs of drug wealth: Japanese motorcycles and stores hawking stereos, late-model pickups, and gold jewelry. Silent men in wrap-around shades and *guayaberas,* the hip-length shirt favored by men in the tropics, sipped coffee in the corner cafés.

In the town of Puerto Asís, we relaxed in a cavernous disco called the Metropolis. The customers were young men with leathery, well-scrubbed hands, the *raspachínes* with a week's pay in dollars wadded in the pockets of their pants. *Raspachín* means scraper, from the verb *raspar*, to pull the *coca* leaves from the bush branches during the harvest. Puerto Asís was the capital of Colombian *coca*, a city of 40,000 created by the boom: farmers who needed supplies, laboratories that needed chemicals, workers who needed food and clothing, sex and drink and music. Under a revolving glitter ball, we drank frozen flasks of *aguardiente*. The disco was filled with beautiful women, in unitards and spangles, heels as sharp as knives. It was a Colombian gold rush, except what those around us pursued was white powder.

Gilberto drank with us. A *coca* farmer, the work of clearing land, burning the dross, and planting seedlings had whittled him to the width of a sapling, toasted by the sun and hard as teak. He was in it for the money. "I tried farming elsewhere, but pffft!" His calloused hand was like the bud of a lily opening. "Nothing. Here, I get paid in cash, dollars. Business is good. If they try to take it away, I fight. Or I'll just move farther away."

I danced with Don Vitervo as the ball threw chips of light on the floor. With the patience of a grandfather, he taught me salsa steps, loosening my *gringa* hips with the firm lead of his shoulders.

Booms were not new to Putumayo. The conquistadors wanted its gold. Then entrepreneurs went after its rubber to feed First World industrialization and World War I. Under the despotic rule of commercial houses like Casa Arana, thousands of Indians were killed in the quest for this lucrative tree sap. In its way, *coca* was more humane. The profits from gold or rubber went almost entirely to the wholesalers. Many early rubber tappers were indigenous people who were virtually enslaved by commercial houses, forced to pay for food or equipment and never managing to earn their way out of debt. In contrast, *coca* was a small entrepreneur's dream. Farmers themselves could invest in bushes and then sell the raw leaves or *base* to the highest bidder. Traffickers also worked with agronomists and plant biologists to improve the alkaloid content in the stock available and increase the leaf yield. In this way, traffickers were like venture capitalists promoting the development of entrepreneurs able to boost quality and production. Hundreds of families moved to the region, attracted by what appeared to be a sure thing.

To the untrained eye, every *coca* bush looks the same. But to Carlos Alberto Palacios, whom I sat with one morning in the town of Mocoa, each is a small novel, with a plot that twists and turns to the rhythm of the people who helped create it. He had been introduced to me as a priest, which he had been up to the week I met him. His calling had ended the day of our meeting, with the birth of his son. Although he had yet to formally renounce his vocation, his superiors in Bogotá were well aware of the impending birth and had removed him from his parish in the town of La Hormiga (literally, the Ant).

A stocky, red-haired man, Carlos Alberto had been born to a peasant family nearby that had raised him to take religious orders. But before entering the seminary, he decided to use some of his father's land to ride the cocaine boom. In that way, he told me, he planned to save a nest egg for his parents' eventual retirement, something he could not hope to do as a priest. First, he planted a bush known as La Caucana, a Colombian native that turned out to be too delicate for the demands of the trade. "To harvest, you needed to remove the leaves from the branch tip down," Carlos Alberto said, meaning that the *raspachínes* had to be specially trained. Although the alkaloid content of the leaves was high, the slower harvest cut into profitability.

Then the traffickers introduced a variety he called La Peruana, from Peru. "It was resistant to most diseases, easy to plant, and you could propagate it easily from new wood, by simply clipping branches and sticking them in the ground." The *raspachínes* could also pull the leaves straight off, meaning that the harvest, up to four times a year, went faster. "A twenty-six-pound sack of leaves meant a kilo of *base*. Refined, that's $1 million dollars. Of course, the farmers got only a fraction of what it might sell for in New York. But for a time, it was enough."

Since few authorities ventured out of Putumayo towns, the FARC was the de facto government, setting the rules and enforcing them. An infraction, like the beating of a wife or a theft, could provoke a warning. A second offense got a stronger response. The third was the clincher. "*Perdonar, avisar, castigar,*" forgive, warn, and punish. Repeat offenders risked exile or an on-the-spot execution. As the *coca* business expanded, guerrillas increased the taxes, Carlos Alberto explained. "They also taxed the chemicals used to manufacture *base* as well as the *base* sold in weekly markets along the streets." Soon, they started buying *base* themselves and sold it directly to traffickers.

There is no reliable record of how much money the FARC collected from the *coca* trade. On a napkin, Carlos Alberto made a calculation that took into account only the most active fields concentrated in Putumayo (there are other fields scattered throughout the country's southern half)—$3 million each month, $36 million per year. Minimum. I have seen other estimates as high as $200 million.

The results in the region were palpable. Guerrillas got better weapons. They marched in crisp camouflage. *Comandantes* got their own vehicles to tear around the roads, blasting salsa.

Carlos Alberto got out of the business when he left for the seminary. By then, it had brought with it other, less welcome developments: murders and men with guns, drunkenness and prostitutes, hundreds and hundreds of boys and young men looking for quick cash earned as a *raspachín* or what came to be known as a *chichipato*, a small-time dealer, or a *traquetero*, one of the middlemen who buys *base* and sells it to the labs. In 1987, Gonzalo Rodríguez Gacha brought MAS fighters to El Azul, a farm near Puerto Asís. There, they attempted to wrest control of the business from guerrillas. They failed, in part because they lacked the numbers and weaponry to roust the FARC. In 1990, the FARC overran El Azul and forced MAS to retreat to the cities (Rodríguez was himself killed in a government raid in 1989).

After his ordination, Carlos Alberto returned to Putumayo to work at a church. He started several projects that he hoped would stop the increase in violence associated with the drug trade. But there was an economic logic to the violence that no community organization or program could detour. During my visit, locals regaled me with stories of Pablito, one of Rodríguez's most feared assassins. Once, Pablito shot five teenage boys on a public bus in broad daylight, apparently mistaking them for other youths accused of robbing trucks. At the time, Pablito ran Puerto Asís like a personal fiefdom, with the full support of the police and local army battalion. Pablito could not venture far from town, however, for fear of the FARC. So his killings were all in town, sometimes within sight of the local police station.

One of the boys' mothers, Rosa, retrieved the bodies from the morgue. I interviewed her in her home outside town, where she was surrounded by grandchildren and chickens. The house was neat and airy, propped on stilts above the floodplain carved each year by the Guamuéz River. "The MAS fighters made the bus stop at about 8 P.M., and right there they killed them. They said, 'Get off, this isn't a robbery, this is the law.' So people began to get off. Pablito, the paramilitary, shot each boy once and there he lay. . . . But one of the boys managed to escape. That was the boy who told my daughters what had happened. There were five boys in all . . . my boy was the last one they killed," she said as she held up his photograph.

For the FARC, the money was a windfall. American consumers spend an estimated $38 billion annually on cocaine. Guerrillas needed only a percentage to prosper. Even as MAS killed suspected guerrilla collaborators in other parts of Colombia, in Putumayo, traffickers like Escobar were forced to deal with guerrillas in order to get the raw material they needed to do business. Growing from a crew of fewer than 1,000 people in 1981, the FARC boasted 15,000 armed and trained fighters by 1996. That paramilitaries like Castaño were also arming themselves largely on the strength of drug money only seemed to spur Marín deeper into the business.

To continue my conversation with Carlos Alberto later in the day, I bought several bottles of Colombian *aguardiente* that featured a label decorated with an outline of the state of Putumayo. Although the liquor came from Bogotá, the distillery labeled it according to the state where it would be shipped and sold, a kind of bow to Colombia's vibrant regionalism. Colombians familiar with *aguardiente* swear they can name the distillery by the taste, which can vary from very sweet to sharp as a slice of fennel. Carlos Alberto took advantage of the label to continue his lesson on the Putumayo. In the light of a fire, he tipped the bottle sideways. With a finger to the shard of land that is the state's body, he pointed out the locations where *coca* cultivation was concentrated. Much of it I had driven through, as seemingly calm and uniform as the American corn belt. His auguries were dire. Violence would increase, he predicted, as the Colombians battled for control of the *coca* fields. Meanwhile, the business itself would endure, no matter what the faraway American ambassador did or thought.

Yet Carlos Alberto was buoyant with joy. That night, his son, Luis Miguel, had been born. Carlos Alberto and the boy's mother had named him Luis Miguel after the Mexican bolero singer. "Luis Miguel is here!" he kept interrupting himself to say.

As he spoke, Carlos Alberto played with the prefix "narco." By the measure of the American ambassador, he is a "narco-priest." Or was, he grinned. "Luis Miguel is here!" There were narco-jets and narco-bars. There were narco-public works. The governments of both Colombia and the United States were "narco-states," since they collected millions in tax revenue from cocaine-linked enterprises. There were narco-paramilitaries, narco-soldiers; narco-weddings, narco-funerals, narco-babies, narco–beauty queens; narco-hospitals, narco–auto dealerships, narco–soccer fields. There were narco-Toyotas, the Camry sedans that Colombians also call *burbujas,* bubbles, for their pop-eyed windows. There were even narco-diplomats, like the American colonel James Hiett, the U.S. embassy military attaché in charge of directing the first efforts at involving the U.S. military in counterdrug efforts. In 2000, Hiett's wife, Laurie, was sentenced to five years in federal prison for conspiring to send $700,000 worth of cocaine from Colombia to the United States through the diplomatic mail. Colonel Hiett himself pleaded guilty to covering up for her by laundering the profits, taking the money she brought home in shoe boxes to pay the couples' credit card bills. His prison sentence–five months–infuriated and delighted Carlos Alberto. So did the fact that Colonel Hiett got to keep his military pension when he retired. A Colombian judge eventually gave Laurie Hiett's chauffeur, convicted of helping her send the cocaine, a sentence longer than the combination of both sentences handed down by American judges to the Hietts (though it should be noted that another Colombian judge gave little more than a slap on the hand to the leaders of the Cali Cartel).

Using Carlos Alberto's semantic logic, Colonel Hiett received a narco-sentence and a narco-pension. Although I later searched the news clips I saved from the case, I never saw the Americans writing or commenting on the case describe it in that way.

ooooo

IN 1997, THE FRUSTRATION WITH THE "WAR ON DRUGS" WAS PALPABLE in the American embassy. I was there to talk with Ambassador Frechette and his team, a ritual stop for me on every trip. The faces that I saw around the conference room table were fatigued. At the time, the embassy was being used as a travel agency for the dozens of congressional delegations arriving to ask why, despite the billions spent, there were more illegal narcotics from Colombia in the United States than ever before. To questions, the team had rehearsed responses (Frechette was known for running a tight ship, and the staff was barred from speaking without his permission). The briefing had the feel of a touring Broadway show on its final, disappointing week. In Cleveland.

I was tired, too. Drug war reports piled on my floor and clogged my e-mail inbox. During my absences from the keyboard, the inbox would start replying that it could accept no more messages, starting a spiral that would keep bounced messages returning like boomerangs. Nothing was new; there was never real progress to report. At times, it seemed to me that the only point of the "war on drugs" was to generate statistics, reports, briefings, and charts that could be hauled out at congressional hearings (when officials inevitably asked for more money) or during American election campaigns (when candidates hoping to look tough on drugs asked for more votes).

Occasionally, the Colombian police would pile seized drugs in a mound and light it, sending a plume of bitter smoke into the Bogotá sky. They never lacked for raw material. Each drug seizure seemed to reveal a hiding place more inventive than the last–in furniture, in waste oil, in coconut cakes, in yachts. At the same time, the most reliable methods were the most obvious: go-fast boats that outran the

U.S. Coast Guard, tanker trucks at the borders, and containerized cargo ships that hid among the hundreds of other vessels that unload at American ports every day.

My interest in the "war on drugs" was narrow and specific. Drugs had an inescapable influence on how people died in Colombia. Men with guns—whether they were guerrillas, soldiers, paramilitaries, or hired assassins—had a connection, one way or another, to the trade. Without it, violence would not vanish, I knew; but the more I followed Colombia, the more I saw that with it, the violence expanded and intensified. Drugs fueled the war that led Amado to attempt to take Josué's life. They were what gave Víctor Carranza the fortune he used to pay hired killers like "Travolta" to kill Josué's colleagues in the Patriotic Union. When the FARC lobbed its gas cylinder bombs at towns, drug money was behind the purchase of the dynamite and the pickup trucks used as launching pads. It would be too much to say that the bullet lodged in Josué's shoulder had been bought with money handed over by a specific American buyer in a specific American city. There were complex and long-standing political disputes at stake, which Josué himself had patiently explained to me.

Yet the link between drug profits, armed groups, and the war was powerfully real to me. Colombia's other, legal products didn't sell. Like other countries left out of the First World boom, Colombia had to find another way to plug into the global marketplace. It was the flip side of globalization, commerce by nations unable to compete with legal products that commanded a decent price. Colombians weren't willing to resign themselves to poverty, to the cheap seat at the world's parade of technological marvels and physical ease. They deploy the next best thing, integration through crime, what Spanish sociologist Manuel Castells has called "the perverse connection."

It is not by chance that Russian mafias deliver Colombian *coca* to European markets. Following the breakup of the former Soviet Union, drug syndicates were quick to recruit Russian technicians left jobless (like the engineers who make the submarines that pack coke in their holds). Crime is one way to pull a people on the brink of economic ruin into the realm where food and warmth and medical care are not just images projected in Hollywood movies. Powderware and gunware fill the busy circuit between Bogotá and Moscow and Pristina and

Paris and Lagos and New York. Like Colombia, Russia has little to offer the "information empires" that rule trade. Both of them, however, can sell what feeds our voracious culture. Each new generation that tries cocaine and heroin comes to it fresh, as if it were an undiscovered country. The lure of illegal drugs to young people is unquenchable, like youth itself.

In some ways, La Violencia had never really ended in Colombia. But what was brewing that year overshadowed even that period's excesses. This time, the Americans were not playing a supporting role, cloaked in Cold War rhetoric. They were front and center, with a purchasing power that made the amount of U.S. military aid being debated seem as irrelevant as a child's weekly allowance. *Coca* was spewing out of the Andes, 550,000 metric tons of raw leaf in 1996 alone. The actual size of *coca* fields shown on the embassy's oversized maps seemed manageable, even tiny. In terms of acreage, it was equivalent to the land devoted only to malt barley in south-central Idaho. But the profits were astronomical–$53 billion annually, calculated on the basis of the average U.S. street price of $175 per gram of cocaine. That was five times the amount of foreign aid spent on the entire African continent. At best, even the most committed drug warriors could only say that American efforts had "slowed the rate of increase"– in other words, shaved some seconds off the run of an accelerating train fueled by their fellow Americans.

For the embassy, it had been a rough summer. The ambassador was embroiled in a diplomatic shoving match with Colombian president Ernesto Samper over the "8,000 investigation." That January, the State Department "decertified" Colombia's anti-drug performance for the second year in a row, a symbolic measure meant to show displeasure with the Samper administration's poor performance in the war on drugs. The Colombians responded by pointing the finger north, accusing the United States of failing to do enough to curb demand.

The Republicans were accusing President Bill Clinton of being soft on drugs and even "sabotaging" the drug war by failing to fight it hard enough in Colombia. Clinton's campaign trail admission that he had tried marijuana but hadn't inhaled enticed some Republicans to portray him as a drug-addled dilettante. It was a cynical, shallow tactic. In fact, little distinguished Clinton's record from that of his predecessor,

George H.W. Bush, or for that matter Ronald Reagan. All favored an emphasis on supply-side eradication and interdiction, even as funding for treatment in the United States—considered the most effective way to reduce demand and therefore the amount of cocaine sent into the country—dwindled. Drug-war scholar Peter Reuter once described U.S. drug policy as "frozen in place" since the mid-1980s.

Instead, American presidents engaged in small changes, tweaks, shifts in language that go virtually unnoticed in the United States but have huge impact in places like Colombia. Bush's tweak was to invite Andean militaries to join the police in fighting the drug war, an initiative Clinton embraced. More firepower was needed, the argument went, to make advances against the cartels. Despite having received millions in security assistance, the police were outgunned. Only the army had the ability to neutralize the well-armed cartels.

The problem for Bush was that the Colombians didn't want to play. The Colombian generals said that the main enemy was Marín, not drugs. In 1990, top Colombian officers came to Washington and told Congress quite pointedly that they intended to use any U.S. aid to fight the FARC. The announcement caused little comment, a sign of how neatly the war on subversion had already melded into the "war on drugs." "The arms are given to the government in order that it may use them in the anti narcotics struggle," commented former U.S. ambassador to Colombia Thomas MacNamara, a Bush administration supporter. "But this is not a requirement." That same year, the United States sent yet another team of military advisers to Colombia, this time to once again revamp the Colombian military's intelligence system. It had been two decades since General Yarborough delivered his scathing report, but little had changed. According to the U.S. Defense Department, the goal was to make the Colombian system more "efficient and effective" in the fight against drugs.

Those in the Colombian military accepted the advice, as always. Then they directed the system not against traffickers but against people they suspected of "subversion." For human rights, the consequences were disastrous. A new navy intelligence network based in Barrancabermeja began to recruit professional killers and paramilitaries as a "hunter-killer" squad that collected information used to murder Colombians, among them peasant leaders, human rights defenders, and people who made the mistake of getting in their way. Called Network 7, its commander, Colonel Rodrigo Quiñones, was later linked by government investigators to at least fifty-seven murders, including the sidewalk execution of the secretary of the main human rights group in the region. Network 7 also set up paramilitary groups that used the name MAS to threaten and kill in the surrounding countryside.

Colombia's use of U.S. funds and advice–and the human rights abuses that resulted–caused little outrage in Washington. To the contrary, officials rejected proposals to place human rights conditions on aid, claiming that they would be counterproductive. Reform, they argued, would come by a kind of osmosis, as Colombian officers saw that good behavior translated into more goodies from the Americans. Assistant Secretary of State Bernard Aronson articulated the U.S. position before the Senate Foreign Relations Committee. "Denying aid or imposing conditions impossible to meet defeats the goals of improving human rights. In the real world, the perfect is the enemy of the good."

A different message was understood by Colombia's generals. The *gringos* would turn a blind eye to abuses as long as the military paid lip service to the drug war. For the politicians, cutting aid on human rights grounds risked making them appear soft on drugs. Especially in an election year, this was unthinkable.

In 1994, President Clinton presented his first budget for the drug war. It differed little from the Bush administration's plan. Of the $13 billion requested, President Clinton asked for a 1-percent increase in spending on demand reduction. But he succeeded in getting something that had eluded President Bush: an agreement by Colombia to drop its opposition to the use of herbicides against *coca*. Drug warriors had long argued that the only way to make headway against drug production was to kill the plants themselves. They had achieved this using paraquat against marijuana in Mexico. In Colombia, the plan was to use glyphosate, sold in the United States as Roundup.

Wasp-like Turbo Thrushes and OV-10 Bronco airplanes–part of the State Department's air wing–were fitted with special nozzles and tanks and shipped south. By 1995, they were crisscrossing the sky over southeastern Colombia. With one swoop over the treetops, they could lay down a veil of white chemical. Within days, *coca* leaves hit by enough spray would crumble into brown flakes. The slender branches would shrivel, and the plant would become a skeleton that buzzed with each breeze.

Predictably, spraying was wildly unpopular. Once, a Colombian pilot showed me where bullets had perforated the belly of a Turbo Thrush. Only the motor and bottom of the pilot's seat was armored. In this case, the bullets had gone straight through the fuselage, allowing the pilot to return to the airstrip and land. In 1996, the FARC helped organize one of the largest peasant mobilizations in Colombian history (and certainly the largest one of its own making) to protest the spray campaign. From farmers defending plots of corn and beans, the guerrillas had become the champions of a new ally, the families that planted *coca* along with corn and beans. Over these Colombians, who had seen their *coca* along with their families and legal crops doused with Roundup, the guerrillas had sudden and powerful influence. An estimated 150,000 people marched on the city of Puerto Asís before being dispersed by the army and police.

In 1998, the FARC delivered a more pointed message when it destroyed an entire town to show its opposition to the spraying. Miraflores was the hub of a huge expanse of *coca* in the southeastern state of Guaviare. The first farmers had been lured there by the government a decade earlier, to colonize the supposedly fertile jungle and relieve overpopulation in the Andes. Government engineers marked open plots, promised fertilizer, technical assistance, and loans, then vanished. Hundreds died as crops failed and disease proliferated, focusing like a death ray on the oldest and weakest. Then came *coca*. Men with *coca* seedlings flew in, gave them to farmers, and taught them how to grow, feed, and harvest them. Suddenly, the farmers didn't need the engineers or their empty promises. Months later, those same men returned, this time with crisp American dollars. They paid cash for the harvest—unheard of, since with legal crops like mangos, farmers often have to wait months to be paid. Then the men flew the *coca* away, lifting yet another burden from the farmers, the hopeless task of transporting their harvest to market over poor roads and without the money to pay the freight on the cargo planes.

By 1998, the 30,000 residents of Miraflores were there for one reason: *coca*. A handful of houses and businesses hugged a single landing strip. Residents ran restaurants, bars, and brothels to serve the thousands of *raspachínes* and *chichipatos* who worked the *coca* fields. Improbably, Colombia's anti-narcotics police also had a base there. It was meant to guard tanks of fuel used to resupply the helicopters that escorted the spray planes.

After dark on August 6, over 400 guerrillas attacked. Armed with rifles, bazookas, mortars, incendiary bombs, and grenades, guerrillas shot over 200,000 rounds over eighteen hours, a *plomacera*–a rain of lead–as one survivor later told me. Blasts ripped the tin sheeting from the mayor's office, the church, and the school. Of the tiny hospital, only four concrete pillars were left standing. Twisted bed frames lay in a smoking pile. Seventeen police officers perished, and forty-one were wounded.

Prior to the attack, guerrillas had ordered 200 roast hens from a Miraflores chicken restaurant, to snack on as the attack developed. Not a word of warning made it to the police.

The issue of a legal alternative to *coca* is a common refrain in the drug war debate, and something that the farmers themselves embrace as a way to oppose the spray. For many, what is called "alternative development"–enticing farmers to eradicate *coca* and plant legal crops–is the spell that will untie the ugly knot of the drug war. If only the peasants had the support they needed to plant something else, the argument goes, the problem would be solved without wars or spray planes. It is an attractive argument. In practice, however, it is as ineffective a strategy as eradication or interdiction. The trade's raw economics doom it. Much of the *coca* grown in Colombia is tended not by farmers on small plots but by men hired to clear jungle land and plant *coca* for big investors. They are not lured by legal crops. For them, *coca* is an investment, not a way of life or a hedge against despair.

Even for the small farmers who dedicate a portion of land to *coca*, alternative development offers little. The premise is that the price of *coca* leaf will not increase enough to tempt farmers back to *coca* growing, as Peter Reuter has pointed out. Yet traffickers can easily–and without losing more than a percentage point of profit–raise the price they pay for *coca*. Ironically, alternative development makes *coca* more attractive, since it forces wholesalers to pay more for raw leaf or *base* to keep farmers in the business. In any case, most of the jungle land used for *coca* is too barren to sustain less hardy crops.

Yet some farmers, eager to avoid arrest or the spray, do sign on to voluntary eradication programs and plant other things. One Colombian cooperative I visited had pledged to uproot its *coca* and accept loans to start vegetable farms. The results were catastrophic. After the first year, the affordable loans vanished. When I visited, farmers faced a 34-percent interest rate that would increase again the next year. Meanwhile, none of the promised agronomists had shown up to teach them the proper use of the pesticides recommended for their new crops. Already, they had lost most of that year's harvest to disease. Water and electricity were expensive, forcing many to depend on rainfall, cutting even further into their yields. Few could afford to bring produce to the markets themselves, so they lost another percentage to the truck drivers. One farmer who had managed to overcome all of these obstacles and deliver vegetables to a market had been stopped and executed by paramilitaries. They accused him of being a Communist since he belonged to a farm cooperative.

The families had begun to abandon their farms for the cities. But even this decision was fraught with peril. In the slums, they had tried to organize a neighbors' association to petition the local mayor for a potable water system. There were delays and broken promises. The people protested. Then they heard rumors that after the protest, they had been identified as guerrillas. Their slum began to be called a *"barrio rojo,"* a pro-Communist slum. Soon afterward, young men from the *barrio rojo* could not find work in town. Their only option was to return to the *coca* fields, still booming. But this time, they were not farmers, but the *raspachínes*, the leaf pullers, lowest of the low.

ooooo

It was not up to Ambassador Frechette to settle the dispute over what worked and what did not in the "war on drugs." His job was to manage the policy as it was handed down from Washington. In 1996, the United States had spent \$44 million spraying *coca* plants. The same year, the acreage devoted to these plants had increased by 32 percent. In other words, one of his jobs was to translate glaring failure into a palatable public face.

His concern about what was happening in Colombia was obvious. At the time, Ambassador Frechette was fending off efforts to commit the United States to the broader war against guerrillas, the only war that his new partners, the Colombian military, really cared about. Even as military leaders rejected any human rights pressure, they were desperate for the helicopters they said they needed to go after the guerrillas. What they particularly wanted were the Black Hawks capable of lifting up to eighteen fully equipped soldiers, flying in bad weather, and negotiating the thin air near the country's tallest peaks. That was where guerrillas walked, not portly drug kingpins.

Washington remained reluctant to commit to direct counterinsurgency. Only the Colombian military and some Beltway hotheads claimed that the FARC was a "cartel." Both Frechette and Colombian police chief Rosso José Serrano routinely iced down these allegations as a ruse that the generals used to wangle money to fight the FARC. In one meeting with a nominee for the post of Colombian defense minister, later recorded in an embassy cable, Ambassador Frechette was categorical about the role the United States was willing to play:

THERE WILL BE NO USG ASSISTANCE FOR FIGHTING THE GUERRILLAS ... [AMBASSADOR FRECHETTE] SAID THAT THE ISSUE RAISES TOO MANY HUMAN RIGHTS CONCERNS AND HAS BEEN A SEARING EXPERIENCE FOR US IN CENTRAL AMERICA.

In 1997, U.S. law for the first time required embassies to screen security force units receiving security assistance anywhere in the world for credible evidence of human rights violations; such evidence would disqualify them from receiving aid. Drafted by Senator Patrick Leahy (D–VT), the measure, called the Leahy Amendment, won congressional support in large part out of concern over the relationship with Colombia's tainted army.

Competing demands left Ambassador Frechette with a difficult task. He had to find some way to spend the new military aid allocated for Colombia's army without having it slop over into the bigger war or go to tainted soldiers. In other words, he had to conjure a miracle. He did it with a felt-tip pen. "The Box is there," Ambassador Frechette said to me, unfolding from his chair long enough to point to a line drawn on a map of Colombia that encircled the country's *coca*-growing bowels. "There are no registered human rights violations by the government in this part of the country. If a unit receives assistance, it has to use it within the Box. If that unit is sent outside the Box, it has to leave the equipment behind."

Only certain units would be equipped by the United States even within "the Box," the ambassador was quick to note. As I later learned, he and his staff had spent much of the year trying to identify Colombian military units that could pass what they called the "smell test." There weren't many of them. At the time, army support for Castaño and his Head Splitters was widespread. A report I prepared for Human Rights Watch concluded that at least half of the brigade-level units in the Colombian army had links to paramilitaries. Ambassador Frechette and his team were trying to make the best of a bad situation, I realized. As yet, Castaño had not sent his paramilitaries beyond the Box's northern border. That meant there were no reports of collusion with the military and the predictable massacres that resulted. So the Americans had taken advantage of adversity by taking a pen to a map and drawing out the limits of Castaño's realm.

I felt like patting the ambassador on the back. He had managed to fit a condom over the drug war. It allowed the Americans to insert without birthing a human rights monster, as Ambassador Frechette knew they had in Central America. At least, they would be able to deny direct involvement. Outside "the Box," the Americans were saying, the war and its atrocities were a Colombian problem for Colombians to solve.

Off the record, one political counselor in the U.S. embassy was more cynical. As long as Castaño was successful against the FARC and stayed out of "the Box," the Americans would ignore him, the counselor predicted. By then, Castaño had pushed the FARC off the Gulf of Urabá and was preparing to take their main camps in the mountains of northern Antioquia, where he vowed to drink coffee by year's end (and did, albeit nursing a bullet to the rear). "Eventually, Castaño will win," the counselor said as the elevator doors opened. "Then he will go away, as he promised." Problem solved.

"At what cost?" I asked.

The counselor shrugged. The cost was to Colombians only. It was a culture of violence. So far, the cost to the United States was zero.

It was not an isolated point of view. In 1997, a congressional delegation led by Representative Denny Hastert (R–IL) visited Colombia. As was their custom, the army generals told the visitors that the FARC was a "drug cartel." I imagine that they hoped to drive a wedge between the ambassador and his congressional guests. The army had even published a book titled *FARC Cartel,* which officers delivered to the members and staff.

In this case, it worked. Representative Hastert, a former wrestling coach, was so outraged by the generals' tales of how they had been prevented from using U.S. aid (by those pesky human rights activists) that he vowed to eliminate human rights conditions from future legislation. The conditions had been placed there, he said, by "leftist-dominated" U.S. Congresses of years past, who "used human rights as an excuse to aid the left in other countries." Representative Hastert closed his remarks by encouraging the generals to bypass the State Department completely and communicate directly with the U.S. Congress.

In a subsequent cable, Ambassador Frechette noted how that remark, paired with the unexpected arrival of a cargo airplane from the United States loaded with weapons that the Colombian army had not been screened to receive, convinced senior Colombian military officers that they had the upper hand in negotiating on human rights. They thought, he wrote, that they "need only take a tough line and wait for the [U.S. government's] insistence on human rights conditions to be overwhelmed by the pressure of events."

Ambassador Frechette was a skilled and resourceful adversary. He ordered the crates left on the dock, unopened. As the generals railed against him, many influential Colombians privately told Ambassador Frechette that U.S. pressure was the only way to get the generals to take human rights seriously. In exchange for what was inside the crates, he demanded that the Colombians remove from the rosters anyone against whom there was credible evidence of human rights abuses. In desperation, one embassy official tried to lure the Colombians into signing a human rights agreement by describing it as equivalent to when a passenger buys an airline ticket and agrees to conditions no one reads on the reverse side.

Purely on its bureaucratic merits, "the Box" was an elegant solution to an impossible problem. Despite the sniping from Representative Hastert, it was backed by the force of law, a law that, in the end, he was not able to change (and later, as Speaker of the House of Representatives, has not attempted to).

Many human rights groups opposed military aid to Colombia altogether. Yet it was this aid, rotting on the dock, that gave Ambassador Frechette leverage to force the Colombian military to admit that links to paramilitaries and their abuses had begun to harm their relationship to the United States. The strategy of offering meat to the starving tiger that was the Colombian military appeared to be working.

For months, Ambassador Frechette held back the aid as Colombia's army failed to demonstrate that it had assigned "clean" officers to the six units proposed for U.S. funding and training. Embassy cables from that period are filled with words describing the Colombian military's efforts to show that it was meeting human rights conditions as "antic," "muffed," and "sheepish." One Colombian defense minister was so shocked by a letter from one general rejecting the human rights conditions that he declined to share it with the Americans. Every time the United States informed the civilian defense minister that the consulate had rejected yet another officer's request for a visa, he would smile, the U.S. embassy reported. He was "happy," according to one embassy cable, "to let the embassy take the heat."

For a while, it proved an entertaining game. But I knew that "the Box" was doomed. It was where the FARC made its *coca* money, a source of strength that Carlos Castaño had vowed to seize. He was the one person who could guarantee that "the Box" would work. But he had no idea that it even existed. To perfect "the Box," I thought to myself, someone should give him a call.

Castaño had been careful not to attack Americans or U.S. business interests, realizing that this would create a serious problem for his group's growth. Ritually, he denied that he engaged directly in drug trafficking, statements designed for an American audience. Castaño had witnessed Pablo Escobar's destruction; indeed, he had helped bring the capo down. Who better than Castaño to understand the lumbering but formidable power of the *gringos* when aroused?

If he did not know about "the Box," how could he keep his men from entering it? It was, after all, only the ambassador's line on an embassy map. As far as I knew (and despite Jesús's musings about Castaño's relationship with the CIA), Castaño had not been granted the privilege of an embassy briefing. The "pressure of events" was controlled not by the U.S. Congress or even Proconsul Frechette. It was Castaño and the Head Splitters. There would be massacres there. What, I asked the ambassador during the briefing, would he do then?

My words, like a meteorologist forecasting rain, dragged through the air. The people whom I sentenced to death with them were still alive somewhere, unaware that they lived in anything called "the Box" or that the number of days they had been allotted on this earth had begun to approach zero, each tick of the clock humming with the sound of diplomatic English.

Frechette, normally tireless, was slumped in his chair. Truthfully, I don't remember how he phrased the answer. He didn't really have one. It was then that I thought that knowing too much about Colombia could be a bad thing for an ambassador. Of course, he knew. "The Box" may have been an elegant solution, a sleight of hand and pen. It was also a little talisman, an amulet, to delay the worst of what was to come.

The members of the team assembled around the table wanted to do their jobs. They wanted to avoid having those twenty-something Capitol Hill aides rake them over the verbal coals in Washington someday. They wanted to go on to bigger and better things, maybe in Belgium or France, any moderately sane country.

"The Box" convinced no one. But for the moment, it was all the Americans had to offer.

ooooo

SIXTEEN DAYS BEFORE THE GOVERNMENTS OF THE UNITED STATES and Colombia finally reached an agreement on human rights (necessary to implement the formal agreement establishing "the Box"), Castaño made it obsolete. On July 15, 1997, 200 of his men pierced its inky border. Thus ended Ambassador Frechette's elegant but irrelevant barrier between Colombia's war and America's "war on drugs."

Not only was Mapiripán, the village that Castaño attacked, in "the Box." To get to it, Castaño had deployed from the Colombian army base used by the Americans to run the spray campaign. On the tarmac that marks the army's "Joaquín París" Battalion–and doubles as the San José del Guaviare municipal airport–the State Department housed its personnel, the Turbo Thrushes, the Roundup, and the technicians and pilots it had hired to select and spray the *coca* fields.

I had been there a couple of weeks before the massacre. The State Department official in charge, Pete Trent, treated the location as if it were a firebase on the Plain of Reeds. His white hair was long and straggly, kept from his face by a hippie-style headband. A Bowie knife jutted from the cuff of his boots. To service and fly the airplanes, the State Department paid a private contractor, Dyncorp. Its technicians were packed into the single room that served as a dormitory and a computer center. They wore freshly laundered clothes and smelled of Old Spice. Trent looked and smelled as if he had just pried his way out of a Vietcong tiger cage.

Truthfully, Trent's fashion sense was arguably more sane than that of his crew, who looked as if they had just punched time cards at the Pentagon. The San José airport was in a sea of FARC. At any moment, guerrillas could lob a gas cylinder bomb at the office complex or, better yet, at the airport restaurant where the Americans ate breakfast, lunch, and dinner. The predictable civilian casualties that would result would not make guerrillas hesitate an instant.

On July 12, paramilitaries landed two chartered airplanes at San José. Later, embassy officials confessed to me that the bustle raised no suspicion. The planes had left Urabá that morning with fifty ACCU fighters and their gear as well as a stack of preprinted flyers announcing that Castaño had formed a "Guaviare Front" to rid the state of guerrillas. In it, residents were cautioned to "distance themselves totally from the guerrillas." How this was to be done in a region that for decades had been home to the FARC was not spelled out. Those who failed to properly distance themselves, however, would be "*ajusticiado*," executed.

At the airport, the paramilitaries unloaded guns, uniforms, and equipment, with help from the army base's intelligence officer and the sergeant in charge of airport security. In the official registry of arriving passengers, soldiers did not record either the arrival of the airplanes or the names of the men who deplaned, required with every other arriving or departing flight. When I had come in at that same airport, I had stood in a long line to show my passport, which a young soldier had dutifully copied ("Kirka Robin," profession *housewife*). The soldier examined the passport photo, then remarked to me that I looked much older in person.

The soldiers did not search the paramilitaries. Instead, an investigation later revealed that they helped them pack the gear into trucks able to navigate the dirt track that took the fighters to the tiny port of Charras, on the Guaviare River. There, they boarded boats. They wore army fatigues and yellow armbands with the letters ACCU. They paused only to clear the checkpoint maintained by the Colombian navy at a river island called Barrancón, where the Colombian military trains. Over the previous weeks, American Special Forces had been training Colombian troops there. Prosecutors believe that a commander at Barrancón, Colonel Lino Sánchez, was the army officer who arranged the paramilitary arrival. In a later declaration to authorities, two anti-narcotics police officers reported that Sánchez had invited them to help "teach the guerrillas a lesson."

Why Mapiripán? It was a marketing center for cocaine and therefore a cash cow for the FARC. On the weekends, Mapiripán bustled with the boys and young men who worked as *raspachínes* and *cocineros*, the laboratory workers. On the banks of the Guaviare River, Mapiripán was easy to reach. Some residents had apparently been warned beforehand of Castaño's plans, among them the mayor and the family of "Alex," the FARC commander in charge of collecting *coca* taxes. By the time paramilitaries arrived, "Alex" had switched sides. To convince his new friends of his sincerity, he had written out a list of the names of the people he had threatened and blackmailed into feeding and clothing his guerrilla troops.

The local judge, Leonardo Iván Cortés, had not been warned. He was at home when paramilitaries landed. They kicked in his door and demanded the keys to his office, where one of the few telephones in the village was located. He handed them over, keeping to himself the fact that he owned a duplicate set. Meanwhile, other paramilitaries began to stop people and check their identity cards against lists of names. People were detained and brought to the tiny market, converted into a jail and interrogation center. That night, the paramilitaries turned off the generator that supplied light to the village, intensifying the terror.

Their intention had been to cut Mapiripán off, enclose it in its own box of terror. But that afternoon, Judge Cortés took advantage of the post-lunch stupor that lulled even the paramilitaries to sleep. He went to the telephone in the hotel. There, he made the first of many calls to San José's army base, not realizing, of course, that the soldiers there had helped arrange the paramilitaries' arrival. The officer he spoke to was Major Hernán Orozco, left in charge after his superior went on vacation. Like Judge Cortés, Major Orozco was not part of the conspiracy. A tall, well-built soldier with a gentle manner of speaking, Orozco had built a successful career largely by keeping clear of trouble, including links to paramilitaries. At the time, his dream had been to win favor with the Americans and maybe gain command of one of the new U.S.-funded units that would fight drug trafficking.

He was unaware that he was to be the fall guy who would take the blame when news of the massacre broke. Colonel Sánchez and the intelligence officer had arranged it so that Major Orozco was left with no troops to respond to calls for help from Mapiripán. Inevitably, however, he would be blamed for failing to respond in time. In other words, Colonel Sánchez was betting on the "Procuraduría syndrome" in reverse, the wrath of the human rights groups taking down the only innocent soldier standing.

Unwittingly, Major Orozco played his role perfectly. He promised Judge Cortés that he would inform the general in charge of the region and request reinforcements. Immediately, he sent a report to General Jaime Uscátegui, the commander of the Seventh Brigade in Villavicencio. Major Orozco described the information as reliable, confirmed, and serious. In a fax, he recommended sending three battalions in three helicopters to Mapiripán immediately.

Nothing was done. Two months after the massacre, General Uscátegui called Orozco to insist that he file a second, fraudulent fax with the same date and registry number. In it, Orozco said the general ordered, he was to minimize the seriousness and reliability of the information he had sent. He was told to leave out any indication that the armed men were paramilitaries. Instead, they were to be suspected guerrillas. The fraud would enable General Uscátegui to justify his own decision to take no action. Uscátegui had reason to tidy his record. At the time, he—and not Major Orozco—was in line to become the commander of a U.S.-funded task force to fight drugs. In other words, he wanted command of the troops in "the Box." Orozco complied.

Confronted later by prosecutors who had obtained both the real and the fraudulent fax, Major Orozco wept and confessed. "I felt that I was obligated to change it in order to save the prestige of a general to avoid scandal, and I was very afraid, because I was receiving veiled threats and I thought I had no other option," he later told journalists.

There was no room for doubt about who the armed men were in Mapiripán. In one of seven telephone calls made over three days, Judge Cortés told Major Orozco that paramilitaries had murdered sixteen people. Among the dead was one of the village's founders, Antonio María Herrera, a refugee from La Violencia. Paramilitaries hung him from a meat hook and dismembered him, then threw his body parts into the river. In a desperate appeal to his superiors at the circuit court, Judge Cortés wrote: "They threw bodies into the river and if the waters returned them to the river bank, they would throw them again into the water, as if they were mongrel dogs. . . . Until yesterday, I witnessed twenty-six murders." The screams made it impossible to sleep at night. "Every night, they murder groups of five or six defenseless people, who are cruelly and monstrously massacred after being tortured. The screams of humble people, begging for pity and help, can he heard everywhere."

One witness later described the panic that seized the village:

Confusion was everywhere, everyone was running from here to there and the uniformed men were stopping them to ask for their papers . . . a group of uniformed men asked my partner and me again for our papers . . . one of them was called Judas, and this Judas said, "These sons of bitches aren't on the list," and we were saved once again. Another one of them was called Nero and another had the last name Sánchez, who appeared to be their commander. Some of the uniformed men had a north coast accent and they were saying to us that they were "Masetos" from Urabá and had come from the Middle Magdalena. Before I was able to return to San José, people in Mapiripán said that at least forty people had been thrown into the river. Later, you could see them floating there.

The paramilitaries killed and beheaded the airport manager, apparently believing that he had alerted the authorities to what was happening. In fact, it had been Judge Cortés. On July 20, Judge Cortés realized that he had to leave with his family. He managed to convince one of the local pilots to fly them out, on credit. When the story broke in the Colombian press, it caused a sensation. It was the first time that Castaño had deployed so far south. Judge Cortés's story was picked up by the magazine *Cambio,* and threats against him forced his family to flee the country.

Like most other massacres, Mapiripán later became a legal case caught like a mammoth in the tar pit of the Colombian justice system. Eventually, both Major Orozco and General Uscátegui were court-martialed. Orozco protested the decision to send his case before a military tribunal, arguing that "it is unthinkable that they would leave a general's prestige even under question, with a guilty verdict, while exonerating a subordinate even if I demonstrate that I am telling the truth."

He was correct. In 2001, Orozco was sentenced to thirty-eight months for the crime of "failing to insist that troops be sent," an absurdity given that Orozco was purposefully left with none. The verdict was a warning to junior officers never to testify against their superiors. Meanwhile, General Uscátegui was sentenced to forty months for "omission"—essentially, failing to act. He served half of the sentence in a military country club. The remaining time was written off for good behavior. It was less than a month for each person murdered in Mapiripán. Colonel Lino Sánchez, who had arranged the massacre, was the only one prosecuted. More than four years later, the final verdict is still pending.

In 2001, Mapiripán was pretty much the same, though under paramilitary control. Instead of charging *coca* farmers a 10-percent tax, as the guerrillas had, Castaño dropped it to 6 percent. Occasionally, I correspond with the survivors. I also correspond with Orozco, now retired, unemployed, and profoundly shaken by the experience. To cover his legal expenses, he had to sell his home and car. While Orozco was in detention awaiting the results of the court-martial, his brother, also an officer, was killed in circumstances he believes may be payback for what happened in Mapiripán.

Once, Orozco had aspired to lead Colombian troops in "the Box,"
since he knew his record, clean of links to paramilitary groups or violations, would make him attractive to the United States. After
Mapiripán, even his passport had been seized. At least until the legal
morass was crossed, there would be no trips for him to the Magic
Kingdom, either. "I am now a man described by *-ado,*" he once wrote
me, referring to the Spanish suffix on words like forgotten, hated,
threatened, rejected, unemployed. "Without warning, the soldier vanished and only the citizen remained, alone, without people surrounding me, without what shapes and gives flavor to a life." His crime was
clear: He told the truth. "In a system like the one that exists in Colombia, the truth ruins everyone's prospects, and accounts for the high lev-
els of indifference and silence, since no one will risk saying anything
for fear of losing what they have."

"The best-laid plans!" one U.S. embassy official told me five months
after Mapiripán. "We thought we could identify an area where we
would not be so close to the paramilitaries. But no more."

When Ambassador Frechette completed his tour in 1997, he left
one last gift for the Colombian army. In an interview with the
newsweekly *Semana,* he said that the United States had evidence that
the army's Twentieth Brigade, the intelligence service, had sponsored
death squads. The statement was a repeat of what has already been
published in the State Department's annual human rights report. But
the fact that the proconsul returned to the charge in his last interview
enraged the generals. The military denounced his words as "absurd."
Then it confirmed their meaning by dismantling the brigade and im-
prisoning its commander on a charge of murder.

The interview caused a beauty of a firestorm. I'm sure that the ambassador, a connoisseur of such things, found it perfectly delightful.

ooooo

CASTAÑO FORCED THE ISSUE. AND, IT MUST BE SAID, THE FARC DID
its part by working up the ladder of the drug business, fulfilling the
American auguries just as they had decades earlier, when Marín
turned to communism as his only hope against American-equipped
and -trained troops. It was like a science fiction story where people live

what they dream and what they fear. Without the American obsession, would there have been a FARC? Would there have been an Escobar? A Mapiripán? On September 10, 2001, while Secretary of State Colin Powell was in Peru, the State Department announced that it had placed Castaño's AUC on the list of foreign terrorist groups. The FARC already had a spot on the list, won when guerrillas executed three Americans in 1999.

Carlos Alberto was sanguine about my questions. It is hard to shock a *coca* grower turned defrocked priest. "The FARC has taken complete control of the business and is forcing out the *chichipatos* and raising the taxes," he had told me quite calmly. "During the weekly market, farmers come and lay out *coca* and *base*. The FARC guerrillas walk by them buying it all up." Eventually, Colombia and the United States formally dissolved "the Box." More precisely, "the Box" became "the entire national territory of the Republic of Colombia, including its territorial waters recognized by the international law, and its airspace."

In 2001, one raid in eastern Colombia netted authorities a Brazilian trafficker who allegedly worked with the FARC's Sixteenth Front. Fernandinho Beira Mar was accused of buying cocaine from a commander known as "Negro Acacio," then shipping the drugs into the United States. A year later, the United States extradited its first alleged FARC guerrilla–Eugenio Vargas Perdomo, known as "Carlos Bolas," captured in Surinam carrying a false Peruvian passport–on charges of conspiring to manufacture and import cocaine into the United States.

It seems to me that the FARC has lost interest in building broader popular support for a political agenda and is simply piling up cash for the slow bleed of endless war. As a young commander, Marín was never distinguished by intellectual brilliance or vision. He distilled survival from certain defeat. Once again, he is proving his talent. This time, the gold in the bowl is a rogue army powered by the transnational trade in illegal narcotics.

It must please him, in his camp, to contemplate what he has done. The empire's taste for oblivion and joy becomes metal and gunpowder in his hands. He nimbly avoids the enemy's blundering strength and instead strikes at the soft and vulnerable thirst for leisure, the sparkling edge of the new and the global and the cool. Only in Burma have guerrillas lasted as long. They, too, feed on our addictions. *Coca* is a marvelous, terrible thing. It defeats ideology, the United States, moral concerns, reason. It is a money-making whirlwind that simply anyone can ride.

My driver Jesús knew that the power to avert the coming hard times did not, ultimately, lie with him or even the president or the generals. He was convinced that all depended on the American ambassador. That personage might be male or female, funny or dour, talkative or as silent as the embassy itself, a bunker with huge metal doors on the way to the airport. He believed Colombia prospered or suffered or died to the rhythm of the ambassador's whims.

Meanwhile, worry kept Jesús up at night, not about himself but for his son. Sometimes, his eyes were red behind those granny glasses and he slept through *La Luciérnaga,* deaf to the peals of laughter coming from the radio. It wasn't that his son was threatening to leave for the drug fields or the armies that fought over them. He was a good boy. After school, he went straight home. He was not allowed to play with friends outside except when his parents were there. Both worked late, so in practice, the boy rarely felt sunshine. As he drove me, Jesús would check in via cell phone. He was afraid of the gangs, the street sellers of *bazuco,* the *bazuco* addicts, the police. Maybe the guerrillas would do something, maybe the paramilitaries would respond. Even if Jesús's son followed every rule and never went outside except to go to school or attend mass, somebody who knew that Jesús earned his pay with the wad of dollars I gave him at the end of each trip could bust into the house to steal it, and with the thoroughness that characterizes Colombian killers, make his son into a *muñeco* on his very own bed. A doll, Jesús reminded me. A dead person.

There was no escape from the war. Not for Jesús, at least. It was its own box. No one, at least no one I knew, could wish it away.

CHAPTER NINE

LA BERRAQUERA

In 2001, I was back near the Metropolis disco in Puerto Asís, the first Colombian city outside Bogotá that I had ever visited. This time, I didn't have a mustard-yellow *campero* equipped with interior Christmas lights and Cuban *son*. I did not know how to find Don Vitervo, the jolly driver who had taught me how to dance on the Metropolis's sticky floor a decade earlier. I wondered if he still lived there. Was he even still alive?

The actual doors of the Metropolis were sealed against the punishing light of noon. The city, never tranquil, had an especially ugly, raw feel. It was the apparent calm that transmits with the subtle vibration of a far-off explosion.

People came and went as they seemed always to do in places at undeclared war, shopping, working, flirting, soothing children. From the parish house where I sat, I could hear the intermittent roar of Japanese motorcycles carrying *parrilleros* and the clop-clop of horses and the carts they drew, carrying farm families in for a day of shopping. Like the other buildings in town, the parish was relatively new, built in the concrete-block style that is both inexpensive and graceless. It gives way quickly to damp and decay. A thousand jungle towns shared this streetscape. I had only a few hours before, for safety reasons, I would have to leave again. The drive back was always the more harrowing, since anyone who wanted to stop a vehicle and remove a passenger could easily mark the moment that the vehicle left town on the single road.

The FARC controlled the countryside. The AUC had taken the cities. In 1998, Castaño had vowed to take the entire state, extending like a sucker on a vine to Colombia's border with Ecuador. His reach was not broad—much of the land between his northern stronghold and Puerto Asís lay firmly under FARC control—but it was tenacious. Castaño meant to take for his own the FARC's wealth, the *coca* that fed and clothed and armed its guerrillas. Several locals told me that he had even come to Puerto Asís to organize the business owners and set the monthly payments to him they were expected to make. It was possible, although I had heard rumors of Castaño's presence in so many places and at so many times that it seemed he was as ubiquitous as the color green.

My eye into the *coca* trade—the former grower, lapsed priest, and new father Carlos Alberto—told me that Castaño's paramilitaries already controlled 30 percent of Putumayo's cocaine business. By year's end, he predicted, they would control 70 percent. Already, the paramilitaries kept many local residents on a kind of unofficial payroll. They needed food, houses, equipment, cell phones, drivers, medical supplies, cars, gas. In the villages where the cocaine *base* was sold, the *chichipatos* and *traqueteros* welcomed them and were comfortable enough to fly in on market days with their women. The women, Carlos Alberto told me, were beautiful beyond description. They wore Spandex and jewels, and walked in clouds of perfume more potent than any jungle bloom.

"A little piece of heaven," he added, contemplatively.

While the ground was being fought over, the skies belonged to the Americans. A month before my arrival, the Americans had begun a new spray campaign in the Putumayo, the "push into southern Colombia" that had motivated an emergency $1.3-billion aid request for the Andes to the U.S. Congress in 1999. Most was meant for Colombia's military and was packaged by proponents as "Plan Colombia." Although it provoked hundreds of news stories and magazine articles, Plan Colombia was a fiction. Announced donations from Europe never materialized. Colombia could not cover its share. Even the American pledge was tricky. Most of the money went to the Connecticut factories where Black Hawks are assembled, not Colombia (even there, the helicopters are leased and can be ordered returned to the United States at any time). The strategy was similar to the one that the United States had tried–and failed with–in "the Box." This time, however, the Americans succeeded in enlisting the Colombian army directly in the war, the first time since 1990 and Casa Verde that Colombian troops received significant U.S. money, weapons, and training.

Led by Senator Leahy, the U.S. Congress had included conditions in "Plan Colombia" that required the Colombian military to break ties with paramilitary groups and prosecute the officers responsible for abuses in civilian, not military courts. It was similar to a tactic used in El Salvador to force U.S. diplomats to pressure their counterparts for human rights improvements. In a last-minute floor maneuver, however, congressmen determined to boost military involvement in the drug war inserted a waiver into the conditions amendment. It allowed the president to suspend the human rights conditions for "national security interest." On August 22, 2000, President Clinton signed the waiver. In doing so, he tacitly admitted that the Colombian military continued to work with Castaño. The Americans would send Colombia the money anyway.

The waiver cleared the way for the first Colombian counternarcotics battalion to deploy near Puerto Asís in December 2000. Its job was to secure the *coca* fields slated for a dose of Roundup, thus preventing guerrillas or irate farmers from taking shots at the Turbo Thrushes and Broncos as they swooped in to drop their loads. Within a year, there would be three such battalions in the field, 3,000 soldiers dedicated to the fumigation campaign. A second brigade was also in the works. These troops would be an army within an army, an American-trained and equipped core in a Colombian shell.

Putumayo was the obvious choice for the battalion's maiden operation. Most of the *coca* supplying the United States with cocaine was there, the fields cherry-red splotches on the satellite maps. I saw the splotches tacked on the walls of trailers parked next to the tarmac at the Americans' new base at Larandia in the state of Caquetá. Ironically, it was less than a morning's drive from the borders of Farclandia. The technicians I had first seen in 1997 in Guaviare–at the airfield where Castaño had landed his men to prepare the Mapiripán massacre–had moved, bringing with them the dozens of barrels of Roundup used to spray the *coca*. There were also Americans at Tres

Esquinas, a base an hour's flight time away (though impossible for Americans at Larandia to reach by land, since it would have meant crossing territory controlled by the FARC). When one helicopter crash-landed shy of the tarmac in 2000, the Americans had to deploy a Green Beret team to rescue the crew, including Americans, from the FARC guerrillas who immediately began to close in for what they surely hoped would be a spectacular kill.

The Americans and Colombian soldiers tightly controlled who could land at the bases. There would be no repeat of Mapiripán. At least, that was what I had been told.

In the months before my arrival, the FARC announced an armed strike meant to shut down Putumayo, to protest the American fumigation campaign as they had in 1996. For over a month, no vehicles could move along the state's few roads. The government airlifted in food, fuel, and medicine. It was unprecedented and a terrifying harbinger of what was to come. By its thirty-sixth anniversary, the FARC was no longer, really, just a guerrilla army, feinting and vanishing. It was an army capable of shutting down a region, of converting its enemy, Colombian soldiers, into terrified security guards for emergency food shipments.

"True believers" ran the U.S. fumigation campaign at Larandia. They were well-intentioned, confident, polite. They had studied Colombia and knew the bones of its history. Yet there was something shallow about their knowledge. As I spoke with them, the word "Colombia" seemed flat and abstract, a concept drawn from a manual. Like a Jurassic-period dinosaur, it could be studied and known as a series of bones that could be cut from the rock, then polished and jointed and covered with skin with theoretic precision. Yet as much as I probed, I rarely sensed an understanding of how this animal moved and ate and shat, or the terror that a human would feel in its grasp.

Pete—the State Department official with the hippie-style headband and Bowie knife whom I had met at the Guaviare airport—was the exception. With his firebase mentality, Pete had channeled something of the reptilian essence of what was happening, the pent-up power of the "apparent" calm (which later burst at Mapiripán). Locombia, some natives called it, Crazy-Colombia. Nothing works as planned. The results are occasionally amusing, often tragic and infinitely worse than anyone ever foresees.

John, Pete's replacement, had the bright confidence of an engineer designing a concept car. A former army officer who had served in Vietnam and El Salvador, John brimmed with details. They would not make the same mistakes they had in Asia or Central America, he assured me. Human rights would be respected. In five years, he predicted, *coca* would be for the history books.

On paper, the spray campaign he directed had a sleek beauty. It made mathematical sense—kill the *coca,* offer the peasants an alternative, punish those who strayed from the true path. Problem solved. They had even offered farmers tiny satellite dishes, to mark plots where no *coca* was grown and thus avoid mistakes by the pilots. It was tough, but humane, forward-thinking, state-of-the-art, meticulous, American. Except it was doomed and as crazy, in its deliberate way, as Colombia itself. In Colombia, beautiful machines become mired in mud, pierced by a thief's bullet, spattered with blood, overloaded with contraband, identified by eyewitnesses, lost, then cannibalized and abandoned as junk. In other words, destroyed.

As I learned upon arrival in Puerto Asís, the spray campaign was floundering less than a month after it had begun. The spraying I had seen in 1997 in the state of Guaviare had only provoked traffickers to bankroll more *coca* elsewhere. In the Putumayo, the planes sprayed even more acres, including over villages and small farms, so the planes were also hitting corn, beans, and yucca. On a videotape made by the state health department, I could see that some farmers had interspersed these crops with *coca* as a way of masking the illegal bushes. Other times, though, the spray planes simply screwed up. Farm animals sickened and died, and people, especially children and the elderly, developed rashes and respiratory ailments they blamed on the spray. U.S. officials countered that there was no proof that the spray was harmful to humans. Indeed, most of the ailments (rashes, diarrhea, reddened eyes, respiratory infections) linked to the spray runs are endemic in the jungle and among the poor, who live in a soup of toxic chemicals used in subsistence farming. Yet the Roundup label for home garden use calls the chemical a hazard to humans and animals and specifically warns consumers not to spray it on water or in the eyes.

The farmers correctly pointed out that installing satellite dishes in their fields was the equivalent of asking the FARC to send their entire families to the firing squad. It simply wouldn't be tolerated. The planes even sprayed jungle where shamans collected the *ayahuasca* vine they use to induce visions (and occasionally charge tourists hefty sums for the privilege of running in their dreams with the now scarce jaguars). A Turbo Thrush doused visiting U.S. senator Paul Wellstone (D–MN), whether by design or mistake it wasn't clear. A Colombian police major told me afterward that it was to show the feisty senator that the spray was harmless.

The day I drove into Puerto Asís, the Putumayo governor was trying to convince 900 families to sign contracts with the U.S. Agency for International Development. In exchange for receiving agricultural assistance and substitute crops, they would voluntarily eradicate *coca*. It was the "alternative development" element meant to soften the eradication effort, the carrot after the stick.

Except it wouldn't work. Most farmers knew it but signed the contracts anyway, hoping, I suppose, for a miracle. Perhaps they thought they could get something to offset what were predictable losses when the Turbo Thrushes came through. But few had any faith that a legal crop could replace *coca*. That was the point the Americans never quite seemed to grasp. The farmers didn't plant *coca* because they wanted to poison America's youth (as the politicians suggested from the floor of the House of Representatives) but because there simply weren't alternatives, subsidized or not.

The soil of the jungle is easily exhausted, a poor medium for most industrial agriculture. There are few roads able to move produce efficiently to any market theoretically able to sell. Anyway, Colombia has plenty of corn, yucca, coffee, and chocolate, already battered by global shifts in price. One crop promoted by the U.S. Agency for International Development was African palm. The tree produces an industrial oil used in cosmetics and soaps as well as an edible oil used for deep frying and products like margarine. Yet even its boosters did not claim that African palm would defeat *coca*. Colombian farms would be pitted against established ventures in Malaysia and Honduras, also struggling for a piece of a static market limited by shifting preferences for oils lower in saturated fat. A U.N.-built heart-of-palm processing plant established in Putumayo in the early 1990s had lain empty for years after its managers belatedly discovered that the fruit spoiled during the prolonged journey from the farm. A 1998 study from the Interamerican Development Bank puts it cruelly: "There is no market in Colombia for legal products from the Putumayo."

The Americans and the police claimed to have carefully mapped areas where alternative crops were being tested, to ensure that they would not be sprayed. But even there, they made mistakes. Lots of them. The spray planes swooped in over fish farms and rubber plantations and heart-of-palm groves, leaving a skin of white powder on what was supposed to be a kind of salvation. Only several weeks after the planes began to spray did the Americans allow a Colombian government team in to evaluate its effects. The team immediately called for the spray to be suspended pending better controls and map coordination. But the true believers pressed on: Victory was only a question of more planes, more army battalions, more helicopters, more money, and more and more potent spray. It was an argument I had heard for as long as I had been working in Colombia. In 1988, Attorney General Edwin Meese came to Peru (then the largest supplier of *coca* leaf) to announce plans to fumigate the Upper Huallaga Valley, plans that, to the Peruvians' credit, they blocked because of the potential harm to the country's poorest residents as well as the fragile Amazonian ecosystem.

In fact, neither the debate over fumigation nor alternative development reduced cocaine imports to the United States, regardless of how much money was spent and how well they were carried out. Less than a year into the spray campaign in the Putumayo, its failure was already clear enough for a U.S. government study to describe the campaign as having made "little progress" and facing "serious obstacles," governmentese for doomed. Most of the alternative development money could not even be spent because the region was too dangerous for the required agronomists, engineers, and project specialists to last more than a couple of days on the ground. It was like funding the construction of a highway overpass in the midst of a bombing campaign. Nice, but irrelevant, and, by the way, potentially fatal for anyone silly enough to ever use it.

Many of the farmers who signed with the governor that day returned to *coca* within several months, selecting for their new plots bushes with a higher resistance to Roundup or planting in areas where the spray planes wouldn't go. The environmental damage–forest cut

down for new plots, pesticides used on *coca* to prevent fungus and disease, the cocaine refining process itself, which dumps thousands of
barrels of sulfuric acid and kerosene into creeks and streams—added to
the harm done by the spray. Or farmers planted in distant spots where
the *coca*'s distinctive wave pattern as seen by the satellites would be
dismissed by the true-believer technicians as anomalies.

Since 1995, when the United States began aerial eradication in
Colombia, *coca* acreage has increased every year, sometimes by as
much as 25 percent. That proved true again in 2001, after the spray
campaign in the Putumayo began. According to the CIA's satellite
data, the spray actually helped foster a boom that pushed *coca* acreage
over 417,000 acres. Some of the newest plots were in the neighboring
state of Nariño, west of the Putumayo. One resident told me the boom
there was an "armed colonization," as traffickers seized land and
brought in armies of killer boys to defend and work it.

Interdiction—another item in the toolbox of drug warriors—has
proved equally ineffective at constricting the drug flow into the United
States. Despite billions spent on intercepting airplanes, "go-fast" boats,
submarines, tanker trucks, and container ships, another U.S. government study concluded that the "enormous profits in cocaine trafficking
make interdiction losses relatively inconsequential, especially in light
of the fact that production and smuggling costs account for such a
small part of street prices." Once the cocaine reaches the United States,
its price soars, between 6,000 to 8,600 percent. That means that losing
raw product en route is affordable, since losses are built into the American street price.

And that was not all of the bad news. In fact, it wasn't even the
worst of it. Spraying—or at least, the Americans' single-minded focus
on eliminating drugs at the source, to the exclusion of most of the
other problems facing Colombia—fueled the war itself. The new American ambassador, the lively and outspoken Anne Patterson, every day
seemed to repeat that the United States was only interested in combat-
ing drugs, not using the war on drugs as a screen for a covert engage-
ment in Colombia's real war. But the relationship between wars was
inevitable and absolutely clear. Indeed, some of my Colombian colleagues argued to me that there was no difference. It was the same
war. Like it or not, the U.S. eradication campaign was enmeshed in it

and exacerbated it. To protect the spray planes, the United States had enlisted the help of Colombia's army. U.S. law required that Americans vet the Colombian troops they chose to train and equip and remove officers or units with human rights problems. Yet even a squeaky-clean counternarcotics battalion could not work in a vacuum. Washington wanted a "clean" army within the dirty husk of Colombia's military, troops that would not embarrass their handlers with atrocities. Many of the Colombia hands are veterans of the 1980s, when the U.S.-vetted, -funded, and -trained Atlacatl Battalion carried out some of the most notorious massacres of El Salvador's war, including El Mozote and the murders of the six Jesuits at the University of Central America.

But inevitably, vetted units had to use regular army bases to house and feed their troops, coordinate intelligence gathering, and plan operations. Intelligence is the main way that paramilitaries and the army work together, the synapse between them. The regular army units in the Putumayo were so penetrated with the AUC that locals had ceased to make any distinction between the two. In one visit, U.N. investigators found soldiers patrolling with paramilitaries, who—with their uniforms and field grime—were distinguishable only by their more eclectic array of guns and footwear.

The commander of the Puerto Asís army brigade was a slender, balding man with a soft voice and a sideways, gentle manner, more like an accountant than a battle veteran. From his office in Puerto Asís, he could see paramilitary fighters come and go from their headquarters, set up across the road at a farm called Villa Sandra. Once, they even held a training camp there, bringing in fighters from across Colombia to perfect their marksmanship and battle readiness. Dozens of visitors asked the general about Villa Sandra and how the AUC could continue to operate literally under the army's nose. He would assume an astonished look, pick up the telephone, and order an immediate raid. This happened several times a month. If visitors bothered to check back, they would be informed that his soldiers had found nothing. It was elaborate theater, like the drug war itself. Every spring in Washington, the true believers troop to Capitol Hill to ask for more money and guns to fight the failed war. Every fall, they get most of what they request.

In 2002, the Bush administration finally acknowledged a fact that was clear to anyone traveling Colombia: The two wars were inextricable, the trunk of a tree and its rotten fruit. The White House asked the U.S. Congress to lift the requirement that all military aid be spent only on counterdrug operations. The request was granted with little opposition. Although the decision simply acknowledged what anyone with eyes could see, it also marked yet another entanglement in a war that would not have such a lethal punch without American consumers.

Not everyone in Puerto Asís suffered from the war. The Metropolis was doing well, I saw. It was the place everyone—paramilitaries, guerrillas, soldiers, traffickers, and locals—danced and drank away the week's wages. The funeral homes thrived. So did the hotels and restaurants that catered to the international visitors like me, drawn to the drama like remoras on a shark.

It was all very *berraco*, I thought as I sat in the parish house. Flies buzzed the metal tops of cans where drops of fruit soda had collected. Putumayo was Colombia's "perfect storm," the confluence of drugs, war, social unrest, and international intervention that acted like cyclones and hurricanes converging on people's lives. Everyone believed that they could win this war, that it was a matter of more guns, more fighters, more radios, more land, and more money. As one Colombian friend put it, it was a "dance of illusions," as if this were a Metropolis special. Another name for it might be "La Berraquera"—*berraco* to the nth degree, an infinity of *berraco*-ness, profound *berrac*-osity, insoluble, like the Bermuda grass even Roundup won't kill. It touched everything and left nothing unchanged. It was everywhere.

ooooo

THE PUERTO ASÍS PRIEST I INTERVIEWED IN THE PARISH HOUSE smoked with mechanical precision, each cigarette serving to ignite the next. I craved Jennifer's aplomb with tobacco, but that week we had parted ways in Cali. On the kitchen table, the priest, "Father Daniel" (I agreed not to use his real name), laid out the registry he kept of burials made on sanctified ground. Although Protestantism has gained many adherents in Colombia, most Colombians still identify themselves as Catholic (whether or not they can remember the last time they attended Mass). When they die, they or their families want them in the Catholic burial ground.

The kitchen table was laid with a white crocheted cloth protected by clear plastic. An older woman, his cook, orbited as she prepared lunch. Father Daniel was no stickler for detail. He told me that he was not interested in being a sleuth, so he never investigated to see whether the deceased had been to Mass recently or had even, ever, been baptized. If the family requested it, he made the necessary arrangements. Therefore, most of the dead in Puerto Asís over the previous year were noted in his registry. At least, he added, the people whose bodies had been found.

Father Daniel thumbed through the registry. It was the kind of blank book covered in plastic one might buy in an office supply store. He had filled it with ink script featuring the person's name and the date of birth and death. Father Daniel also described the cause of death, when he knew it. On a few, he had written "natural causes," *muerte natural*. Most, though, were murdered: by firearm or what in Colombia is called *"arma blanca,"* a "white" or metal weapon, usually a machete. In Puerto Asís, murder appeared to be the leading cause of death for all age groups, including children, and both genders.

Murder happened for political reasons, as the paramilitaries and guerrillas fought each other through the civilians and the perceived support individuals gave, willingly or not, to the enemy. It had also become, Father Daniel said, the way people solved rivalries over a lover or disputes over property. Practically everyone was armed. Although the legal purchase of guns is more restricted in Colombia than in the United States (the military is the only authorized dealer), the black market readily supplies anything from ancient revolvers to MAC-10s. Especially in the lowlands, every household has a machete. Even a minor altercation can turn homicidal.

Colombia's familiarity with sudden, violent death, the deaths of its most famous and accomplished citizens, has spawned a curious art form. As I learned through stops in cemeteries in many of the places I visited, graves were often as expressive as museum sculpture gardens. For instance, I once visited the cemetery where one of Pablo Escobar's most ruthless killers is buried. Tyson Brances Muñoz Mosquera was La Quica's older brother, killed in 1990 by police. When I arrived, it was a typically brilliant afternoon, broiling in the sun and cool in the shade. Families interring loved ones were grouped in tight knots around the above-ground niches, some thrown open like bread ovens for the day's new caskets. I always expect to be assaulted by the smell of death in such surroundings. But instead it was flowers—gladioli, daisies, freesias, and roses—that broadcast a thick aroma.

From an alcove protected by bulletproof glass, a boom box blared round-the-clock salsa. I found Tyson's mausoleum by following the music. The mausoleum also had a small and visible room that was decorated as a part of a family home, featuring memorabilia from Tyson's favorite soccer team and photos of children. Tyson was not a thinker, and of course he couldn't have been, given his chosen profession. Yet the display moved me, if only because of the pulsing and deliberate life it represented. Even in death, Tyson was vibrant, a speeding rocket that explodes in light and sound. I had the strong sense that if Tyson had been standing there next to me viewing the tableau, he would have been satisfied that his mother had carried out his orders exactly as told, placing there everything he deemed important.

Within the week, the diocese would fly Father Daniel out of Colombia for studies in Europe. He had begun receiving death threats for doing just what he was doing with me, showing me the registry and talking about who was killing whom. He wouldn't tell me who was threatening him. He said he didn't know. The week I visited, he had received printed invitations to his own funeral, a Colombian style of threat that dates back to La Violencia. Father Daniel's registry was the essence of La Berraquera, the way the conflict had become every day, soaked like smoke into the fabric of life. It was everywhere—in the way people talked to each other, the way they moved (always on edge, surprised by nothing), the way they thought.

Father Daniel reminded me of the case of a local pediatrician who had just left the city. While in her office one morning, she had examined a one-year-old boy who had a high fever. She admitted him into the local hospital. But the next day, the family checked him out against her advice. At home, the boy worsened. Again, his parents brought him to the hospital, where the attending physician paged her to come to the hospital.

As the pediatrician entered the examination room, the doctor saw that the family had brought several men with them. They were paramilitaries. Immediately, the men accused her of failing to treat the boy properly the previous day. The threat was direct. If she did not cure him, they would kill her.

Later, the boy's mother pulled the pediatrician aside. It was a terrible misunderstanding, she said. While in the hospital the day before, she explained, a nurse had failed to find a vein in the infant's dehydrated body to insert the needle for the intravenous drip. The boy had screamed for hours. Distraught, the parents had decided to take him home. When the boy's grandfather heard the story, he went to the paramilitaries to complain. "They think they are the superheroes and can solve any problem," someone familiar with the story had told me.

It was not the first time the pediatrician had seen armed men in the hospital. She later told government investigators that it was common for both the guerrillas and paramilitaries to accompany comrades into the examination and even the operating rooms, to ensure good care and, perhaps more important, the patients' survival, since it was also common for their enemies to enter the hospital to shoot patients in their beds. The misunderstanding between the infant's family and the pediatrician could not be resolved. She was marked as incompetent and, worse, complicit. She had botched the infant's treatment, the paramilitaries argued, because she knew that his family was linked to them. That could only mean that she was a guerrilla using medicine and her position as the boy's physician to kill. The paramilitary leader issued an order to kill her, because he believed she was a guerrilla infiltrated into the hospital.

The pediatrician was innocent, of course. But this accusation was quite serious. She reported the incident formally, thus confirming for the paramilitaries their conclusion. To them, that was the final evidence that clinched her guilt as a guerrilla. Only a guerrilla would go to the authorities, the thinking went. Anyone innocent would simply choose the far more reliable method of vanishing without a trace. The pediatrician was forced to leave Colombia for her safety.

La Berraquera also provoked messier crimes. In the same hospital, an elderly woman dying of cancer had caused a melee in the emergency room when she accused the hospital's director of mismanagement, poor medicine, theft, homosexuality, bestiality, and other failings that were rooted well back in his pedigree. Pain had loosened her tongue, and more pain had sharpened it like a machete. She threatened the nurses with scissors. She screamed for long minutes. She was so loud that even the administrative staff could hear her (provoking giggles and glances that made the hospital director seethe). The woman had the force of her body's last energy and untreated pain that nothing but oblivion could ease.

Finally, someone–the hospital director, it was surmised, though no one knew for sure–called the paramilitaries. The "superheroes" came by in the pickup truck that everyone recognized. A nurse left the woman in her wheelchair at the curb. Two hours later, her body was found in a ditch.

Of course, it wasn't only the paramilitaries doing such things. I also interviewed the health department's team of malaria specialists, called *malarios,* men hired to track down malaria cases and fumigate homes where there were outbreaks. One of the specialists told me how he had run out of gas one evening, just when he was about to head back to the city for dinner. These unforeseen but inevitable problems can be a death sentence in Colombia. In areas like the Putumayo, no one travels after dark. That is when the armies and the thieves are about, like cockroaches in the kitchen.

A kindhearted woman took the *malario* in for the night. She prepared a bed in a storeroom, to hide him from inquisitive eyes. He ate with her family, then went to sleep.

In the middle of the night, he said, he woke up to shouting. The local FARC commander had seen the *malario*'s motorcycle. What was it doing there, he wanted to know. Its owner had taken a truck into town to buy a part, the woman lied. She knew that if she revealed the *malario*'s location, he would be shot. Somehow, she convinced the guerrilla commander to move on. The next morning, the *malario* was able to fill his tank and leave.

He happened to pass by the woman's house again fifteen days later. It was burnt to the timbers. When he asked what had happened, he was told that the guerrillas had accused the woman of harboring paramilitaries. They meant him. The guerrilla commander had returned the next day and burned the family alive in the house where the *malario* had been given shelter.

ooooo

AFTER I FINISHED MY CONVERSATION WITH FATHER DANIEL, I RE-
turned to the parish hall where some locals were waiting. They had
been brought by Germán, the municipal official whose job was to receive reports of human rights abuses.

Germán was an international legend. Tall and handsome, he wore
cowboy boots and spoke with an accent characteristic of southern
Colombia, a purr of the r's and a singsong way of connecting words in
a kind of spoken aria. It made his pronunciation of my first name
unique, turbulence preceding the flat air of the second consonant, "Ha-
RU-hhhhu-bin!" He was every journalists' and human rights workers'
dream, a conscientious public official who told all with little apparent
concern for his own safety.

Germán had arranged for several residents to speak with me there
in the parish, where a visit would raise few suspicions. The first was a
taxi driver who had found himself enmeshed in a paramilitary killing.
Some fighters had gotten into his taxi—and paid the fare—with a third
man, whom the driver realized was a captive accused of some mis-
deed. What the man had done was not clear. The driver said that the
third passenger had been silent during the brief journey. The driver de-
posited the three men outside a farm the paramilitaries had been using
to house and train their forces. It was a stone's throw from the army
base, and he described how soldiers had waved them through the permanent checkpoint at the base entrance. Later, the guerrillas apparently linked his taxi to the third passenger's murder. Through the
grapevine, the taxi driver learned that the guerrillas accused him of
working for the paramilitaries. His wife's beauty shop had been van-
dalized. The next step, he feared, was a shot in the head for them both
and an entry in Father Daniel's registry.

It would have been a remarkable story anywhere but Colombia.
There, it was routine. Daily activities compromised people, not allegiance to any one force. The taxi driver and his wife wanted out. They
were hoping I could get them to Miami.

I had been fielding an increasing number of these requests. Some
Colombians had begun to link the troubles that everyone who lived in

a war zone faced to what they saw as an unexpected opportunity, a fast-track visa to the United States. Otherwise, a visa for most was an impossibility. To this taxi driver, misfortune seemed almost like a gift, a way to reach the nirvana of the Magic Kingdom and Miami's Mall of the Americas or a steaming bowl of *sancocho* (a Colombian stew) in Queens's Little Colombia. In their mind's eye, I imagined, the United States was just a safer and more prosperous Colombia, where everyone spoke Spanish and jobs were for the taking.

The United States is stingy with asylum and does not offer any financial or language assistance to the few newcomers who manage entry. Some European countries offer support, though Colombians there had told me horror stories about being housed in giant refugee camps where even their shoes were taken from them upon arrival. In contrast, Canada allots families that qualify for asylum a place to live, financial support, and language training. Yet for Colombians, Canada's geography makes it into a kind of hell. Once, I had visited in Quebec a prosecutor whom I had helped leave Colombia. The day I arrived, the wind chill was a steady $-40°F$. In my rental car, I briefly wondered if a flat tire along the highway would cost me my life. The road signs warned of errant moose. What was "moose," I wondered, in Spanish?

The prosecutor was in a tiny apartment in a complex that looked flattened by snow. The door opened with a poof of tepid air, which froze into ice crystals quicker than I could blink. He told me that he had no car, so he, his wife, and his two-year-old daughter had to walk the three miles to French class. The daughter had developed a terror of her stroller. It meant a cryogenic immersion twice daily.

Some exiles moved on, embraced new lives. Others lived in a kind of twilight, still tied to Colombian events and dramas like a tube feeding them essential nutrients. I would hear from them occasionally, people I had last seen in bars or hotel lobbies as they handed over the papers or audiotapes that had almost cost them their lives. E-mails or calls would come in from Salamanca or Stockholm or Vancouver.

Most of the time, I had to disappoint Colombians anxious to flee north. Asylum requests only worked in the most extreme cases, when Colombians literally faced a life-or-death choice. For people like the taxi driver, La Berraquera was just normal life. Nevertheless, I had no doubt that his indiscretion would follow him like paper stuck to a shoe sole. Someone, somewhere, would see him and remember. Or see him and remember in error, putting him at the mercy of the same kind of misunderstanding that led to the pediatrician's exile. The only thing worse than being killed for the crime of living in La Berraquera was being killed because someone made a mistake about what you were doing when La Berraquera struck.

ooooo

THE NEXT PERSON GERMÁN BROUGHT TO THE PARISH HALL WAS "Pilar." In a report I later wrote, I could not use her real name. Her family lived in Puerto Asís (as it happens, they were eventually forced to move) and would have been endangered. Pilar was exceptionally beautiful. She had *ojos zarcos,* as they are called in Colombia, the flecked hazel-green irises of her eyes outlined in black. Her lustrous black hair was barely tamed by barrettes. She wore her jeans and T-shirt tight. Her short stature was accentuated by the stiletto heels on her boots.

Pilar herself had already decided to leave Colombia, for anywhere, really, the true sign of a successful candidate for political asylum. Unlike the taxi driver and his wife, Pilar had not parsed the relative merits of Miami versus New York, nor had she dreamed about possible jobs or trips to Disney World or the new status among her friends that living outside Colombia would give her. What was at stake was her life.

She had chosen to talk to me before leaving because she didn't want her story to go unheard. That was all. She wanted to make it matter. It was an elemental human desire, one I had come across often in Colombia. Her story was the one thing she thought she could save from La Berraquera, the intact teacup in the rubble of what her life once had been.

Pilar lived with her partner, who was a doctor, and her child from a former relationship. She began her story with an encounter at the Metropolis. One night, she told me, she had met a man there and danced with him. He introduced himself as Dario. They talked, and Pilar mentioned that she was between jobs. Several days later, she saw Dario in a local restaurant. This time, he was dressed in a military uniform. With him was an army officer assigned to the local base. Dario offered her temporary work as a bookkeeper. She thought it was something extra the Colombian army might be doing—contracts for locals in order to boost community relations. With a borrowed laptop, she began doing his weekly accounts.

The expenses were largely the kind that any army incurs: salaries, food, weapons, funeral expenses, informants. But when she delivered the floppy disks and printouts to Dario, she realized that she was not working for the army. Dario had given her the address of a house in town, where men in civilian clothes lounged with their weapons on display. It was then that she saw that the income did not come from the government; it was what the paramilitaries made from drug trafficking and extortion. Dario was the paramilitaries' financial chief in Putumayo. Like the taxi driver, Pilar had stumbled into working for the AUC.

For a while, she imagined that she could maintain a certain distance and perhaps, when the time was right, announce that she was leaving for a new job. Pilar didn't count on the fact that Dario had become enamored of her *ojos zarcos* and her tantalizing hair. As the weeks passed, she realized that she had started down a path that ended in Father Daniel's registry.

Her story was a treasure trove for me. Because she had been responsible for the paramilitaries' accounting, she knew their financial structure: not only how they got money, but who got paid. A new recruit received the equivalent of $275 per month, plus a stipend for food. An urban fighter got $350. There was a separate category for the payments made to local army and police officers, divided by rank. Pilar sometimes made the payments herself, walking the money to the local express mail service, Servientrega, to send to wives or lovers living elsewhere.

As she talked, Pilar demonstrated a talent for remembering facts and figures. At first, I had been skeptical about her explanation of how she had begun working for the AUC. Anyone who had lived in Puerto Asís for more than a month would likely have recognized Dario immediately at the Metropolis. Why would the army, surrounded by the guerrillas, contract out its bookkeeping so haphazardly, especially to a potential FARC informant? Clearly, there were parts of Pilar's story— a possible love affair with Dario that she regretted or a political affinity with the AUC that she feared revealing to me—that were hidden.

Yet each element of her story eventually checked out with other information I had received and with Germán's own investigations. For
instance, he had checked on the parcels she had mailed through
Servientrega, the cellular phone numbers for Dario, the names of the
paramilitary commanders in the city and surrounding towns. Everything fit. Pilar had even helped Germán clear up the mystery of a missing law student, someone he had begun to look for after receiving a
visit from the student's worried father. The father had come to Germán's office to present the formal report necessary to start a missing-
person investigation. His story was unusual. Weeks earlier, the man's
daughter had received a call from her husband, an army captain stationed in the Putumayo. The captain told his wife that he was in trouble and needed her to come and help him.

She borrowed money for airplane fare from her father and flew to
Puerto Asís. There, she planned to catch a bus that would take her to
the town where her husband was stationed. The airline, Germán
found, showed that the woman had registered as a passenger who had
arrived at the airport. So had the army, which keeps a separate list of
arriving and departing passengers. Then the woman vanished.

Germán counseled the father to post flyers with his daughter's photograph, which he did. That was where Pilar entered the story. During
one conversation with Dario, he told Pilar that some army officer had
fooled the paramilitaries into killing an innocent person. As Dario told
it, this officer had a new lover, so he wanted to get rid of his wife. The
officer lured his wife to Puerto Asís. At the same time, the officer told
Dario that the army had information about an important FARC guerrilla, a woman, arriving on the flight that day. The officer gave Dario a
description of his wife. Dario ordered his men to pick up the woman at
the airport. They had killed her and, Germán surmised, buried her at
Villa Sandra, opposite the army base. Only when Dario saw the father's flyers did he realize that the army officer had used them to break
his marital chain.

Pilar's downfall had been her beauty. Increasingly, she said, Dario
pressed her to leave her partner and move in with him. She refused.
Dario threatened to kill the doctor or bomb Pilar's house. She convinced him not to. But she knew that her time was running out. As
careful as she had been to distance herself from Dario, she knew that

the guerrillas would eventually find out that she had been working for the paramilitaries. Several days before I arrived, three guerrillas had come to her house. They gave her three days to pack up everything and vanish. They knew everything.

There was one last thing Pilar wanted me to know before she left for the airport. Dario was going to kill Germán, because he had been talking to people like me. In fact, she was worried that the taxi driver, who had just left, would be angry enough about not acquiring an immediate visa and ticket to the United States that he would tell Dario that I was in the city and talking with Pilar. The speculation ended the interview on a unique note.

I talked to Pilar several times after that, in Bogotá and later, when she and her family and even Germán had found a safe haven far from La Berraquera's path. She lived her tragedy, told her story, and got out alive. She was a lucky girl–and she knew it.

ooooo

SOMETIMES, MY TRIPS TO COLOMBIA GENERATED THEIR OWN *berraqueras*. Behind me, like tornadoes and siroccos and Santa Ana winds, the effects of my work tipped the precarious lives of the people who had given me their stories. They concluded that enough was enough. They got visas. They resigned. They vanished. They left apartments and careers abandoned. They embraced new lives as cooks and busboys and paralegals in Miami, Vancouver, and Madrid. Once, I saw one such man in the immigration line in the Mexico City airport, leaving Colombia behind like a dirty blanket. He was wise enough to cover his Colombian passport with a newspaper until the final moment of presenting it to be stamped, fearful that he would be pulled out by police and strip-searched. Not, of course, because he was a human rights defender who had risked his life to tell the truth, but because he was Colombian and therefore suspected of muling drugs.

Or the people whose stories shaped my nightmares rededicated themselves to the path that Josué had chosen, at the point in his life when he accepted his destiny. To visit these friends and colleagues, I cleared metal detectors, introduced myself to bodyguards, was filmed by surveillance cameras, found secret locations. I promised not to tell. I spoke in allusion, metaphors, even, with friends I initiated, in a version of Star Trekese. The Federation was the United States, the Klingons were the Colombian military, and the Romulans were the FARC, cruising the edges of the known universe and engaging in complex and devious alliances. Castaño and his gang could only be the Borg. It was our version of Navajo code talk, incomprehensible to outsiders but a complete and evocative dialect for those in the know. It also often made us laugh.

In *The Sorrow of War*, the Vietnamese novelist Bao Ninh wrote of the "appalling paradox" of the loss of the best among us. "Not a new phenomenon, true," he acknowledged. "But for those still living to know that the kindest, most worthy people have all fallen away, or even been tortured, humiliated before being killed, or buried and wiped away by the machinery of war, then this beautiful landscape of calm and peace is an appalling paradox. Justice may have won, but cruelty, death, and inhuman violence have also won."

Colombia loses its best. Mediocrity rules. After the annihilation of the Patriotic Union, all that was left in the FARC were the ones who loved war. They are the perfect match for their enemies, so similar that Colombians who live this drama every day sometimes have difficulty telling them apart. Colombia's political trends are like a satellite stuck in a forgotten orbit. Each trip around the planet leaves it a bit shabbier, pieces spinning off into the cosmos. A peace president (López) is replaced by a war president (Turbay) who is replaced by a peace president (Betancur) who is replaced by a war president (Barco) who is replaced by a peace president who turns to war (Gaviria) who is replaced by a war president who turns to peace (Samper) who is replaced by a peace president (Pastrana) who is replaced by the war president to end all war presidents, Álvaro Uribe, elected in 2002.

During his campaign, Uribe promised to double the size of Colombia's military and enlist a million civilians in an effort to block the advance of the FARC guerrillas and hurt their ability to mount the kind of operations that crippled the country. As if in delicate coordination, the FARC responded by knocking out power to Medellín and Cali, bombing the cables that connected Colombia to the Internet, and blowing key bridges to smithereens. On Uribe's inauguration day, guerrillas greeted him with mortars fired from a house over a mile from the Presidential Palace, killing nineteen people there and in a home (three children) and a flophouse in between. A pointed critic of Pastrana's failed peace plan, Uribe said he would only negotiate with the FARC if it first agreed to a cease-fire. In other words, never. Colombians understood that what Uribe really meant was that he would bloody and bow the FARC until a negotiation—or, more precisely, surrender—was their only viable option. In other words, never.

Uribe doesn't look like a warrior. A former Antioquia governor, Medellín mayor, and senator, Uribe wears wire-rimmed spectacles and is boyishly slender, a policy wonk more fluent in the language of government than war. For most of his career, he was a loyal member of the Liberal Party. But he chose to run for president as an independent (as Jorge Eliécer Gaitán had), defeating the official Liberal candidate.

In other ways, the contrast between Gaitán and Uribe is stark. Gaitán was a son of the working class struggling for recognition. Uribe's father was a land dealer who amassed a fortune. Growing up, Uribe went to elite schools and took Miami vacations, competed in the horse shows, attended charity balls and dinners to celebrate the beginning and end of the bullfighting season that are part of the *paisa* elite's social whirl.

The Liberal faithful accuse Uribe of links to drug trafficking, but so far they cannot prove it beyond the inevitable contact that anyone living in Antioquia during the 1980s might have had, particularly if that person had interests in land and politics. In 1984, Colombian police seized a helicopter at Tranquilandia whose registry number corresponded to a machine purportedly owned by Alberto Uribe, Álvaro's father. Investigators once identified a brother's telephone number stored in one of the cell phones used by Pablo Escobar. But on the day the calls were logged, the family claims that the brother was mute, hospitalized with throat cancer. Álvaro claims that the telephone had been "cloned," a technique used by Medellín criminals to steal cell phones to make free calls. As a boy, Álvaro had rubbed shoulders with the Ochoas. He shared their passion for Paso Fino horses. But the friendship was not a product of the 1980s, when the Ochoa boys were trafficking. It began decades earlier between the boys' great-grandfather and Alberto Uribe.

The Uribes also suffered political violence. In 1983, the FARC tried to kidnap Alberto Uribe at Guacharacas, a family ranch. Alberto had time to pull out his gun but was killed. In 1995, the ELN burned Guacharacas to the ground and killed its foreman. During the presidential campaign, the FARC tried to kill Uribe twice, most spectacularly by setting off a remote control bomb in the city of Barranquilla (a bad-luck town for candidates, since it was also the destination of Carlos Pizarro when one of Castaño's assassins shot him). The forty-pound bomb flattened the tires of Uribe's bulletproof car and killed three fishermen nearby. The candidate and his companions were shaken, but unharmed.

Asked repeatedly about allegations of his family's links to drug traffickers, Uribe denied them with *paisa* bluntness. "I'm no asshole," he once told a journalist. Persistent questions provoke Uribe to tantrums, one of the few cracks in his earnest persona. Once, he walked out on a *Newsweek* reporter pressing him about airport licenses issued to traffickers while Uribe ran Antioquia's civil aviation office. He is fiercely loyal to both family and longtime friends, some of whom have been less scrupulous in their behavior. For instance, Uribe has publicly embraced notorious thugs, among them General Del Río. Uribe was governor when Del Río made his fame as the so-called "pacifier" of Urabá, won by helping Castaño carve a merciless advance. No massacres were ever linked directly to Uribe. But he remained silent as his advisers publicly attacked Apartadó mayor Gloria Cuartas as a secret guerrilla supporter.

I had first met Uribe when he was governor and promoting the idea of using civilians in the fight against guerrillas, something he would later incorporate into his presidential platform. Uribe studied at Harvard and knew how to phrase his pitch for *gringa* ears. The plan, he told me, was like the neighborhood watch committees that he had seen in Cambridge. These groups even had a pleasing name—"*convivir,*" to live together. *Convivir* groups, Uribe said, would organize only to defend themselves. They would be closely monitored by the government.

In fairness to Uribe, the idea was not his. It had been proposed by Ernesto Samper, a fellow Liberal. But among Colombia's governors,

Uribe most actively promoted it. During his tenure in Antioquia, seventy-seven *"convivir"* groups were formed, including some within the city of Medellín itself. During my first meeting with Uribe, I sat in his spacious and tastefully decorated office at the top of one of the skyscrapers that mark Antioquia's government office complex, La Alpujarra. Uribe's assistant served cappuccinos dusted with nutmeg. The civilians who belonged to *"convivir"* groups were, in his words, *"gente de bien,"* good people. I couldn't finish the fragrant drink.

Uribe's plan would have pleased President Valencia in 1964, when the Colombian army tried and failed to catch Marín at Marquetalia. In the 1980s, the same idea–to enlist civilians in the war–had become MAS. Wasn't the governor running the risk, I asked, of making the same mistake? How was his idea of self-defense different? Even Pedro Marín got his start at war as "self-defense." One columnist in the daily *El Tiempo* raised the same concern in this way: "Colombian history, it would seem, doesn't move in a progressive line but a vicious circle. We always return to our past mistakes, not to correct them but to perfect them."

Uribe waved off each question. He had studied conflict resolution, he told me, had consulted with the United Nations. He was a modern man, a forward-thinker. He thought beyond the bones of Colombia's past.

I spent the next weeks collecting the cases that proved him wrong. These were not "neighborhood watch committees," but a vehicle for creating yet another irregular army. One *"convivir"* in La Ceja, Antioquia, was so infamous that people advised me to not even drive through town. Several well-known paramilitaries, among them one of Castaño's closest allies, set up *"convivir"* groups in other states and obtained legal weapons from the government (to augment the illegal arsenals they bought on the black market). President Pastrana ended the *"convivir"* program after it became clear that a number of these groups had either melded into the AUC or had become independent criminal enterprises, kidnapping, stealing, and extorting money from the people they were supposed to protect.

In 1999, President Pastrana also cashiered General Del Río because of his links to paramilitaries. That same year, the United States canceled Del Río's visa, reportedly on the grounds that he had taken part in "international terrorist" activities through his support for paramilitaries.

But Uribe remained loyal. At the general's retirement dinner, Uribe praised him as a national hero. As president, Uribe maintains him as an adviser. Among the first decisions made by Uribe after taking office was to reintroduce the "state of siege" legislation first invoked in 1965 to repress dissent. Uribe also ordered his generals to begin recruiting civilians to spy on suspected guerrillas and work with the army to catch or kill them, a direct throwback to the decisions that had led to the formation of paramilitary groups.

Men like Del Río and the ideas he represents send some Colombians into despair when they contemplate what an Uribe term will mean for Colombia. It is ironic that despite Uribe's reputation as a leader who can deliver greater security, his record in Antioquia is poor. During his term as governor, the rate of murders for political reasons (unrelated to combat) more than doubled, reaching a peak in 1996 of 1,431 people. Although Castaño never publicly endorsed Uribe, their affinity was evident. Throughout Colombia, the AUC told people to vote for Uribe and threatened voters who supported other candidates. The left despised him with equal virulence. Before election day in 2002, I was inundated with e-mail messages promising apocalypse if Uribe won. One correspondent made a desperate plea: "If you care about Colombia, don't vote for Uribe. He will lead us into the abyss!" To his enemies, Uribe is a murderer, a pusher, a dictator, a bully, a liar, an oligarch, a closet paramilitary, an open fascist, a disaster. For these many Colombians, negotiation with the FARC is the only option. The guerrillas' struggle, they argue, is rooted in a legitimate battle to promote a fair distribution of the country's wealth. To solve the country's problems, then, an accord must be reached that guarantees a remaking of Colombian society that is equitable.

Certainly, there is injustice aplenty in Colombia. But in the presidential election, voters chose Uribe by unprecedented majority. Turnout was robust. His support cut across class, party, and geographical lines. Predictably, Uribe won among Colombians most interested in security, including the residents of the capital and Colombians voting from Miami and Madrid, many exiles because of kidnapping fears. Yet he also won among average Colombians sick to death of the slow bleed of "ya pasó."

There are many disturbing things about Uribe's plan, and the friends and associates he will entrust with carrying it out. There are people among them whose definition of *"gente de bien"* only reaches as far as the boundaries of their ranches. The man nominated to fill the combined posts of interior and justice minister was a lawyer, who, along with Uribe, had feted General Del Río after that officer's dismissal from the army. But it would be a mistake to see Uribe's election only through that lens. Elections are never as much about the candidates and their teams as about the people who elect them. There was wisdom in the vote as well as despair. Colombians saw the guerrillas not for what they were, a movement to redress specific land grievances, but for what they are, criminal enterprises riding the frothy surf of globalization. That the paramilitaries ride the same surge is a given and causes no argument. If anything, the election showed how deeply most Colombians cling to another path, how firmly they reject both the guerrillas' and the paramilitaries' excuses for mayhem.

Ultimately, however, the fate of Colombia is not entirely in the hands of its citizens. Much rests on American drug consumers, unaware of the harm they do or the repercussions of their buying habits. Colombians, at least, know that this will not change, that the entity to their north will continue to behave irresponsibly, satisfying its own needs and desires and oblivious to the harm it can cause. So Colombians, to the best of their ability, are making the hard choices necessary to preserve hope. To Colombians, Uribe does not offer good or even tolerable times. His promise is war, and enough of it to go around. On the day after the presidential election, the FARC ridiculed Uribe's first appearance before the media after being declared the winner. He was funereal and pasty-faced, "cold as a wind from the deepest tomb." Developing their familiar flair for the mortuary, they continued: "For every Uribe vote, there will be a grave," one communiqué promised.

Surprisingly, I found the FARC's description of Uribe accurate. Moreover, it comforted me. I had seen the photograph. Uribe looked as if he had just been told that his fortune was lost, his family murdered, and his arrest imminent. What human wouldn't feel stone-cold terror when handed Colombia in an electoral basket? Only a monster would have greeted the morning with a broad grin. That would have filled me with foreboding.

On my last visit in 2002, the air force reported that unidentified craft were overflying Bogotá, prompting fears of a September 11–style attack. In the countryside, guerrillas told hundreds of mayors and municipal officials to resign or face an execution, then proved the seriousness of their threat by killing officials who refused. In response, Bogotá's mayor, Antanas Mockus, refused a bulletproof vest and donned a paper one instead, with the heart cut out. For a man who had ridden to his wedding on an elephant and married in a circus cage containing seven live tigers, it was a restrained gesture. Yet even such theater could not cut the tension pervading the country. The mystery pilots were, people feared, no Islamic fundamentalists but purveyors of an all-too-familiar terror. The fact that the blips turned out to be a virus in the computer system comforted no one. What, then, people asked, had the people who were supposed to be protecting them missed?

With Uribe's win, war became Colombia's polestar, its dreadful chief executive. Whether this direction would bring relief or further woe was the topic of debate in circles far beyond Colombia. Just as it had in the 1950s, the United States was enmeshing itself in Colombia's war. Except this time, we were fighting on both sides: fueling illegal armies with our purchases, then fighting them with our charity. I found most of these discussions hollow and without texture. Often, I found myself wondering what Josué would have thought.

Once, Josué had asked me to accompany him on the drive from Villavicencio to Bogotá. I was his protection, something more than the pistol resting on the front passenger seat next to his driver. At the time, it was possible to believe that the simple presence of a foreigner, particularly an American, would make for a peaceful trip over land to the capital. It was just before Christmas. In the trunk, Josué had packed gift boxes of *aguardiente* and rum. He brought one box into the back seat for us to sample during the three-hour journey.

At first, Josué was tense. Frequently, he looked behind the car as the driver navigated the crowded streets. He was trying, I guessed, to read the motions of the pedestrians and motorcycles for threats of killer boys that the driver might miss. Once we were in the mountains, he relaxed. There, Josué told me, he had a deal with the owners of the restaurants that punctuated the road all the way to Bogotá. If they saw unusual activity, for instance, strangers gathered for an ambush, they had a way of warning Josué's driver to stop and turn around. Josué sealed this deal with gift boxes of liquor. His protectors were not political supporters of the Patriotic Union, but customers. They appreciated the perks that only the distillery's manager could deliver.

We tested the quality of that season's product sip by sip. The car strained on the steep grade that marked the climb out of the plains. Often, guerrillas would mount one of their "miraculous fishing expeditions" along this very road. But that day, our luck was good.

Josué opened the *aguardiente* first. I confessed that its licorice taste was too sweet for me.

"Correct!" he said with a tongue thwack.

He chose an aged rum. It was the Colombian drink, I told him, that I liked just as much as the country's coffee. The cold on the heights was intense. At least I thought it must be. It was hard to tell since the rum warmed my body to the fingertips. Halfway to Bogotá, I was pleasantly soaring. Not even the usual nausea provoked by Colombia's hairpin curves disturbed me.

A thick fog drew close to the ground, hiding the broader horizon. The grass was dense and lime green. What I knew lay in the distance was converted into a mystery land with its wonders shrouded. Anything could have been there–towns, tanks, beauty queens, armies, the dead, wild parties. My fear blossomed, then focused on that pistol grip, worn with use. Then I let my fear go, like a scarf in the wind. It was during this drive that Josué told me the rest of the story of his death and rebirth. Afterward, each time we met, he would elaborate on and fine-tune its elements. He also told me that everything mattered, what I did and what he did and what we all did and everything that we wanted to do, but couldn't. We didn't always perceive how it mattered in the rush and triumphs and defeats of the day. Somewhere, though, it was marked, he said. It was a number on a line. To him, it meant progress.

Sometimes, I confessed to him, what I did felt like less than zero. I mean literally negative, more harm than good. The number on the line went backward, into what was imaginably worse.

Josué shook his head. He raised a paper cup of rum and smiled. "Don't doubt," he said. "To give up is more terrible than death."

Josué had his own opinion about why Colombians fight. This was it: Colombians do not believe that another way is possible, that life can be different. It was a lack of imagination. It was the absence of faith.

These are weirdly religious thoughts for a man who embraced a secular life. Yet there it was, faith. You had to believe, as Josué did, that something else was possible on the earth, at the precise place where he had been born and raised, which he believed to be the most beautiful spot life offered. If someone or many someones stand up and point to another path, and convince others, then perhaps change is possible. God didn't stand at its end; life did.

To me, the obstacles seemed insurmountable. Not the least of them was the United States. The casualties of our war on drugs are not limited to the addict, the teen pusher, the abandoned baby, the college student too addled to stand. America's consumer habits pay for the bullets that cut down people like Josué as well as the gas cylinder bombs that fall on churches filled with refugees and the chain saws that dismember farmers and the rockets that slam into houses. Even if there were Colombians willing to stand up for something different, the other Colombians who fight over the money that America pumps into their country shoot them down. New people rise. They, too, fall.

It is a human story, not new to the world. Yet it was new to me.

When Josué and I arrived in Bogotá, it was late afternoon. The smoke of grilling sausage filled Avenida Jiménez. Josué dropped me near my hotel. I watched the taillights of his car disappear.

I knew that Josué would likely die violently, perhaps in that same car. Before leaving for a brief exile in Switzerland, he had said to friends that he did so only to "delay my death a little bit." He refused to leave permanently. Colombia was in his veins, like a shot of rum.

I never did ask him about my amulet.

On October 12, 1996, a Saturday, Josué went home to Villavicencio. He did the normal things one does on a weekend: shopping, a walk, a trip to the gym. For Josué, it was as strange as a flight to the moon. He had not been home for weeks, surrounded as he was in a parallel world of death threats and men with quick eyes following him.

His daughters were excited. They hadn't seen him in so long. That Sunday morning, Josué rose early. He got a machete and went across the street to a field to cut down weeds. In the cleared space, he set up a pup tent for the three of them to play. That day, Josué had another foreigner with him, an American lawyer named Michael. Michael had been infected by the passion that seizes many who visit, seduced by Colombia's beauty, the intelligence of its people, and their sense of fun and life even in the midst of so much death. *Rumba* and death: joy and the end of days.

The assassin who had come for Josué didn't even glance at Michael. Michael told me that he saw that the man had a mustache and curly black hair. The man looked only at Josué.

Josué saw him and ran. It was not just his first reaction, that animal instinct that impels us to save ourselves. Over the years, Josué had tamed that, like many Colombians who live with the daily knowledge that any of the moments that make up an average day could be their last. He was doing something more specific. He was running away from his girls.

"Run, run, run!" he yelled at Michael, pointing away.

He meant run with the girls. Run away from me. It was the logic of geometry, to force the path of the bullets directly to him and away from them. He was the apex of the triangle. He wanted the man to aim at him and him alone. He wanted to give him a human target.

That day was my birthday. I don't remember who called to tell me the news. Josué did not linger. The assassin found his mark, as they usually do. Josué wasn't lucky twice. When I heard the news, a ball of hatred rose up in me. It was as powerful as the fear I had felt on that long ride with Josué. I let it go, too. Not just a gun killed Josué. It was also hatred. That day, I chose to deny it the power to arm me with my own hate.

When a life ends, it is a lovely book that closes forever. The answers are the ones you have already read. One can look back at a life as if it were a text, search out nuance and shading and words that reveal themselves unexpectedly in light of new events. But it is not the same. It is exegesis, not life, the interpretation of texts, not the flash of a glance or the sound of words.

I am incapable of absorbing the true measure of loss in large number. I feel small tragedies. This is my little vial of grief. This is the one I lost, my heart tells me. This is the story I know.

COLOMBIANS SAY, AT TIMES WITH PRIDE AND AT TIMES WITH EVIDENT frustration, that their history and relationships are complex, often contradictory, and paced at breakneck speed. "A day in Colombia," a Swedish diplomat once told me, "is like a year in Stockholm."

In these pages, I have tried to identify what I believe to be relevant moments and figures and trends. This book is not, nor was it meant to be, a comprehensive study. I have left much out and much that is of importance by necessity gets token treatment. What I hope readers come away with is a heightened sense of how and where Americans connect to Colombia and why that relationship needs urgently to change. Its grace notes I owe to the many Colombians and others I talked and traveled with. Its faults are my own.

I wrote this early in the mornings, on weekends, during a sabbatical, and on days off from Human Rights Watch, an organization that I admire and support. There are many challenges to human rights in the world. This organization meets them with energy and creativity and a will to make change, elements that keep vibrant the hope that what we are doing matters, even on the gloomiest days. My special thanks go to Ken Roth, the Human Rights Watch executive director, and José Miguel Vivanco, director of the Americas Division.

Many colleagues and friends assisted me in the research I did for this book or were patient readers of early drafts, among them Roxana Althoz, Ana Carrigan, Lisa Haugard, Winifred Tate, Daniel Wilkinson, and Coletta Youngers. Cynthia Arnson and Jennifer Bailey were both occasional travel companions and readers. I owe a lot to my many colleagues and correspondents in Colombia, some mentioned in these pages and some, by request, left anonymous. Colombia can be a disheartening place. Josué is beyond my thanks now; but he stands in this book for the many Colombians who continue to work for a different future.

Paul Wolf's excellent and determined research on the murder of Jorge Eliécer Gaitán helped me add color and verve to the book's opening chapters. I admire his initiative in tackling a subject new to him and illuminating a part of history that remains too little examined. In Washington, the people who have embraced the human rights cause—Senator Patrick Leahy and Tim Rieser, especially—are my private superheroes. Lest I err in failing to cross the aisle and the Capitol grounds, I was also enriched and educated by many long conversations with Colombia veteran Gil Macklin, whose perspective I greatly value.

I would like to give special thanks to Herbert "Tico" Braun and Iván Orozco, two readers who gave this manuscript in its rough form close, constructive, and passionate reads, with comments to match. I also had perceptive readers in Anne Allison, Charlie Piot, Frances Starn, and Randolph Starn.

I had angels along the way, among them Peder Zane, the book review editor at the Raleigh *News and Observer,* whose support was the oxygen that nourished this book in its earliest stages. Mickey Choate, my agent, helped my idea grow into something tangible. Robert Kimzey, my editor, perceived in it something that went beyond the day's headlines and was worth a second look, the charm that led to these pages.

Books are born in the mind, but they become creatures of schedules, missed appointments, exhausted Saturdays, empty milk cartons, hot dog dinners, and laundry left heaped on the dining room table. My husband, Orin, and my children patiently bore it. Without their support, I could not have finished. Without them, I would not have wanted to.

Colombia has a rich literary and artistic tradition. Its cities have many book-stores filled with the latest American and European best-sellers, along with the newest Latin American and Colombian works. Its theaters, Internet cafes, art exhibits, and concert halls are filled. Lamentably, this traffic does not, as yet, flow as deeply the other way. Few of Colombia's historians, journalists, and novelists have had their work translated into other languages accessible to non-Spanish-speaking readers. Authors like Arturo Alape, Marín's biographer; Alfredo Molano, Colombia's answer to Studs Terkel; and Antonio Caballero, a sharp-eyed analyst, were essential source material for history and contemporary analysis.

Along with my own research, I drew on Colombia's vibrant press, particularly magazines such as *Semana* and *Cambio* and the newspapers *El Tiempo, El Colombiano, Vanguardia Liberal,* and *El País* (Cali). Colombia's struggling but highly accomplished film industry has also produced excellent movies about the country and its history, among them *Cóndores no se entierran todos los días* (Francisco Norden, 1984), about La Violencia; *Rodrigo D: No futuro* (Víctor Gaviria, 1990), about Medellín's killer boys; *La estrategia del caracol* (Sergio Cabrera, 1993), about slum dwellers fighting eviction; and *Soplo de vida* (Luis Ospina, 1999), a murder mystery.

There are some web sites in English that contain valuable information on specific aspects of Colombian history or contemporary life. Among them are Paul Wolf's site, containing his research on Jorge Eliécer Gaitán's murder and its aftermath (available: www.icdc.com/~paulwolf/gaitan/gaitan.htm); the Colombia Project site on current U.S. policy toward Colombia (available: www.ciponline.org/colombia/); Peace Brigades International, a nonprofit organization of volunteers who work with human rights defenders in several countries, among them Colombia (available: www.peacebrigades.org/); and the National Security Archive, which has a treasure trove of declassified U.S. documents on the evolution of U.S. policy toward Colombia (and many other parts of the world) (available: www.gwu.edu/~nsarchiv/). The Inter-American Commission on Human Rights, which can examine specific cases involving allegations of human rights violations, maintains a list of the cases related to Colombia (available: www.cidh.oas.org/DefaultE.htm). Frontline:

Drug Wars, a collaboration with National Public Radio produced by Martin Smith and reported by Lowell Bergman, features fascinating material on the early players in the rise and fall of the Medellín Cartel. The transcripts of the series, broadcast in 2000, are on the PBS web site (available: www.pbs.org/ wgbh/pages/frontline/shows/drugs/). Finally, much of the work on Colombia published by Human Rights Watch is also on the Internet (available: www.hrw.org/).

All of Colombia's illegal armed groups have their own web sites: the AUC (available: colombia-libre.org/colombialibre/pp.asp); the ELN (available: www.eln-voces.com/); and the FARC (available: www.farc-ep.org/).

Alape, Arturo. *La paz, la violencia: Testigos de excepción.* Santafé de Bogotá: Planeta, 1985.
_____. *Las vidas de Pedro Antonio Marín Manuel Marulanda Vélez Tirofijo.* Santafé de Bogotá: Planeta, 1989.
Álvarez García, John, ed. *Camilo Torres: His Life and His Message.* With an introduction by Dorothy Day. Springfield, IL: Templegate Publishers, 1968.
Arango, Carlos Z. *FARC: Veinte años de Marquetalia a La Uribe.* Santafé de Bogotá: Ediciones Aurora, 1984.
Aranguren Molina, Mauricio. *Mi confesión: Carlos Castaño revela sus secretos.* Santafé de Bogotá: Editorial Oveja Negra, 2001.
Asencio, Diego, and Nancy Asencio, with Ron Tobias. *Our Man Is Inside.* Boston: Little, Brown and Company, 1982.
Bergquist, Charles, et al. *Violence in Colombia: The Contemporary Crisis in Historical Perspective.* Wilmington, DE: Scholarly Resources, 1984.
Betancourt, Dario, and Martha L. Garcia. *Matones y cuadrilleros: Origen y evolución de la violencia en el occidente Colombiano.* Santafé de Bogotá: Tercer Mundo Editores/Instituto de Estudios Políticos y Relaciones Internacionales, 1991.
Betancourt, Ingrid. *Until Death Do Us Part: My Struggle to Reclaim Colombia.* New York: Ecco, 2002.
Bowden, Mark. *Killing Pablo: The Hunt for the World's Greatest Outlaw.* New York: Atlantic Monthly Press, 2001.
Braun, Herbert. *The Assassination of Gaitán: Public Life and Urban Violence in Colombia.* Madison: University of Wisconsin Press, 1985.
_____. *Our Guerrillas, Our Sidewalks: A Journey into the Violence of Colombia.* Niwot: University of Colorado Press, 1994.
Broderick, Walter J. *El guerrillero invisible.* Santafé de Bogotá: Intermedio, 2000.
Carrigan, Ana. *The Palace of Justice: A Colombian Tragedy.* New York: Four Walls, Eight Windows, 1993.

Castro Caycedo, Germán. *Colombia amarga.* Santafé de Bogotá: Círculo de Lectores, 1987.

———. *En secreto.* Santafé de Bogotá: Planeta, 1996.

Comisión de Superación de la Violencia. *Pacificar la paz: Lo que no se ha negociado en los acuerdos de paz.* Santafé de Bogotá: IEPRI/CINEP/Comisión Andina de Juristas, CECOIN, 1992.

Duzán, María Jimena. *Death Beat.* New York: HarperCollins, 1994.

Escobar Gaviria, Roberto. *Mi hermano Pablo.* Santafé de Bogotá: Quintero Editores, 2000.

Gallon Giraldo, Gustavo. "La república de las armas: Relación entre fuerzas armadas y estado en Colombia: 1960–1980," *Controversia* (CINEP, 1983).

García Durán, Mauricio. *Procesos de paz: De la Uribe a Tlaxcala.* Santafé de Bogotá: CINEP, 1992.

García Márquez, Gabriel. *News of a Kidnapping.* New York: Knopf, 1997.

———. *One Hundred Years of Solitude.* New York: Harper and Row, 1970.

Grabe, Vera. *Razones de vida.* Santafé de Bogotá: Planeta, 2000.

Gugliotta, Guy, and Jeff Leen. *Kings of Cocaine: Inside the Medellín Cartel–an Astonishing True Story of Murder, Money, and International Corruption.* New York: Simon and Schuster, 1989.

International Commission of the FARC-EP. *FARC-EP: Historical Outline.* Canada: International Commission of the FARC-EP, n.d.

Landazábal, General (retired) Fernando. *El equilibrio del poder.* Santafé de Bogotá: Plaza and Janes, 1993.

Lara, Patricia. *Las mujeres en la guerra.* Santafé de Bogotá: Planeta, 2000.

———. *Siembre vientos y recogerás tempestades: La historia del M-19, sus protagonistas y sus destinos.* Santafé de Bogotá: Planeta, 1986.

Leal Buitrago, Francisco. *El oficio de la guerra: La seguridad nacional en Colombia.* Santafé de Bogotá: Tercer Mundo/IEPRI, 1994.

McClintick, David. *Swordfish: A True Story of Ambition, Savagery, and Betrayal.* New York: Pantheon Books, 1993.

Medina Gallego, Carlos. *Autodefensas, paramilitares y narcotráfico en Colombia.* Santafé de Bogotá: Documentos Periodísticos, 1990.

———. *ELN: Una historia contada a dos voces: Entrevista con "el cura" Manuel Pérez y Nicolás Rodríguez Bautista, "Gabino."* Santafé de Bogotá: Rodríguez Quito Editores, 1996.

Meta Civic Committee for Human Rights. *Ceder es más terrible que la muerte: 1985–1996: Una década de violencia en el Meta.* Santafé de Bogotá: Abogados Democráticos, ASCODAS, Comisión Intercongregacional de Justicia y Paz, ILSA, 1997.

Molano, Alfredo. *Los años del tropel: Crónicas de la violencia.* Santafé de Bogotá: CEREC/El Áncora Editores, 1985.

_____. *Trochas y fusiles*. Santafé de Bogotá: IEPRI/El Áncora Editores, 1994.

Morris, Hollman. *Operación Ballena Azul: Las armas del Cantón Norte*. Santafé de Bogotá: Intermedio, 2001.

Pax Christi-Netherlands. *The Kidnap Industry in Colombia: Our Business?* Utrecht: Pax Christi-Netherlands, November 2001.

Pizarro Leongómez, Eduardo. *Las FARC: De la autodefensa a la combinación de todas las formas de lucha*. Santafé de Bogotá: Tercer Mundo Editores, IEPRI, 1991.

Proyecto Nunca Más. *Colombia, nunca más: Crímenes de lesa humanidad*. Santafé de Bogotá: Proyecto Nunca Más, 2000.

Rempe, Dennis. "Guerrillas, Bandits, and Independent Republics: U.S. Counterinsurgency Efforts in Colombia 1959–1965." In *Small Wars and Insurgencies*. London: Frank Cass, 1995.

Rivera, José Eustasio. *La vorágine*. New York: Editorial Andes, 1929

Rubio, Mauricio. *Crimen e impunidad: Precisiones sobre la violencia*. Santafé de Bogotá: Tercer Mundo Editores, 1999.

Salazar, Alonso. *Born to Die in Medellín*. London: Latin America Bureau, 1990.

_____. *La parábola de Pablo: Auge y caída de un gran capo del narcotráfico*. Santafé de Bogotá: Planeta, 2001.

Salvatierra, Pedro. *Confesiones de un secuestrado: Crónicas del Sumapaz*. Santafé de Bogotá: Intermedio, 2001.

Samper, Ernesto. *Aquí estoy y aquí me quedo: Testimonio de un gobierno*. Santafé de Bogotá: El Áncora, 2000.

Sandoval, Marbel. *Gloria Cuartas: Por qué no tiene miedo*. Santafé de Bogotá: Planeta Colombiana Editorial, 1997.

Thoumi, Francisco, et al. *Drogas ilícitas en Colombia*. Santafé de Bogotá: Ariel/United Nations Development Program/Colombian Justice Ministry, 1997.

Uribe, María Victoria. *Matar, rematar, contramatar: Las masacres de La Violencia en el Tolima, 1948–1964*. Santafé de Bogotá: CINEP, 1996.

Valencia Tovar, Álvaro, and Jairo Sandoval Franky. *Colombia en la Guerra de Corea: La historia secreta*. Santafé de Bogotá: Planeta, 2001.

Vallejo, Fernando. *La Virgen de los sicarios*. Madrid: Editorial Santillana, 1994

Villamizar, Darío. *Un adiós a la guerra: Memoria histórica de los process de paz en Colombia*. Santafé de Bogotá: Planeta, 1997.

Villarraga, Álvaro S., and Nelson R. Plazas N. *Para reconstruir los sueños (una historia del EPL)*. Santafé de Bogotá: Progresar/Fundación Cultura Democrática, 1994.

PublicAffairs is a publishing house founded in 1997. It is a tribute to the standards, values, and flair of three persons who have served as mentors to countless reporters, writers, editors, and book people of all kinds, including me.

I. F. Stone, proprietor of *I. F. Stone's Weekly,* combined a commitment to the First Amendment with entrepreneurial zeal and reporting skill and became one of the great independent journalists in American history. At the age of eighty, Izzy published *The Trial of Socrates,* which was a national bestseller. He wrote the book after he taught himself ancient Greek.

Benjamin C. Bradlee was for nearly thirty years the charismatic editorial leader of *The Washington Post.* It was Ben who gave the *Post* the range and courage to pursue such historic issues as Watergate. He supported his reporters with a tenacity that made them fearless, and it is no accident that so many became authors of influential, best-selling books.

Robert L. Bernstein, the chief executive of Random House for more than a quarter century, guided one of the nation's premier publishing houses. Bob was personally responsible for many books of political dissent and argument that challenged tyranny around the globe. He is also the founder and was the longtime chair of Human Rights Watch, one of the most respected human rights organizations in the world.

ooooo

For fifty years, the banner of Public Affairs Press was carried by its owner, Morris B. Schnapper, who published Gandhi, Nasser, Toynbee, Truman, and about 1,500 other authors. In 1983 Schnapper was described by *The Washington Post* as "a redoubtable gadfly." His legacy will endure in the books to come.

Peter Osnos, *Publisher*